BRINGING ZION HOME

BRINGING ZION HOME

Israel in American Jewish Culture, 1948–1967

EMILY ALICE KATZ

STATE UNIVERSITY OF NEW YORK PRESS

Published by
STATE UNIVERSITY OF NEW YORK PRESS, ALBANY

For information, contact
State University of New York Press, Albany, NY
www.sunypress.edu

Production, Laurie D. Searl
Marketing, Michael Campochiaro

Library of Congress Cataloging-in-Publication Data

Katz, Emily Alice, 1975– author.
   Bringing Zion home : Israel in American Jewish culture, 1948-1967 / Emily
Alice Katz.
       pages cm
   Includes bibliographical references and index.
   ISBN 978-1-4384-5465-8 (hardcover : alk. paper)
   ISBN 978-1-4384-5464-1 (pbk. : alk. paper)
   ISBN 978-1-4384-5466-5 (ebook)
   1. Jews—United States—Attitudes toward Israel.   2. Israel and the diaspora.
3. Jews—United States—Social life and customs—20th century.   4. Israel—
Public opinion.   5. Public opinion—United States.   I. Title.

DS132.K38 2015
956.9405'2—dc23   2014007253

10 9 8 7 6 5 4 3 2 1

For Thad

CONTENTS

ILLUSTRATIONS

ACKNOWLEDGMENTS

I am deeply grateful to a host of individuals and institutions for helping to bring this project to fruition.

I undertook the labor of transforming my dissertation into this book while teaching at the University of California, Irvine, where I have benefited from conversations with colleagues and have been inspired by the intellectual curiosity of my students. As a faculty advisor for the UC-Irvine branch of the Olive Tree Initiative, I have developed rewarding intellectual partnerships and friendships with Daniel Wehrenfennig, Daniel Brunstetter, Arturo Jimenez, Paula Garb, and Susan Seely. Their support has been essential.

Thanks are due to archivists, librarians, and staff at several institutions, including the American Jewish Archives, American Jewish Historical Society, the University of California-Irvine, Hadassah, the Library of the Museum of Modern Art, Yeshiva University Museum, and the Library of the Jewish Theological Seminary. I am particularly grateful to Susan Woodland, senior archivist at the American Jewish Historical Society (formerly of the Hadassah Archives); Barbara Simon (formerly of the America-Israel Cultural Foundation); Kevin Proffitt and Gary P. Zola of the American Jewish Archives; Ruth Goodman and Ruth Schoenberg of the Israeli Dance Institute; and Rhoda Seidenberg and Bonni-Dara Michaels of Yeshiva University Museum for their expert advice and enthusiastic assistance.

This project has been enriched by formal interviews and informal conversations with a number of individuals. I would like to thank the following people for sharing their thoughts and their time with me: Clara Frieder, Barry and Irene Friedman, Ayalah Goren, Judith Brin Ingber, Gila Zalon, and Gideon Paz.

Crucial financial support for the dissertation came from several institutions. A Recent Doctoral Recipients Fellowship and a Dissertation Completion Fellowship from the Andrew W. Mellon Foundation/ACLS Early Career Fellowship Program provided funding in the last phase of dissertation writing and first phase of revisions toward the book manuscript. Support for dissertation writing was also provided by the Foundation for Jewish Culture's Maurice and Marilyn Cohen Doctoral Dissertation Fellowship and a Doctoral Fellowship from the Memorial Foundation for

Jewish Culture. I am also grateful to have received a Loewenstein-Wiener Fellowship from the Jacob Rader Marcus Center of the American Jewish Archives. The Charles H. Revson Fellowship in Advanced Jewish Studies provided financial assistance at several points during my graduate studies; I thank the Graduate School of JTS for designating me the recipient of that and other fellowships throughout my time as a graduate student.

A section of chapter 4 was published in my article, "It's The Real World After All: The American-Israel Pavilion–Jordan Pavilion Controversy at the New York World's Fair, 1964–1965," in *American Jewish History* 91, no. 1 (March 2003), and appears here with permission from Johns Hopkins University Press. A portion of chapter 5 first appeared as "Introducing Israeli Art: Communal and Critical Encounters in Postwar America," in *Images: A Journal of Jewish Art and Visual Culture* 3, no. 1 (2009). It is reprinted here with the permission of Brill.

My heartfelt thanks to Professor Jack Wertheimer, my dissertation advisor, whose careful reading, incisive critiques, and refreshing insights—well beyond graduate school—have strengthened this book in innumerable ways. David Roskies, Alan Mintz, Shuly Rubin Schwartz, and Barbara Kirshenblatt-Gimblett served, along with Jack, as dissertation committee members, and it was their thoughtful comments that provided a first, crucial bridge from dissertation to book. I am indebted to BKG, too, for including me in the Working Group in Jews, Media, and Religion of the Center for Religion and Media at New York University, where fellow members exemplified the rigorous, creative study of Jewish culture in its myriad forms.

Over the years, I have benefited from the questions and comments of colleagues who encountered my work as panel chairs and audience members at various conferences. I would like to extend a special thank you, however, to Riv-Ellen Prell, Ari Y. Kelman, and Jenna Weissman Joselit, who went above and beyond the call of duty, reading portions of this book along the way and providing helpful comments. Jenna not only offered an in-depth critique of chapter 3, on Israeli folk dance in America, but also pointed me toward the Hadassah fashion shows as a worthy subject. I thank Margaret Olin and Steven Fine for helping to refine my thinking on the material about Israeli art in America.

I am grateful to SUNY Press, and particularly to James Peltz, for extending me this opportunity and expertly shepherding the project through to publication. Jessica Kirschner and Rafael Chaiken provided excellent editorial support. I am indebted to my anonymous reviewers, whose insights and critiques helped me to see my work with fresh eyes and (I hope) to sharpen the manuscript in important ways. It was a pleasure working with Laurie Searl, production editor at SUNY Press; thank you to Alan V. Hewat for his careful copy editing.

The love and support of my parents, Lenore and Joel Katz, have allowed me every opportunity. They have been eager, thoughtful readers of mine for as long as I can remember, and I treasure their continuing interest in my work. My sister Marisa, intelligent, witty, and encouraging, is also a beloved friend, and reminds me by example that the work we do matters.

My children Lincoln and Willa have enlivened my world immeasurably; I love them beyond reason. I look forward to reading, thinking, talking, debating, and laughing with them both as they grow up.

Thad, my collaborator in all things for twenty years now, has made everything in this life richer, deeper, and brighter. I cannot imagine my life without him and I am boundlessly grateful for his love and support. This book is dedicated to him.

ONE

INTRODUCTION

Postwar American Jewry Reconsidered

In the fall of 1962, a contributor to *Women's League Outlook*, the magazine of the women's branch of the Conservative movement in American Judaism, rhapsodized about the wide adoption of Israeli folk dance among American Jewish youth. She wrote:

> Visit any group of young Jewish girls and boys, from Bangor, Maine to Corpus Christi, Texas, from Vancouver, Canada to San Diego, California—the length and breadth of the country, and see how those children dance a hora and sing Israeli songs. . . . We, the middle aged folk of today, had nothing like it in our youth. As Jews, we lost our identity in . . . the jitterbug. A special Jewish dance for the young? Unthinkable, when we were young, except at Jewish weddings.[1]

To the author, American Jewish youth's championing of Israeli folk dance signaled a willingness to appear different from the surrounding American culture. She chided those nostalgic for the immigrant Jewish culture of yesteryear, writing, "We don't have to feel sorry for our children. . . . [T]hey are building up a much richer and much prouder life as Jews" than the previous generation had done.[2] The field of dance, from the author's perspective, was a powerful incubator for postwar Jewish life. Israeli folk dance both shaped and reflected a new kind of American Jewish dignity; Zionism and Israel, her essay suggested, were most significant to American Jews as guarantors of a vibrant American Jewish culture rather than as vehicles for political liberation, the protection of persecuted Jews, or the revitalization of the Jewish religion.

Bringing Zion Home shines a spotlight on the phenomenon described above—broadly speaking, the extensive promotion and consumption of Israel in the American Jewish cultural realm. In this book, I address a question that historians have not yet fully answered: How, exactly, *did* Israel surface in American Jewish culture in the immediate postwar decades, and what does this reveal about the nature of postwar American Jewish culture more generally? Examining the fields of publishing, the arts (dance, fine art, and music), and material and consumer culture, all together, I contend that Israel served as an increasingly significant touchstone in the American Jewish imagination in the two decades after Israel's founding.

Most specifically, I argue that many American Jews encountered Israel in the early postwar decades primarily through their roles as cultural impresarios, tastemakers, and consumers.[3] They became active organizers of and participants in Israel-related cultural practices, including writing and reading about Israel; teaching and performing Israeli folk dances; promoting and consuming Israeli fashions and objects; and arranging and attending exhibitions of Israeli art and concerts by Israeli musicians. I find that a diverse and growing spectrum of actors—including journalists, Jewish educators, Zionist and synagogue youth, Hadassah members, business entrepreneurs, collectors, and arts foundations, to name a few—envisioned the cultural sphere as the front line in the campaign to win the hearts and minds of postwar Americans, Jews and non-Jews, to the cause of Israel. In so doing, these actors remade American Jewish culture in the postwar era.

With this study, I hope to elaborate, enrich, and nuance a story that we often think we already know. Over time, a kind of shorthand has emerged to describe the American Jewish relationship to Israel in the first decades of the postwar era. This narrative prominently features massive outpourings of support for Israel among American Jews during 1948 and 1967, during Israel's pivotal wars with its Arab neighbors. Scholars of postwar American Jewry are right to draw attention to the substantial and unprecedented contributions of American Jews, primarily in financial and political terms, on Israel's behalf in 1948 and, even more so, in 1967. While it is natural for historians to be drawn to "momentous events such as the birth of . . . Israel and, along with it, the role played by the American Zionist movement in the birthing process," as historian Rafael Medoff has acknowledged, this has led to relative neglect of other sorts of engagements with Israel in less "dramatic" moments.[4]

So, too, has popular memory of the 1967 Arab-Israeli war and its aftermath implicitly shaped our understanding of American Jewish imaginings of Israel in the earlier postwar decades. According to this narrative, American

Jewry, fearing a second Holocaust in 1967 as Israel faced off against the surrounding Arab nations, embraced the Jewish state unapologetically in a moment of mass catharsis and reoriented their communal agenda to reflect Israel's now central importance to them.[5] In this light, the period between 1948 and 1967 appears as a doldrums, undistinguished by bold political actions or astonishing philanthropic largesse. The problem with this story is that it undervalues Israel's impact on American Jewish culture—high culture, popular culture, and material culture—in these years. In neglecting the cultural sphere, as such, we are in danger of missing a prime arena in which American Jewry first explored its relationship with the state of Israel.

To focus squarely upon American Jewish culture as a field of inquiry does not mean, however, that "culture" existed as a thing apart, an enlightened realm unsullied by political or economic realities. To be sure, many of the actors who appear in this book described their cultural engagements with Israel as deliberately nonpolitical in nature. Focusing attention on Israeli art and fashion, for example, helped some American Jews mediate potentially awkward political entanglements with the Jewish state at a time when the United States was weighing the advantages and disadvantages of an alliance with Israel. The boundary dividing cultural and political transactions in this field, however, was fluid, and the book seeks to navigate the explicit and implicit relationship between culture and politics among postwar American Jews, particularly in relation to Israel.

In anticipation of Israel's tenth anniversary in 1958, for example, a group of prominent American citizens calling itself the American Committee for Israel's Tenth Anniversary Celebration spearheaded the planning of commemorative events in the United States. The American Committee encouraged local communities to organize musical concerts featuring the work of Israeli composers, arrange exhibitions of Israeli art at local museums, sponsor presentations of books about Israel at libraries and schools, and create window displays "saluting Israel" at local department stores, among other things.[6] The organizers of the 1958 celebrations framed such cultural programs as an accessible, noncontroversial means of bringing Israel into the American public sphere—of spotlighting Israel's achievements in a "non-political, non-partisan setting," in the words of the American Committee.[7]

The term *non-political* bears scrutiny, however. Herbert H. Lehman, the general chairman of the American Committee for Israel's Tenth Anniversary Celebration as well as a retired U.S. senator and former governor of New York, was eager to cast the Jewish state as an American partner in the Cold War. In seeming contradiction to the American government's more sustained attention to postwar Europe and Asia as prime theaters for battling communism, Lehman—still a consummate politician—insisted that Israel was central to America's strategic interests. He argued that "[t]he peace of mankind and the preservation of freedom and of civilization itself hangs on the forces at work and the events which are taking place in the Middle East." Lehman promised that, in the commemorative year then unfolding, the American Committee would call attention specifically to the "danger of continued Communist success in breeding unrest and conflict in the area."[8]

For Lehman, and presumably for his fellow members of the American Committee (including organizational leaders, clergy, politicians, artists, journalists and educators, both Jewish and non-Jewish), Israel presented a clear contrast to the destabilizing forces at work in the Middle East. The Jewish state was a dynamic symbol of "man's capacity to create and build, despite danger and adversity, given the will and the passion for creation— and for freedom," as Lehman put it, linking creative aptitude and achievement, broadly speaking, with political freedom.[9] The American Committee endeavored to disseminate this idea by means of special cultural and religious events to be planned and observed by a wide swath of the Jewish and Christian populations in the United States. Rabbi Irving Miller, chairman of the group's Committee on Community Organization, stressed that the celebrations should be "all-American, involving all facets of community life . . . in hundreds of communities large and small."[10] The point, it appears, was to generate a sense of broad consensus, deploying Israel-positive messages largely in educational and cultural forums rather than in explicitly political arenas. Yet for Herbert Lehman and his fellow members of the American Committee, as for many of Israel's American Jewish advocates (as we shall see), culture and politics were intimately intertwined.

Although the occasion of Israel's ten-year anniversary afforded a heightened public platform for Israel-themed cultural and educational programming in the United States, the activities championed by the American Committee were not rare, isolated experiments. By the time of Israel's tenth anniversary in 1958, Israel-focused cultural activities had already become quite familiar to many American Jews, a phenomenon that only intensified in the course of the 1960s. Yet, even in light of existing scholarship on American Jews and Israel between 1948 and 1967, lacunae in this cultural history still exist. In their important surveys of American Jewish history, scholars such as Edward S. Shapiro, Jonathan D. Sarna, and Gerald Sorin, among others, have noted that postwar American Jews were, at the very least, enthusiastic supporters of Israel who created communal networks, spaces, and times for primarily philanthropic engagements with the Jewish state.[11] To the extent that such surveys address the cultural sphere, however, they frame Israel as a subconscious influence on American Jewish culture at most, something to be mentioned in passing.

Shapiro, for example, has written that, until the crisis of the 1967 war, "not even [American Jews] themselves realized just how important Israel had been to them," and he points to the popularity of Leon Uris's *Exodus* and Otto Preminger's film adaptation of that book as "clues" that, in fact, American Jews had developed an intense emotional bond with Israel in the preceding two decades.[12] Sarna has looked at the 1950s as a period of "incubation," regarding the impact of both the Holocaust and Israel, in contrast to the period after the Six-Day War, when these themes "moved on to the center stage of public life." Before 1967, according to Sarna, Israel had a "subtle" influence on American Jewish life by means of such practices as the sale of Israeli goods in synagogue gift shops and the "spread of Israeli dances among young people."[13] Meanwhile, Stephen J. Whitfield has written that, in the late 1950s (and specifically at the time of *Exodus*'s publication), "American Jewish interest in Israel was slight . . . levels of philanthropy and tourism were—by later standards—low, and . . . ethnicity was suppressed or disdained as an embarrassing residue of the immigrant past."[14] My exploration of American Jewish culture in the first postwar decades challenges the notion that Israel was, for American Jews, merely an afterthought.

I have premised *Bringing Zion Home*, as a historical project, on the notion that it is worth investigating specifically cultural engagements—i.e., the adoption of Israeli folk dance, to name one prominent example—delineating the processes by which these practices took hold and assessing their influence. This is the first book-length study of these explicitly cultural practices. To be sure, there has been much significant scholarship on aspects of the relationship, since 1948, between the United States, American Jewry, and Israel. These include examinations of Israel's place in the thinking of postwar Jewish leaders and intellectuals and studies of the organizational sphere that American Jews created in order to raise funds and advocate for Israel, for example.[15] Few scholars have fully tackled the subject of Israel's significance in this period in the wide-ranging "cultural realm" per se, however—that is, in the arts and in popular and material culture.

Three books do merit particular attention as noteworthy forays into the question of Israel's role in postwar American Jewish culture. Historian Deborah Dash Moore devotes a chapter to the subject in her pioneering work on postwar American Jewry, *To The Golden Cities: Pursuing the American Jewish Dream in Miami and L.A.* She argues for the importance of Los Angeles and Miami Jews in positioning Israel—especially via Hollywood films and Israel Bond campaigns—as an object of nearly universal American Jewish veneration. Providing substantive details about these Jews' Israel-related practices in the first postwar decades, Moore contends that, for these pathbreaking Jewish communities, an "imagined Israel displaced New York as the source of authentic Jewish culture."[16]

Meanwhile, in *Eye on Israel: How America Came to View Israel as an Ally*, Michelle Mart mines representations of Israel in mass media, popular fiction, and film, arguing that the unambiguously heroic depictions of the Jewish state found within them satisfied the muscular political and cultural agenda of Cold War America.[17] Though Mart pays close attention to how American Jews and Israelis were represented in popular media in this period, she is largely uninterested in developments within the American Jewish community, leaving room for further work on this subject. Most recently, in his book *Our Exodus: Leon Uris and the Americanization of Israel's Founding Story*, M. M. Silver has focused upon Uris's bestseller as a masterly public relations coup for post-1948 Zionism, the first truly compelling Zionist narrative of Jewish history for a mass audience. Silver argues that by "projecting his own personal problems and existential dilemmas" onto the story of Israel's founding, Uris transformed recent history into an Americanized fable of "Judeo-Christian union in a post-Holocaust melting pot."[18] However, although Silver concedes that *Exodus* "did not emerge ex nihilo," he presents few examples of American Jews' engagements with Israel in the cultural realm.[19] Even with these important contributions to the historical record, then, there is still much to learn about Israel's place in American Jewish culture.

AMERICAN JEWRY AND ISRAEL AFTER 1948

By the close of the 1940s, the internecine battles over Zionism that had plagued and stymied the organized American Jewish community in the interwar period and the World War II years seemed, for most, a distant memory. In response to the acute crisis of Israel's War of Independence, American Jews forged, in the words of one historian, "a unity of purpose on a scale unprecedented in the modern history of the Jews."[20] American Jewry proved instrumental—in terms of both money and influence—to Israel's emergence on the world stage as a full-fledged nation. Indeed, Israel quickly became a philanthropic common cause among American Jews, to the extent that Israel's leaders now bypassed American Zionist organizations altogether, focusing fundraising appeals on the vast population of supporters in the American Jewish community not formally affiliated with Zionist groups.

Israel appeared to have many sympathizers in the American public sphere. Pro-Israel sentiment was expressed in "resolutions passed by state governments, rhetoric of members of Congress, political platforms, and speeches of leading politicians from both major parties," even before Israel's independence, revealing "an enormous groundswell of support" for the Jewish state, as Peter L. Hahn has shown.[21] President Harry Truman, whose foreign policy approach to Israel was somewhat inconsistent, was personally sympathetic to Israel's needs, a position rooted in his Protestant Christian religious convictions and sense of moral responsibility toward the

Jewish state in the wake of the Holocaust.[22] In Congress, the granting of a $221.5 million loan package between 1949 and 1952 constituted a significant gesture of goodwill in the first years of Israel's existence, a practice that continued well after the first postwar decades. The American press was filled with enthusiastic reports and positive editorials on the subject of Israel, describing the country as a land of hardy pioneers and as a place of redemption for the surviving remnant of European Jewry. Favorable attitudes toward Israel in the elite press—specifically, the *New York Times* and the *Washington Post*—even surpassed the degree of support for Israel in the American public at large.[23]

American supporters of Israel, Jewish and non-Jewish, often argued that there was a natural congruence between the national characters of America and Israel, a common love of freedom and democracy and a shared generosity of spirit and resources. In this formulation, analogous myths and historical sagas pointed to a deeper harmony of interests that formed the basis of a special relationship between America and Israel. These themes, and the deeply felt faith in American pluralism that informed them, had strengthened the various strands of American Zionism before 1948, from the pragmatic Progressive-era version endorsed by Louis Brandeis to the spiritual and cultural Zionism of rabbi-intellectuals such as Solomon Schechter and Mordecai Kaplan as well as the small but influential moderate wing of Labor Zionism in the United States.[24]

In the context of a postwar America facing new geopolitical challenges, the likeness took on new nuances. Many explicitly or tacitly agreed with Jacob Blaustein, president of the historically non-Zionist American Jewish Committee, who intoned that "with our aid, Israel, like our own United States, can become a positive force for democracy and for international peace and order."[25] No mere rhetorical flourish, this statement encapsulated exactly how many of Israel's American supporters (including Herbert Lehman of the American Committee for Israel's Tenth Anniversary Celebration) understood that nation's strategic value in the Cold War era— as "both a haven for the persecuted and a doughty democracy surrounded by and threatened with destruction by totalitarian Arab regimes allied . . . with an expansionist Soviet Union," in historian Arthur Goren's analysis.[26]

Yet it is easy to forget that, at the time, the nature of American Jewry's long-term relationship to Israel was unclear and potentially problematic. The emergence of Israel was a unique event, without precedent within the American Jewish experience. Aside from a small population of European émigrés and Holocaust survivors, postwar American Jews no longer constituted an immigrant community. America was home, a land freely chosen by immigrant parents and grandparents, most of whom had arrived from Central and Eastern Europe in the nineteenth and early twentieth centuries seeking better economic opportunities and relief from persecution. The ties, real and symbolic, that connected American Jews to the lands of their close ancestors were fast receding into communal memory. Suddenly, third-generation American Jews were faced with the reality of a new nation-state, one that declared itself the true homeland of world Jewry, the end to two millennia of exile.

Moreover, Israel's status among American political elites was in fact far from clear. While this is not a book of diplomatic history, it is worth bearing in mind how shifts in the political discourse and in American Jews' access or lack of access to the highest echelons of government power may have shaped their approach to, and renderings of, Israel. Though members of the U.S. Congress and the American public expressed sympathy for the Jewish state, the White House and State Department continued to debate whether Israel was a strategic asset or a liability in the Middle East. In 1956, Israel provoked the ire of the Eisenhower administration by covertly arranging and then executing an aggressive military campaign, with the help of France and Britain, to halt Egypt's nationalization of the Suez Canal. In the waning years of the 1950s, the United States' relationship with Israel was tentative at times and generally inconsistent; as the American government weighed Arab nations and Israel as potential allies against the Soviet Union, American Jewish leaders made the case for Israel's strategic value and its security needs while wielding little actual influence with the Eisenhower administration.[27]

This scenario changed, to some extent, with the administration of John F. Kennedy, the first American president to articulate the notion of a "special relationship" between the United States and Israel.[28] Kennedy and Lyndon B. Johnson, both of whom courted Jews as a prime Democratic constituency, expressed steadfast American support for Israel's continuing independence. In contrast to Kennedy, however, Johnson had positioned himself as an outspoken friend of Israel early in his career, and it was under Johnson's administration, especially after 1967, that the ties between the United States and Israel evolved into a clear patron-client relationship. Yet in terms of foreign policy, both Kennedy and Johnson sought, above all, to guarantee America's strategic interests in the Middle East and in the Cold War generally.[29] In sum, for much of the period under consideration, American Jews could safely assume the good will of much of the American public toward Israel while being less sure that their vision of appropriate U.S.-Israel relations always cohered with that of the government.

In these circumstances, Israel's true import, in terms of sustained influence on American Jewish life, was impossible to predict. While the establishment of Israel "clearly marked a turning point in Jewish history," as the *American Jewish Year Book* announced in its review of the year 1947–48, "the significance and long-range implications of this event could not . . . be fully appraised" while matters were still so fresh and so volatile.[30] Larger questions loomed about Israel's impact on American Jewish life.[31] On the one hand, widespread support for and sympathy with the Jewish state heralded a new, enhanced role for Israel within the American Jewish mainstream. In the Jewish organizational sphere, this trend was exemplified by Hadassah, the Women's Zionist Organization of America, whose pragmatic and popular brand of Zionism helped transform Israel into a fixture of suburban Jewish life in the 1950s. Other sectors of organized American Zionism fared less well, however, experiencing a steep decline not only in membership but also, more critically, in influence.[32] Put simply, political Zionism faced an unprecedented crisis of purpose in the United States after 1948. The paradox was immediately apparent: as the American Jewish masses embraced Israel as a nearly universal communal cause and as the Israeli government assumed sovereignty in its political affairs, the leaders of American Zionism found themselves sidelined as activists and intermediaries.[33]

It is difficult to say with precision what "counts" as Zionism in this context. For hardline Israeli Zionists such as Israel's first prime minister, David Ben-Gurion, and some American Zionist intellectuals, to be a Zionist meant putting the state of Israel at the very center of Jewish political, economic, and organizational life.[34] Certainly, relatively few American Jews or Jewish organizations fit that description in this period. In the words of one historian, "The conversion of American Jews to full-fledged Jewish nationalism . . . never really materialized."[35] Yet historians sometimes use the term *American Zionism* more broadly, as shorthand for pro-Israel sentiment and behavior among a wider segment of the American Jewish population. In this book, I try to be as specific as possible in designating "card-carrying" Zionists as such and distinguishing hardline Zionists from those whose "love of Israel" was less ideologically precise—a description that fits the great bulk of the American Jewish population in the postwar period, even among those who actively promoted Israel's interests in the American sphere.

Mainstream American Zionism had, from the beginning, been premised on the notion of the American exception, the idea that the long-term insecurity and periodic persecutions that had characterized Jewish life elsewhere in the Diaspora had dissolved in the light of American freedom and democracy. According to this conception, Israel, like Jewish Palestine before it, was first and foremost a place of refuge and rehabilitation for Jews of other nations, not of America. At the same time, however, American Jews shared a religious, cultural, and political heritage with the people of Israel; the new state of Israel clearly meant something more to American Jews than did any other foreign nation.

Israel *seemed* to be an acceptable object of pride and interest within the context of American culture, but might support for Israel, misconstrued as political fealty to another nation, ultimately be a liability? The notion of a "dual loyalty" divided between America and Israel continued to hover at the periphery of the national discourse after 1948, occasionally emerging into the light, as in the pages of *Reader's Digest* in 1949 and *Commentary* in 1950.[36] Those figures who publicly rejected the dual loyalty charge, such as rabbi and Zionist leader Abba Hillel Silver and Harvard historian Oscar Handlin, argued that the maintenance of bonds between hyphenate Americans and their nations of origin—or affinity—was a valid, healthy facet of American life. Such assertions surely heartened American Jews, but hardly laid the matter to rest: anxiety about the dual loyalty charge fed the rancorous response to David Ben-Gurion's repeated calls for American Jewish immigration to Israel, for example, necessitating the so-called Blaustien–Ben-Gurion Understanding of 1950. (In it, the Israeli prime minister affirmed, in writing, that American Jews' only political loyalty was to the United States.)[37]

In contrast to the community's hardline Zionists, who did not view Jewish nationalism as inherently compatible with American interests, many American Jews sought to position Israel as a "natural" fit with American interests and values. American Jews' turn to culture, and their engagement with Israel within the cultural realm, cohered well with the American discourse of consensus at mid-century. In this period, as Wendy Wall has argued, elites in the spheres of business, politics, religion, and culture eschewed conflict in the public sphere and developed a shared public lexicon that stressed American virtues such as "freedom" and "diversity" as a source of national unity in the Cold War (even as these elites actually disagreed about what those terms meant).[38]

Applying Wall's insights to the cultural phenomena at hand, we can begin to trace the ways in which many of Israel's American Jewish supporters insisted that "culture" was a forum for the public good, a site of consensus rather than conflict. If "culture" was, ostensibly, a vehicle for furthering human aspirations, safeguarding individual freedom, and encouraging mutual education, who could argue with that? Certainly, by the late 1960s one could no longer pretend that American culture was a placid, harmonious meeting ground for diverse social and economic groups with sometimes conflicting agendas. By that time, too, American Jews had begun vociferously contesting Jewish communal ideals, goals, and methods, as historian Michael Staub has illustrated.[39] Even in the face of increasingly fractious debates about the values and aims of the postwar Jewish community in the course of the 1960s, American Jews did seem, for a time, to shape "culture" into a safe haven from which they could map their relationship with Israel, on the one hand, and with America, on the other.

Whether reading "Israel books," dancing Israeli folk dances, promoting Israeli goods, or sponsoring presentations of Israeli art and music, American Jews were careful to articulate that their behavior fully aligned with American mores and goals. As true believers in "diversity" as a chief American value—an idea that loomed large in the mid-century discourse of consensus—Israel's American Jewish impresarios viewed their cultural engagements with Israel as legitimate expressions of American identity. They premised their behavior on the idea that a reasonable degree of cultural difference buttressed democratic claims and maintained cultural vitality, enriching American life even as it aided America's cause in the larger postwar world.[40]

REASSESSING POSTWAR AMERICAN JEWS AND THEIR CULTURE

The basic social and economic patterns of American Jewry in the first postwar decades are beyond debate: namely, increasing professionalization, affluence, and large-scale suburbanization.[41] In electing to buy houses in the burgeoning suburbs, as a vast and increasing majority of American Jews did in this period, young families left behind the cramped ethnic neighborhoods of their youth and "created a lifestyle and a cultural milieu built around family life, recreation for couples, and the educational and social needs of their children."[42] Formal Jewish institutions—especially suburban synagogues, founded by migrating Jews as one-stop social, ethnic, educational, and religious venues—and local Jewish social networks made up of other young families fulfilled these needs for many. Faced with unprecedented opportunities for individual advancement and a new landscape in which to chart their lives, American Jews stood at the threshold of a new era, one that "as a whole was defined by choice," as historian Hasia Diner has argued.[43]

Interpreting the ensuing cultural gestalt is a more contentious undertaking. Indeed, the development at the heart of this book—that is, Israel's emergence as a substantial and nuanced influence on American Jewish culture—has been obscured, in part, by a foggy critical discourse about American Jewish culture in the first postwar decades, a combination of contemporaneous pessimism, popular memory, and later scholarship. American Jews of the postwar period have often been taken to task for their political and social conformity, intellectual and spiritual vacuity, and rank materialism; similar indictments extend to their engagements with Israel in these years, which have commonly been characterized as trivial, trite, and vulgar. As American studies scholar Riv-Ellen Prell has shown, Jewish intellectuals and social scientists writing at the time bemoaned the new suburban milieu as "a community without a culture," in contrast to the seemingly organic, unself-consciously Jewish environment of the (now moribund) ethnic urban neighborhood.[44] Condemnations of Jewish suburbanites and their practices bore the influence of postwar intellectual preoccupations with conformism and mass culture as dangerous societal forces while also revealing specifically American Jewish concerns about authenticity and the viability of Jewish life in a posturban, postimmigrant setting.[45]

Products of suburban Judaism—that is, American Jewish baby boomers—coming of age in (and helping to shape) the political, social, and cultural ferment of the 1960s voiced this critique most forcefully, both at the time and afterward. Indeed, the generational identity of many American Jewish baby boomers has hinged upon the notion of resolute rejection of the allegedly shallow, stultifying Jewish culture of the 1950s. This narrative gained increasing authority as Jewish baby boomers moved into positions of power and became the gatekeepers of communal memory.[46] Hasia Diner has written compellingly about this phenomenon, making the case that the Jewish activists of the boomer generation, who saw in "their parents' institutions, practices, and ways of thinking . . . all that was shallow, compromising, and wrong with America and its Jews," helped shape the mistaken notion that pre-1967 American Jewry was silent on the subject of the Holocaust.[47] The boomers' condemnations of the mainstream American Zionism of their suburban childhoods—the accusation that Israel did not enter into postwar Jewish life in meaningful ways—appear to follow a similar logic.

Such voices within the academy, too, have cast the feasibility of postwar American Jewish culture into doubt. In recent years, for example, some scholars have accused postwar American Jewry of cultivating a "culture of retrieval" based on nostalgia for the immigrant milieu and have indicted this cohort for prizing individual achievement and societal integration over Jewish commitments.[48] Postwar American Jewish culture continues to provoke anxious misgivings among some of the most astute observers of the American Jewish experience.

Rather than engaging in a "discourse of elegy,"[49] that traces the dissolution of American Jewish life and culture, some scholars have instead analyzed the altered landscape of postwar American Jewish culture in light of its innovative adaptation to new realities. Cultural historian Jeffrey Shandler has written persuasively, for example, of the postwar period as one of "new opportunities" (i.e., an expanded array of public cultural venues) and "new paradigms" for American Jewish culture. On the latter subject, he has described the increasing importance of "culture" in the postwar period as a category for defining and constructing Jewishness, akin to the highly elective nature of religious self-definition rather than to the "ethnic, national, political and especially racial identities," that constituted Jewishness in America before World War II.[50]

In reassessing American Jews' early encounters with Israel, this study adopts Shandler's perspective. It argues *against* the idea that culture is, by implicit or explicit definition, "natural" and not constructed. In contrast, I view culture as a sphere of activity that, like politics or philanthropy, may be deliberately created, organizational in nature, and chiefly public in expression. It is perhaps fair to say that, for most American Jews of the postwar era, Jewishness was not "almost as natural as breathing,"[51] as one historian has characterized Jewish identity in the pre–World War II period. This does not mean, however, that Jewish culture ceased to evolve or to matter within the postimmigrant milieu. In analyzing the cultural channels through which Israel entered the lives of many American Jews, this book illustrates, to the contrary, that postwar Jewish culture—selected and selective—became a purposeful group project of increasing import.

THE TURN TOWARD CULTURE

Historical evidence suggests that postwar American Jewish culture was a fertile and growing field as well as an increasingly public endeavor. Just as suburban pioneers deliberately reconceived the synagogue and posed formal affiliation as an answer to the erstwhile, informal "Jewish street," so too did American Jews construct new and expanded formal cultural arenas in response to the challenges of postwar Jewish life.

The publishing world, for example, was one such site of invention and growth. In the same years that the American Yiddish newspapers, once influential and ubiquitous, faded from prominence, Jewish organizations and intellectuals established major journals of opinion such as *Commentary*, *Midstream*, and *Congress Weekly* as public platforms for assessing and debating American Jewish culture and politics (including American Zionism and relations with Israel).[52] In the postwar period the Jewish Book Council, founded in 1943, reached growing audiences with its Jewish Book Month programs, while major American libraries set about augmenting and improving their Judaica collections.[53] At the same time, Jewish subject matter was becoming increasingly visible in the realm of popular fiction: in 1955, Herman Wouk's *Marjorie Morningstar*, the story of a young Jewish woman's coming-of-age in 1930s New York, became a national best-seller. Three years later, Leon Uris's *Exodus*—which presented the saga of Israel's birth from the ashes of the Holocaust—achieved even greater popularity.[54]

In this period, too, preeminent Jewish institutions and organizations created new programs and venues as part of their mission to enrich American

Jewish life, secure its longevity, and educate the wider public about Judaism and Jewish culture. The Jewish Theological Seminary beamed programs on Jewish themes over the radio and airwaves during its broadcasts of *The Eternal Light* and oversaw the opening of a refurbished Jewish Museum on Fifth Avenue, New York's museum mile, in 1947.[55] In 1945, the Jewish Music Council, a new subsidiary of the National Jewish Welfare Board, instituted its Jewish Music Festival as an annual, nationwide event. Fifteen years later, in 1960, the Council of Jewish Federations and Welfare Funds established the National Foundation for Jewish Culture as "the central address for the total Jewish cultural enterprise in America."[56] As historian Stuart Svonkin has noted, even the American Jewish Congress, an organization that then applied itself primarily to protection of civil liberties, began sponsoring cultural events such as book fairs and music festivals as part of an expanded program to "promote a healthy self-knowledge and positive identification of Jews with Judaism."[57] The postwar period also witnessed a renaissance in synagogue architecture and in the design of Jewish ceremonial art.[58]

This cultural flourishing within the American Jewish community mirrored the broader American moment; by many accounts, the postwar United States was experiencing a surge in cultural life. While the consumption of mass culture—television, popular music, and so on—exploded most forcefully as a national trend, so too did interest in the arts seem to be swelling. In his contemporaneous study of postwar America "at work and play," published in 1959, business economist A. W. Zelomek found increased interest and demand among American audiences in the spheres of literature, music, dance, and art, as measured by growing figures in sales and attendance.[59] Examining an array of evidence, sociologist Alvin Toffler agreed that America was experiencing "a great expansion in culture consumption."[60] Americans were not only buying books and attending museums in unprecedented numbers, he argued, but they were also "active amateurs" who made time to paint, play music, and study dance in their everyday lives.[61] August Heckscher, appointed special consultant on the arts to John F. Kennedy in 1962, captured the optimistic strains of this cultural uptick when he wrote that "it is through the enjoyment of art . . . that public happiness is ultimately attained."[62]

A number of factors shaped this broad cultural revitalization. Rising affluence after years of fiscal sobriety meant that, finally, people were able and eager to spend money—not only on an expanding array of modern, mass-produced goods, but also on tickets to the local symphony and art museum (as well as the sports arena).[63] The slightly decreased workweek of the first postwar decades and the widespread adoption of annual paid vacations were crucial, too, in this regard, granting middle-class Americans leisure time heretofore reserved for the moneyed elite.[64] The culture boom was also indebted to the surge in education, characterized by exploding matriculation numbers in colleges and universities following the passage of the GI Bill in 1944.[65]

American Jews exhibited these patterns to an even greater extent than their non-Jewish compatriots, positioning this minority population as key cultural producers and consumers.[66] While the New York intellectuals associated with *The Partisan Review* and *Commentary* were among the most celebrated and influential American Jewish cultural arbiters of the postwar era, growing numbers of rank-and-file American Jews, too, partook of the cultural opportunities at hand. "The burgeoning number of American Jews who attended college in the post–World War II era created a new kind of widely shared literacy, informed by the scope and sensibilities of liberal arts curricula," a phenomenon that these Jews carried into their postcollege lives as middle-class citizens.[67]

Beyond the magazine offices of New York and the halls of academe, the increasingly affluent and educated American Jewish masses applied themselves with vigor to the acquisition of culture. Alvin Toffler noted in his book *The Culture Consumers* that American Jews—young, well-educated, and financially secure—made up a disproportionately large portion of the new "culture public."[68] Jewish women, it seems, were particularly avid culture consumers. Noting that, "many suburban Jews are interested in and thoroughly enjoy the theatre, ballet, the opera, museums—indeed, all forms of art," sociologist Albert Gordon cast Jewish women as the motivating factor in such behavior.[69] Likewise, Gordon found Jewish women to be the primary adult readers and learners, particularly in regard to Jewish subject matter, in the suburban Jewish household.[70] Cultural commentator David Boroff also cited the significance of Jewish women in this role (which, as a reversal of traditional male stewardship of Jewish learning, he considered "a melancholy and inescapable truth"): "They buy the books," he wrote, "they act as tastemakers, and, with missionary zeal, they get their husbands to read worthwhile books."[71] So, too, did Jews ensure their children's exposure to Jewish culture. In suburban Nassau County, for example, synagogue classes embarked on field trips to New York to visit Jewish exhibitions, performances, and other sites at which students could explore aspects of Jewish culture."[72] As these and earlier examples suggest, American Jewish women and men—pursuing specifically Jewish and more general cultural offerings alike—deliberately shaped "culture" both as a public project and as a personal, familial, and communal preoccupation in the postwar years.

I argue in this book that this cultural impulse was bound up with multiple, interrelated agendas. On the one hand, adopting Israel as a focus for such activity allowed American Jews to create what they felt was an authentically Jewish culture in postwar America, a major desideratum of the posturban, postimmigrant milieu. On the other, American Jews shaped their stewardship of Israeli culture into a means of polishing their social and cultural status outside the Jewish community and thus of hastening integration into middle-class American life. Equally significant, American Jews felt they were contributing to America's welfare: in these years, influential cultural and political elites positioned "culture" as both an engine of American dominance and as a purveyor of peace in the Cold War. These elites "represented the Cold War as an opportunity to forge intellectual and emotional bonds" with people in Europe, Asia, Africa, and Latin America; it was through the creation of such ties, as Christina Klein has argued, that the U.S. government insisted that the "economic, political, and military integration of the 'free world' [would] be achieved and sustained."[73] The State Department and the United States Information Agency worked in tandem to send American art exhibitions, films, musical artists, and dance troupes all over the world; Congress's passage of the International Cultural Exchange and Trade Fair Participation Act in 1956 illustrates how central cultural diplomacy had become as a strategy for winning the Cold War.[74] To many American Jews, cultural patronage of and exchange with Israel seemed to offer an opportunity for them to advance America's interests abroad, or, at the very least, to proclaim that they were trying to do so.[75]

In this light, it is no wonder that the cultural sphere served American Jews as an appealing locus for exploring their relationship with the new nation of Israel. The chapters that follow detail the key cultural arenas in which American Jews did this. First, I consider Israel's place in the publishing world. I trace the appearance of an ever-growing corpus of "Israel books," particularly nonfiction, intended for popular audiences, which presented American readers with a body of seemingly authoritative (and highly partisan) accounts of Israel's birth and early years. Its authors, from journalists to self-proclaimed housewives, introduced an Israel at once heroic and quotidian to American Jewish audiences and established Israel as a mainstay of the postwar publishing industry.

From here, I move from words to "things"—that is, from books to bodies and objects. I consider the popularization of Israeli folk dance in the postwar United States through the efforts of Jewish educators and choreographers, American Zionist youth, and non-Jewish aficionados of international folk dance, each of which had particular (and sometimes contradictory) goals in mind. This chapter explores how Israeli folk dance provided participants a legitimate means of exploring Jewish difference, both in the American Jewish community and on the public stage, within the context of Cold War cultural politics. Turning next to material and consumer culture, I trace how two American Jewish organizations propagated support for Israeli-made goods—from bathing suits to Hanukkah menorahs—as a means of aiding Israel, acting as tasteful middle-class consumers, and spreading American-style capitalism and democracy. Though members of Hadassah, synagogue sisterhoods, and the America-Israel Chamber of Commerce and Industry thought of their activities as nonpolitical in nature, I find that, as promoters of Israeli goods, these influential American Jewish organizations increasingly blurred the boundaries between economic, cultural, and political advocacy on Israel's behalf.

In the last chapter, I return to the realm of "high" culture to examine the stewardship and critical reception of Israeli fine art and music. I pay particular attention to the contrasting values and expectations of American Jewish "boosters" of Israeli culture, including (prominently) the America-Israel Cultural Foundation, and those of the critical establishment in the postwar United States, asking, How did each "community" understand the significance of Israel's cultural endeavors? This chapter illuminates how and why some American Jews, fueled by a combination of cultural aspiration, ethnic pride, entrepreneurial savvy, and political commitment, worked diligently to introduce Israeli culture to American audiences in the 1950s and 1960s.

I argue throughout the book that follows that the promotion and consumption of books, dance, fashion, household ornaments, music, and art presented sanctioned, satisfying avenues for American Jews to grapple with Israel's role in American life. So, too, did the cultural realm appear to provide a neutral, mutually beneficent arena in which American Jews might introduce Israel to their non-Jewish neighbors. Through the channels described in this book, American Jews argued for Israel's "natural" place in American Jewish culture—and in American culture more broadly.

It is true that Israel rose to the top of the political and philanthropic agenda of the American Jewish community only in times when Israel faced serious existential threats—chiefly in 1948 and 1967, and, to a lesser extent, during the Suez-Sinai War of 1956. This study challenges the view, however, that Israel "by no means came to preoccupy American Jews in the 1950s," as one prominent historian has written, or that postwar American Jews "did not see Israel as a source of strength or inspiration for their own needs," in the words of another.[76] It holds with those who cite *Exodus* (the 1958 book and 1960 movie) as a major touchstone in American Jewish culture and a breakthrough moment for Israel's popularity within and beyond that culture. But this book reassesses even that narrative by providing the context for the success of *Exodus*. It argues that what might be termed "the *Exodus* phenomenon"—the rapid mainstreaming of Israel in American Jewish life—

was *not* based upon a single incident but, rather, grew out of a cumulative body of cultural imaginings and practices.

Israel, in contrast to the Holocaust, presented American Jews a vision of Jewish destiny rife with hope and possibility. It offered them a positive opportunity to reimagine and reshape the Jewish present and Jewish future. American Jews explored this opportunity not only in the spheres of political action and philanthropy, as has been well documented, but in the realm of culture. This book argues that, as "culture" grew ever more central to Jewish life and discourse in the early postwar decades, Israel became essential to the creation of that culture. In bringing Zion home, American Jews attempted to secure a place for themselves in the American landscape.

TWO

BEFORE *EXODUS*

Writing Israel for an American Audience

In the introduction to *Palestine: Land of Israel*, published in the United States in 1948, journalist Pierre van Paassen cast his eye over the vistas of the Holy Land, comparing the landscape encountered by nineteenth and early-twentieth-century European travelers to that which greeted the contemporary visitor. "In less than thirty years' time," he proclaimed, "the Land of Israel has undergone a transformation which is indeed nothing less than wondrous. . . . With a loving care and ceaseless effort . . . the Jews have recovered what seemed but a few years ago irremediably lost beneath layers of rock and sand and neglect."[1] Van Paassen's rapturous introductory essay on the Zionist redemption of the land was followed by more than one hundred pages of photographs by Herbert Sonnenfeld capturing, in black and white, a spectrum of Jewish life in Palestine: the boulevards of Tel Aviv and the irrigation ditches of a Negev kibbutz; the port of Haifa and a prayer hall in Jerusalem; the "husky young chalutz," scythe in hand, the "immigrant lad" in prayer shawl and phylacteries, and the "proud, fine-featured" descendent of Spanish Jews, in his beard and fez.[2]

As early as the 1920s, American readers had glimpsed the Zionist "rehabilitation" of Israel through the eyes of influential public figures such as Horace Kallen and John Hayes Holmes, both of whom had written laudatory books about brave and steadfast Zionist pioneers in Palestine.[3] The mid-1940s had seen a spike in nonfiction works by both Jews and non-Jews; among them was Walter Clay Lowdermilk's *Palestine, Land of Promise*, published in 1944, which became a best-seller. Political scientist Samuel Halperin has shown that Zionist organizations such as the Zionist Organization of America sometimes subsidized Zionist-friendly books and certainly promoted them vigorously during an increasingly well-coordinated campaign in the 1940s to shape American public opinion in favor of a Jewish state in Palestine.[4]

Now, however, the context had changed. The Land of Israel had become the State of Israel. Copies of *Palestine: Land of Israel* hit American shelves in the fall of 1948 with an editor's note appended: the Zionist dream had come true, and Israel was a full-fledged nation. The photographs that followed stood now as "a simple yet dramatic chronicle of a nation in the making"; it was the story, the editor rhapsodized, of "a heroic people who, after centuries of oppression and exile, have at last achieved nationhood."[5]

Palestine: Land of Israel was one of more than three dozen books about Israel published in the United States in the first several years after the establishment of the Jewish state. (In contrast, nonfiction books published between 1947 and 1951 about Pakistan and Burma, nations that had also recently gained independence, numbered three each, in total.)[6] A "popular hunger and pressure for information" appeared to be driving the profusion of books about Zionism, Israel, and the recent Israeli War of Independence, according to one cultural commentator in the American Jewish community.[7] Remarking on the phenomenon in *Commentary* magazine, Milton Himmelfarb wrote, similarly, that he saw "no sign that the flood of books [about Israel] pouring off the presses will abate soon."[8] The profusion of nonfiction titles about Israel that had appeared by the early 1950s suggests that, for publishers at the very least, the American appetite for Israel was vast and unslakable.

Indeed, this was precisely the scenario conveyed by the *Jewish Book Annual*, a yearly roundup of Jewish book news and bibliographies published by the Jewish Book Council. While the large volume of titles on Palestine/Israel published in the year 1948–49 reflected Israel's significance in global affairs at that time, there seemed to be no slowdown in publications even as Israel receded from the headlines. Far from wearying of the subject, publishers continued to bring out title after title on Israel. "Either there has been a delayed reaction in the writing and printing of these books, all inspired by the events of a couple of years ago, or the publishers still have confidence in public receptivity," wrote Carl Alpert in the 1951 *Jewish Book Annual*.[9] Almost all of the major American publishing houses were now invested in the topic, he noted. Reviews of—and advertisements for—"Israel" books appeared regularly in American Jewish publications in this period, from journals of opinion such as *The Reconstructionist* and *Commentary* to mass-circulation magazines such as *Women's League Outlook* and the *National Jewish Monthly*.

In part, the receptivity to books on Israel mirrored an upswing in interest in Jewish books generally in the immediate postwar years, a prime example of the turn toward culture among American Jews in an effort to secure the long-term viability of Jewish life in America.[10] It is essentially impossible to tally the precise number of Jewish books being purchased and read by American Jews at this (or any) time. According to data collected by the Jewish Book Council, however, it appeared that a growing number of American Jewish organizations, institutions, and individuals were participating in Jewish book–related programming and turning to the Jewish Book Council for resources and advice (such as bibliographies and reviews) on building communal libraries and home collections.[11] These phenomena suggest that American Jews shared the Jewish Book Council's goals of stimulating Jewish knowledge and developing "a Jewish cultural atmosphere in the home."[12]

One of the Jewish Book Council's primary projects in this regard was to encourage American Jews to devote time to reading both Jewish classics and contemporary publications, including literature from and about modern-day Israel.[13] The council promoted a "home ceremony" in honor of Jewish Book Month, for example, comprising a medley of Jewish publications, including adaptations of Israeli songs and poetry.[14] Jewish community centers celebrating Jewish Book Month in the early 1950s arranged "Israeli programs" along with other special events for their constituencies.[15] And in a public event that implicitly merged politics and culture, Abba Eban, Israeli ambassador to the United States, held forth on "the Renaissance of Hebrew Literature in Israel" before an audience at the Library of Congress in 1950.[16]

Publishers and booksellers, too, stood to gain from a ready-made audience of Jewish readers of Jewish books, including books about Israel. *Publishers' Weekly* carried announcements and news about the special market for Jewish books, apprising retailers of such events as the Dexter-Davidson Jewish Community Center's second annual book fair (in Detroit, in 1953), which promised the participation of twenty-five publishers, many visiting authors, and attendance numbers in the thousands. The emphasis, the editors assured its industry audience, would be on "get[ting] more books into the home."[17] In a talk before the Women's National Book Association reprinted in *Publishers' Weekly*, Mortimer Cohen—a rabbi as well as the editor of the Jewish Book Council's magazine *In Jewish Bookland*—counseled bookshop owners to court Jewish readers with special Jewish interest book sections and promotions. And "Jewish books" did not simply mean religious tomes. "When a Jew speaks about Jewish books, he means books about Palestine, novels about Jewish life, Jewish history, books about Jewish education, Jewish cook books," he explained. Cohen noted further that, in the campaign for Jewish readers, Jewish organizations were significant allies. Hadassah, the National Council of Jewish Women, and other organizations "are all potential 'book carriers,'" he advised, "and all, or most of them, have their own publications which frequently mention books."[18]

While "Israel books" comprised one genre among many in the postwar Jewish publishing scene, they also seemed to constitute a special phenomenon in the Jewish book world. Beginning in 1950, the Jewish Book Council devoted a special section of its *Jewish Book Annual* to "American Books on Zionism and Israel." Although some evidence pointed to a slackening of Jewish book consumption in the early 1950s,[19] the appearance of "Israel" books seems, in fact, to have continued unabated, defying the news of a possible Jewish publishing slump. Indeed, judging from the annual lists of titles in the *Jewish Book Annual*, the roster of new publications about Israel either held steady or increased slightly from year to year through the late 1950s.

Several books about Israel published in the years immediately following Israel's establishment counted among the most noteworthy nonfiction titles on the subject. I turn to three of these books in this study: Robert St. John's *Shalom Means Peace* (1949), Ruth Gruber's *Israel Without Tears* (1950), and Molly Lyons Bar-David's *My Promised Land* (1953). I considered two major factors in selecting these particular works: the elevated status of the individual authors as professional writers and public personalities and the attention granted to these books and their authors by American Jewish publications and the mainstream media.[20] The limits of space, too, are a factor. Although books such as Jorge Garcia-Granados's *Birth of Israel* (1949), James G. McDonald's *My Mission in Israel* (1951), and I. F. Stone's *This Is Israel* (1949) fit the rubric detailed above, I have included only limited references to these books, for comparative purposes, due to space constraints. All these books, long neglected by historians, were certainly among the first to position Israel, implicitly and explicitly, as an American partner in the postwar world. Significantly, these titles are among the earliest, most visible attempts within the publishing world to position the new state of Israel as an appropriate focus of attention for American readers—and as a subject worthy of continued consumption (as publishers hoped).

"Tough Jews," to borrow Paul Breines's resonant phrase, abound in the pages of the most popular nonfiction books about Israel, with American Jews (as well as non-Jewish Americans) depicted as heroic fighters alongside their Israeli counterparts.[21] Historian Michelle Mart has argued that coverage of Israel in the American mainstream media in the 1940s and 1950s was surfeit with masculine representations of Israel. According to Mart, hypermasculine rhetoric and images about Israelis were premised upon and reinforced a gendered discourse about the Cold War. In contrast to earlier renderings of Jews in American popular culture as weak and cowardly, images of Israelis in *Time, Life,* and *The Saturday Evening Post* (among others) as manly, disciplined fighters positioned that population, and American Jews by extension, as "like us"—that is, like other (non-Jewish) Americans.[22]

I wish to complicate this scenario, however, by drawing attention to a new type of "Israel" literature, exemplified by Molly Lyons Bar-David's *My Promised Land*, which I call the "American housewives in Israel" subgenre. Though this writing, too, was thick with masculine images of fighters and leaders, books about the Jewish state written by (and for) American women translated the contemporaneous Israeli experience for the postwar American housewife. This literature focused upon the quotidian demands of child rearing and household management during the Israeli struggle for independence and in the early years of statehood. Bar-David's book in particular offered (presumably female) American readers an intriguing combination of historical drama and homespun vignette, arguing implicitly that the home front in Israel was as riveting a setting as the front lines. Even books that were not written explicitly from this perspective—including Ruth Gruber's *Israel Without Tears* and James McDonald's *My Mission in Israel,* for example—included anecdotes and metaphors about Israel that drew upon the assumed experiences and perspective of the American housewife.[23] Considering that American Jewish women appeared to be the chief consumers of Jewish books in the postwar household, one must take this subgenre into serious consideration in order to grasp how contemporary readers encountered and perceived Israel.[24]

Crucially, the books under consideration in this chapter presented Israel as essentially analogous to the United States. To be sure, nonfiction about Israel in this period almost invariably alerted the reader to the picturesque and exotic aspects of life there—a practice that extended back to the popular travelogues of the Holy Land published in the United States in the nineteenth century.[25] By and large, however, the authors of these books measured their experience of Israel with a postwar American yardstick and insisted that the two nations were comparable in many telling ways. In a practice rampant in contemporaneous writing about Israel, for example, authors underscored the compatibility of the two nations, often by invoking shared historical themes such as the settlement of the frontier, the battle for independence, and the absorption of immigrants. They also conjured the Israel of biblical tradition (Jewish and Christian), a staple of the American religious imagination.[26]

Thus, while all of the authors under consideration attempted, in one way or another, to hold a mirror up to contemporary Israeli life, their books are, in the end, a more accurate reflection of American sensibilities in the late 1940s and early 1950s than of Israel itself. Much like their successor on the fiction lists, *Exodus,* the major nonfiction books about Israel in the early post-state period presented images of Israel that appealed to American audiences and were compatible with American ideologies—not only political, but cultural, in the broadest sense. Of the hundreds of books on Israel published in the United States in the late 1940s and 1950s, it appears that only a handful adopted a pro-Arab or anti-Zionist perspective or expressed serious misgivings about Israel.[27] On the whole, American books about the Jewish state, including those examined here, depicted Israel as an enthralling moral, spiritual, and social experiment. Their authors and publishers assumed that American Jews and others would make buying and reading such books a priority—a supposition that many thousands of readers seemed to share.

TWO BOOKS BY AMERICAN JOURNALISTS IN ISRAEL

By the 1940s, a new breed of American public personality—the professional journalist—was alighting on the stretch of contested ground that would soon become the modern state of Israel. In the "'Golden Age' of American foreign correspondence" (the years just before, during, and after World War II), professional journalists such as Dorothy Thompson, John Gunther, William L. Shirer, and Walter Duranty translated events in Europe for Americans and sharpened the public's knowledge of and interest in international affairs.[28] By 1948, some American foreign correspondents were employing the tools of their trade—in many cases, honed in war-torn Europe—to capture a roiling Middle East at the crossroads. Although few media outlets apparently assigned reporters to the region full time until the Arab-Israeli War in 1967, the mainstream press in the United States lavished attention on Israel in the years surrounding that nation's birth. Articles and editorials on Israel's fight for independence, its role in global and regional politics, its national leadership, and its continuing conflict with the Arabs, for example, appeared in the *New York Times, Washington Post, New York Herald Tribune, The Atlantic, The New Republic, The New Yorker, Newsweek, Time,* and *Life,* among other publications.[29]

The book format, however, offered journalists a chance to roam more widely, interview more extensively, and ruminate more expansively than did newspaper or magazine articles. From the presumed perspective of organizations such as the Jewish Book Council, moreover, the medium provided a more lasting cultural and educational impact, as a permanent part of the family or communal bookshelf, than a daily newspaper or weekly magazine could. Journalists Robert St. John, I. F. Stone, and Ruth Gruber all produced book-length treatments of Israel in the 1940s, as did George Fielding Eliot, a former military intelligence officer for the United States who had become a commentator and writer on military affairs on radio and in the press.[30] St. John's book, published in 1949, was among the first of the "'eyewitness' journalistic literature" genre to achieve "a high degree of popularity" among American readers.[31] As a popular journalist—he had scooped the announcement of the end of World War II while reporting for NBC, and his first book about Yugoslavia, *From the Land of the Silent People* (1942), was a bestseller—St. John reached a wide swath of the American public in the 1940s and 1950s.[32]

St. John had been a reporter in southeastern Europe in the 1930s and 1940s, arriving in Israel in the wake of its independence, and the Holocaust—glimpsed in passing—was intimately tied to the moral calculus of *Shalom Means Peace*. St. John was explicit about the role that the mass murder of European Jewry played in piquing his interest in the Jewish state. As he wrote in his foreword to the book, St. John, living in Bucharest at the time of a massacre of local Jews by the fascist Iron Guard, considered his brief encounter with the murder of Europe's Jews "merely [his] introduction to the disease of anti-Semitism."[33] "I remembered the abattoir of Bucharest when I decided to go off to witness the birth of a nation in the Middle East and watch its struggle to keep alive," he continued. And while St. John arrived and departed from Palestine "convinced that nationalism is one of the root evils of modern civilization," he firmly believed that the international community had left the Jews of Palestine no feasible choice for survival (3).

Other notable "Israel books" published contemporaneously with St. John's constructed a similar moral framework. Indeed, historian Hasia Diner has noted the important role of books such as Stone's *This is Israel* and Gruber's *Israel Without Tears* as a means of communal advocacy among American Jews on behalf of Holocaust survivors.[34] Both Jorge Garcia-Granados's *The Birth of Israel* and I. F. Stone's *This Is Israel,* for example, dealt directly and repeatedly with the genocide of European Jewry and presented it as evidence for the necessity of a Jewish state. Garcia-Granados, whose book detailed his experiences as a member of the United Nation's Special Committee on Palestine in 1947, wrote of his encounters with Holocaust survivors both in Europe and in Palestine as he gathered facts for UNCSOP. The author presented the case for moral restitution most bluntly when describing a visit to a kibbutz comprised of child survivors. Asking, upon his departure, what he could do to help them, the children reportedly declared in unison, "Give us a Jewish State."[35] Stone, meanwhile, had written extensively about Jewish DPs and the effort to smuggle Jews illegally to Palestine after World War II for *PM* magazine and in his book *Underground to Palestine* (1946). In *This Is Israel,* based on his eyewitness experiences in Israel from March 1948 through the first months of Israel's independence, Stone referred continually to Hitler, the Nazis, the death camps, and crematoria in determining Israel's right to take up arms for independence.[36]

These precepts—that the Nazi genocide necessitated the establishment of Israel, and that the Israelis had no alternative route to survival than to fight for an independent Jewish state—underlay St. John's narrative throughout the book. Beneath these two fundamental beliefs lay a third: that Americans had a moral responsibility to support the state of Israel. To this end, St. John focused particular attention on a number of Americans who had heeded the call to arms on Israel's behalf.[37]

The author thus introduced readers to Monroe Fein, a former GI who had grown up in a "typically middle-class, Middle-Western Jewish family" in Chicago (32). A Navy lieutenant in the Pacific in World War II, Fein found that life as an office manager of a publishing house in postwar Chicago lacked meaning. "The war had made some sense," Fein told St. John. "I had a good idea what I was fighting for. Now I needed to find something else I could believe in" (33). Fein was made chief officer of the *Altalena*, an Irgun ship bound for Palestine with more than eight hundred European Jewish refugees as well as a stock of war weaponry, in violation of a truce between the Irgun and the Haganah. Among the passengers were some sixty English-speaking volunteers, mostly former GIs, like Fein. The *Altalena*'s entrance into Israeli waters near Tel Aviv was, famously, a disaster; according to Fein, miscommunication between the Israeli government and the crew of the *Altalena* was to blame for the deadly exchange of fire that broke out between the Irgun-manned *Altalena* and the Haganah. St. John also wrote about Jerry Rosenberg, a veteran of the Canadian navy, who told the story from the Haganah's perspective. Though, in the case of the *Altalena* incident, these young American Jews had clashed violently, St. John emphasized that such differences could be smoothed over. Their commonalities, to St. John, outweighed their differences. What mattered was that Rosenberg and Fein and others like them enlisted to fight in the Zionist cause because, in the words of one, "it was right that people in America . . . should help" in the creation of the Jewish state (43).

St. John introduced readers to other young American men who viewed Israel as a just cause, not all of them Jewish. As he wrote:

> In the summer of '48 the lobby of the Park Hotel . . . in Tel Aviv looked more like the living room of a fraternity house on some American campus than anything else. During the day there was seldom a time when there weren't at least fifteen or twenty young men sitting around speaking English in the dialects of Brooklyn, Chicago, Atlanta, Memphis, or Boston. . . . Their faces were eager, fresh, and alert. If you were to ask them point-blank, a majority would tell you that they were not Jews and had no Jewish connections . . . and the subject was never mentioned unless . . . questions were asked, which rarely happened. Even then, the non-Jews seemed to resent [the question]. (57)

St. John pressed one such young man, an Irish American named Joe Murphy, to explain his decision to fly for the Israeli Air Transport Command. What, the author prodded him on several occasions, had led him to fight on Israel's behalf? St. John reported Murphy's halting answer:

> I don't know whether I can make you understand how I feel. . . . It's just—well—it's just that I don't like to see people pushed around. These Jews have been pushed around for a long time. I saw up in Europe what they did to them. . . . These people have a right to a place to live and this is their old home. So. . . . But don't get me wrong. I'm no god-damn idealist. I don't go in for that stuff. I'm just a hard-boiled Irishman. (63)

Likewise, another Irish American GI, Jimmy Kilgore, had come to fly planes for Israel. His impressions? "He liked this place. Liked the people. His Jewish friends back home in Jasper [Alabama] hadn't lied to him. He was glad he'd come. And he was definitely coming back!" (272). So reported St. John, offering one more portrait in a gallery of young Americans with a can-do attitude and an eagerness to aid in the cause of Jewish independence.

As prominently as St. John featured intrepid fighters such as Monroe Fein and Jimmy Kilgore, he leavened the masculine imagery with a decidedly more "feminine" embodiment of commitment to the cause of Israel. Through the figure of Zapora, a young woman who appears in the last third of the book—and one of the people to whom the book is dedicated—St. John provided an alternative portrait of selfless devotion to Israel's well-being. Zapora's calling, it seems, was making the case for Israel—in "personal" rather than "ideological" terms—for the foreign correspondents, diplomats, pilots, and miscellaneous other visitors (including St. John) for whom she acted as travel agent, tour guide, and voluble friend. "Thousands of foreigners saw Palestine through Zapora's eyes," St. John wrote, explaining her influence. "Thousands who might have hated, went away with a clearer picture of what this thing called Israel . . . really meant" (231). St. John crafted Zapora as his primary ambassador to his American readership; he clearly hoped that his readers, too, would fall in love with the indomitable, irrepressible Zapora—and thus with Israel itself.

The irony, as St. John and his subjects saw it, was that Israelis believed fervently in the concept of peace but couldn't yet realize it. Zapora, like the other personalities featured in St. John's book, espoused the view that circumstances beyond their control pushed peace-seeking Israelis into war, and that no one else could be relied upon to protect the Jewish state. The phrase "shalom means peace" appeared as a refrain throughout the book, an allusion to the good will of the Israelis as well as their insistence on

the dearth of viable alternatives to war. "[The Israelis] . . . say shalom and
they . . . want peace," St. John explained early in the book, "[b]ut they are
determined not to be pushed around any longer" (18).

St. John's feelings about Israel in *Shalom Means Peace* were as straight-
forwardly positive as those he ascribed to his subjects. The author's sentiments mirrored those attributed to the young GI, Jimmy Kilgore, whom he
had interviewed for the book: like Kilgore, St. John liked the place (Israel)
and he liked the people (Israeli Jews). Introducing hardy American fighters
and determined Israeli citizens, taking the pulse of cosmopolitan Tel Aviv
and ancient Jerusalem, visiting kibbutzim and factories, St. John was an
eager student of the Israeli experience.[38]

St. John presented his sympathy for Israel as a result of his reporting
rather than as an a priori affinity. Yet his recounting of his path from fascist
Europe to newly born Israel signaled, from the first pages of the book, that
the author already viewed Israel's emergence as appropriate restitution for
the Holocaust. He demonstrated throughout the book that he believed fervently in Israel's right to exist and to defend itself. What's more, St. John's
style of reporting—one critic called it "readable, glossy journalese"[39]—did
not lend itself to analyses of the political complexities of the Israeli situation. "People, not politics, are St. John's primary interest," wrote a critic in
the *Los Angeles Times*, who found *Shalom Means Peace* to be "fresh, vital,
and enthusiastic."[40] Its value, according to reviewer Gerold Frank, was as
"the first book [on Israel] which is concerned almost wholly . . . with the
people of Israel—their way of life, their sense of humor, their hopes for the
future."[41] From a critical standpoint, *Shalom Means Peace* was breezy and
accessible at best and flagrantly biased at worst. Indeed, Herbert Poster noted
in the *American Jewish Year Book* that St. John's partisanship was "observed
by some critics and, in certain instances, severely rebuked."[42]

The publishing industry expected the book to do very well among
American readers. Alice Hackett, in her regular "Forecast for Buyers" column in *Publishers' Weekly*, detailed Doubleday's marketing strategy—rolling
out advertising to coincide with St. John's book tour, beginning in February
1949, and launching a "big campaign in regular book media"—and she predicted success. "Like his 'From the Land of the Silent People,'" she wrote,
"Robert St. John's new book is great reporting, illuminating the larger per-
plexing issues in Israel and also giving an account of the day-to-day lives
of people in conflict struggling to forge a new nation." Designating the
book "[c]onsistently absorbing and vivid reading," she assured buyers that
Shalom Means Peace would "reach a large audience, always being increased
by [St. John's] lecture tours."[43] The book did, in fact, sell very well, making
it a candidate for the national bestseller list in spring of 1949. *Publishers'
Weekly* confirmed in early April that St. John's appearance on the lecture

circuit was increasing sales, with bookstores reordering copies at a rate of 250 books a day. Later that month, Doubleday reported fifteen thousand copies had already sold.[44] Of course, such numbers cannot tell us how many of the readers were Jews or non-Jews. There is no doubt, however, that the thousands of readers who purchased *Shalom Means Peace* in the first months after its publication encountered a vision of Israel as an eminently likable, new American friend.

Jewishness was hardly a prerequisite for veneration of the Jewish state, as Robert St. John's *Shalom Means Peace* made clear. Nevertheless, *Israel Without Tears*, penned by an American Jewish woman journalist, Ruth Gruber, implicitly offered American readers an insider's perspective on the subject. Gruber began her career with the *New York Herald Tribune* in 1935, reporting from Europe and the Soviet Union. Her first book, *I Went to the Soviet Arctic*, was published by Simon and Schuster in 1939. In the immediate aftermath of World War II, she turned her attention to the plight of Jewish displaced persons, reporting on (and photographing) Palestine and Israel for the mainstream and Jewish press.[45] In 1948, Gruber published a book, *Destination Palestine*, about the earlier travails of the refugees in Cyprus awaiting permission to enter Israel—the same subject covered by Leon Uris, from a fictional perspective, ten years later in *Exodus*.[46]

With the emergence of the state of Israel, Gruber turned her attention squarely to the life and times of the Jewish homeland. Written in a lively, conversational tone, packed with information on everything from Israeli jokes to the new *sabra* physique, with settings ranging from Shabbat on the beaches of Tel Aviv to Druze weddings, *Israel Without Tears* depicted Israel as "healthy . . . robust . . . [and] full of vinegar and salt."[47] Comprehensive in breadth and partisan in perspective, *Israel Without Tears* served as a journalistic Baedeker for Americans curious about contemporary Israel—its historic struggles and triumphs, its landscape, the texture of everyday life in its cities and settlements.

Artist Saul Steinberg illustrated the jacket, and the drawing that graced the inside of the front and back endpapers visually summed up the Israel that Gruber presented in the pages of the book: a jazzy, bustling, and up-to-the-minute society—in short, a Middle Eastern counterpart to postwar America. That Steinberg was chosen as illustrator says much about the book's intended readership. The Romanian-born artist, who had established a reputation in the United States by the early 1940s for his drawings for *Life* and the *New Yorker*, had been feted by the Museum of Modern Art as one of fourteen great American artists in a seminal group exhibition at that museum in 1946. The production team behind *Israel Without Tears* must have presumed that Gruber's target audience comprised middle-class Americans with a taste for contemporary art as well as curiosity about current events

in the wider world: that is, a culturally savvy readership. (Indeed, *Publishers'
Weekly* especially noted Steinberg's artistic contribution nearly every time it
reported on the book's publication.)

Gruber was quick to point out that, underneath the razzle-dazzle of
the "modern, progressive Republic of Israel," lay a country with a soul and
a purpose (16). "A robust reality has arisen out of the pale dreams and
tears of the ghetto," she declared, evoking the classic Zionist rehabilitative
project, "a pioneer land whose meaning lies in the simple word home"
(15). Similarly, Gruber recounted, Israel was forging "a new type of man,"
different from those of the Diaspora, "a tiller of the soil in peace, a fighter
in war," under whose guidance the land of Israel was becoming the Middle
East's gateway to contemporary (Western) civilization (16–17). The birth
of Israel was nothing short of a modern miracle, she insisted, one brought
about in love and in anguish by its citizens, a "people who have known
death and outwitted it" (18). For Gruber both ancient and recent history
loomed large, and, as with St. John and other authors, the Holocaust was
vitally important in providing justification for the Jewish state. The "key
to Israel," the author announced, was "that it was built on a Biblical vision
and the cremated bones of six million dead" (18).

Gruber endeavored to translate the significance of contemporary Israel
into terms Americans could understand. So, for example, she depicted the
absorption of displaced persons into Israeli society as an intensified version of
the great American project to integrate its immigrant populations: the melting pot, in other words, on high heat. Americans back home were participating in a postwar housing boom with the help of their federal government;
Israelis too were building, Gruber was careful to note, as their government
"threw up new homes all over the country, using American techniques,
and even import[ing] the fabulous American Tournalayer machines, using
a housewife's baking technique, pouring the house in a steel frame and let-
ting it set" (80). In Gruber's portrayal, Israel was a kind of Levittown on
the Mediterranean, a place where absorption into productive life was swift
and healthy. People "could forget the past . . . [and] become normal citizens
again, with a fair chance at happiness" (81). Israel, in other words, was
a version of the American dream—portrayed in an idiom of middle-class
domesticity that Gruber's audience would well understand.

To be sure, *Israel Without Tears* was not only a report on the growth
of a new postwar nation with much in common with the postwar United
States. It also afforded American readers a view of the idiosyncrasies of
the Jewish state. Gruber was particularly interested in providing readers a
glimpse of the mosaic of religious and ethnic communities in Israel (including the many varieties of Jewish inhabitants). Her method, though, was to
highlight local color without alienating her American readers. According

to the book's rhetoric, the familiar ultimately trumped the unfamiliar. From a certain angle, Gruber found, even the most exotic of locales eventually called to mind American sites. The international hubbub and freewheeling street markets of Jaffa evoked Orchard Street in New York's Lower East Side, while Beersheba (Be'er Sheva), a burgeoning desert town of new immigrants and soldiers, was "Israel's Wild West" (194). Haifa and Tel Aviv were contemporary cities, home to industrial workers and sidewalk cafes, factories, and modern apartment blocks.

Gruber devoted an entire chapter of *Israel Without Tears* to the Americanization of Israel, apparently already well underway. "Israel has Yankee ways," she declared, and the cities of Israel were apparently awash with evidence: milkshakes at the "Brooklyn Ice Cream Bar," laundromats with American-made washing machines, American cars on the streets, Hollywood films in the cinemas (72). Even that most Israeli of institutions, the kibbutz, appeared suspiciously familiar if an American visitor looked closely enough. At Kibbutz Kfar Blum in the Galilee—founded by Zionist youth group Habonim in 1943, with American members playing an instrumental role—Gruber found that

> the girls wear sandals and American playsuits, the boys T-shirts and American loafers. They cut their dark bread . . . in an American bread-slicer, peel their Cyprus potatoes in an American potato peeler, and squeeze their Jaffa oranges in American juicers. They sleep in cots under American . . . quilts and watch American movies projected once a week from an American projector by an American engineer from Buffalo. The children's favorite character is Mickey Mouse, who is called in Israel "Mickey Mahoo," which means "Mickey—what is he?" (75)

Gruber chalked up the sudden ubiquity of American exports, from kitchen implements to movies, to the advent of large-scale American aid. She cited a recent $100 million loan from America as a particular boon to the industrial and agricultural sectors, resulting in a wave of American-made trucks, tractors, and combines trundling down roads and through fields. American investors, too, were making an impact, Gruber reported. Indeed, the Israeli government had established a "Center for Investors" to help Americans navigate the infamously labyrinthine Israeli bureaucracy.

Like St. John, Gruber highlighted what she saw as the bravery and fighting spirit of the Israeli people. Gruber devoted a chapter of *Israel Without Tears* to the front lines of Israel's War of Independence, recounting the story of Negba, the "fortress kibbutz" in the country's southern desert that had withstood an onslaught by the Egyptian army and air force from May to July of 1948. Though she hadn't witnessed the battle firsthand, Gruber provided readers a gripping account. Strafed with bombs and machine gun fire, shelled by tanks, Negba burned, but its residents prevailed, ultimately pushing back the Arab forces. "The lesson we learned," Gruber quoted a participant in the battle, "is that if you have your soil, if you never leave it, they cannot conquer you" (193). As with St. John, Gruber lauded the tenacity of the Israelis in defense of their homeland. A year after the war, Gruber found Negba blossoming once more in the desert. Here, too, the journalist detected America's fingerprint: the kibbutz had been rebuilt, in large part, with American equipment.

Gruber also reminded potential visitors of the special significance of a visit to the Holy Land. "What you need to put in your baggage," Gruber advised, "are humor, humility, and the Bible" (212). The Bible was the one true guidebook to the modern land of Israel, Gruber found. "Jerusalem, Saffed, Tiberias, Nazareth," she wrote, "Bible names that we learned in childhood—are living places here, where people eat and drink and sleep and fall in love and die. There is a tie to this Land in each man's heart. And every return to it is a return to the Bible" (212). Or, in the words of a Ministry of Tourism leaflet handed out to newly arrived travelers disembarking at the Lydda airport, Israel offered visitors the spectacle of "the people of the Bible re-constructing the Land of the Bible" (225).

Israel Without Tears, then, was both a travelogue and an exhortation for Americans curious about everyday Israel in the first few years of its existence. Written by an American Jewish journalist for a broad Jewish and non-Jewish audience, the book offered an overview of the life of the Jewish state from ground level, from a highly sympathetic perspective. It stressed deep cultural affinities between the two nations, including, prominently, the Israeli use of middle-class American technologies and cultural forms. The book made the effects of American aid not only visible but also praiseworthy, casting a nascent patron-client relationship between the United States and Israel as a natural and positive development.

On the one hand, Gruber seemed to be positioning herself as a neutral observer: she always referred to Israelis as "them" and "they," for example, even using the third person in discussing Jews as a group ("The Jews were back, running their own government").[48] Gruber did not discuss her background or status as an American Jew in *Israel Without Tears.* At the same time, however, Gruber adopted the Israeli majority's point of view about matters of defense and Israel's civilizing mission in the Middle East. So, too, did the breezy authority of her voice, her ease with Jewish customs and her grasp of Israeli humor, mark Gruber as an insider. The author presented herself as an unimpeachably American narrator who was, nonetheless, an intimate friend of the Israeli people.

A. A. Wyn, Gruber's publisher, expected Jews to constitute her core readership and targeted Jewish organizations, including Hadassah, the Zionist Organization of America, and the American Jewish Congress, in promoting the book. Gruber, who had returned to the United States in December 1949, spoke "constantly" before Jewish audiences and at travel agencies across the country in the months leading up to its release (which was moved from spring to fall of 1950).[49] Alice Hackett of *Publishers' Weekly*, alerting book industry professionals in late October to the imminent publication of *Israel Without Tears*, lauded it as "[a] bright, expert travel book" that offered "[l]ots of material not in other books," such as jokes and light anecdotes, as well as shining a light on the phenomenon of Israeli Hebrew. She noted that the book was "of course," of "special Jewish interest."[50]

Reviews following publication were good, overall: the book review section of Gruber's home newspaper, *The New York Herald Tribune*, for example, found *Israel Without Tears* to be "a gay, warm book, written all in a glow, with both delightful and moving characterizations of life in Israel." *The New York Times*, too, gave the book a positive review.[51] "All friends of the new Israel—both Christian and Jewish—should read this book," wrote a reviewer in the *Churchman*, well attuned to Gruber's attempt to write about Israel for a broad audience.[52] This statement in particular points to the presumed readership for Gruber's book—that is, those who already counted themselves as sympathetic to the Jewish state. Where Gruber excelled was in employing the genre of the travel book, an emblem and repository of middle and upper-middle-class culture since the nineteenth century, to present Israel as a thoroughly modern counterpart to the postwar United States.[53]

WOMEN'S DIVISION: AMERICAN HOUSEWIVES IN ISRAEL

Accompanying a feature story in the July 1957 issue of *Good Housekeeping* was a full-page photograph of a woman in profile, her hair pulled back, a floral apron tied around her sturdy, middle-aged frame. In the photograph, she leaned slightly forward over a kitchen sink, absorbed in the task of scrubbing and rinsing dishes by hand. The woman was none other than Golda Meir, then foreign minister of Israel. The caption alongside the photograph of the well-known international statesperson read: "Her own dishwashing? It's not the first time, and it won't be the last. The Foreign Minister, who was once an American housewife, [and] has no sleep-in help, often does her own tidying up."[54]

The article, narrated by Meir herself, allowed readers of the monthly bible of the domestic arts in America a glimpse of her high-profile career, detailing a typical workday as foreign minister: breakfast conferences, a session at the parliament, meetings with cabinet members and colleagues in the

Foreign Ministry, and various other appointments throughout the day. The heart of the article, however, was devoted to Meir's manifold entertaining duties at her home in Jerusalem. Guests at mealtime included visiting foreign dignitaries ("especially from the United States"), members of the local diplomatic corps, Israeli academics and artists, coworkers, and friends (68). Meir carefully described to *Good Housekeeping*'s readers how she planned her dinner parties, from choosing a menu during a period of food rationing to overseeing seating arrangements. "My entertaining, as well as that of all Israeli ministers, has to be much simpler than that in many other countries," she explained earnestly. "We are intent on putting every dollar we can into the development of our country" (71). Her distinguished visitors didn't mind the reduced scale of the entertaining, she insisted.

The portrait that emerged in *Good Housekeeping* was one of a woman who, if not exactly the pinnacle of elegance, knew how to balance work and domestic duties, and to execute both with gusto—no mean feat, as the magazine's readers would appreciate.[55] Simultaneously a high-ranking government official, a busy hostess, and a dutiful mother and grandmother, Meir presented to readers a portrait of womanly fulfillment that would have been tantalizing indeed to those postwar American women who sought an equitable solution to the demands of work and home life. Above all, however, this portrait of Meir as an accessible housewife in the American mode—well informed, resourceful, conscientious, content—offered readers of *Good Housekeeping*, Jewish and non-Jewish, a vision of contemporary Israel at once comforting and inspiring. If Israel's domestic front was being stationed by a million Golda Meirs, *Good Housekeeping* implied, the country was in good hands.

Meir was not, of course, a typical housewife, American or Israeli. Yet the profile of Meir in *Good Housekeeping* demonstrated the appeal of this story for the American women that made up the magazine's readership. Here was an erstwhile American housewife applying her considerable skills in an unusual and challenging setting, far from American shores, and without benefit of postwar American luxuries. As it turned out, women intrigued by the day-to-day life of an American housewife in Israel had plenty of other reading material to choose from in the 1950s and 1960s.

Hadassah Newsletter was one source of such information, providing members of the women's Zionist organization with accounts of the tribulations and joys involved in making a home in the new Jewish state. Writing in the pages of *Hadassah Newsletter* in March 1952, for example, Nell Ziff Pekarsky, a former national president of Junior Hadassah on leave in Jerusalem with her rabbi husband and two children, shared her hard-won wisdom as an American housewife in Israel. Pekarsky described how she had perfected the art of shopping under austerity measures, learning to wait in long lines, always carrying her own shopping bag, and trading desired goods with fellow homemakers. "Sometimes I find myself reflecting on the difference between life here and in the States," she wrote, musing on the subject for her American readers:

> I wonder what I did with all my time when I didn't have to stand in queues, run to the plumber to try to get him to come for some emergency in the bathroom, or deliver messages by foot to people who don't have a telephone. I am ashamed to think of my complaint that I didn't know what to serve my family on an evening for dinner. I blush when I remember how much food I used to dump into the garbage can each day.[56]

Pekarsky translated her experience in Israel as a critique of the postwar American lifestyle, with its excessive choices and emphasis on disposability. In this light, Israel—and the Israeli kitchen in particular—provided a proving ground for the "spoiled" American housewife.

In fact, *Hadassah Newsletter* devoted sustained attention to the subject of keeping house in Israel, in war and in peace. A sidebar in *Hadassah Newsletter* published in April 1948, for example, a month before Israel's declaration of independence and the formal outbreak of war, had dismissed the notion that a "mere" housewife had nothing to contribute to the defense of the Jewish people. This reprinted exhortation from the Haganah, warning against panic and, more specifically, against buying on the black market, was addressed to the Jewish housewives of Palestine. By reprinting the exhortation, however, the editors of *Hadassah Newsletter* clearly intended this proclamation to inspire their American Jewish cousins. "Your kitchen and your table are defense posts most vital to our fight," ran the message. "Upon you—your skill, adaptability, and devotion—depends the feeding of the embattled Yishuv. . . . In the new day that is coming, the people will remember not only the soldiers, but their mothers and wives—the women who stood on guard in the Jewish home in days of emergency and hardship. Will you be among them?"[57] Thus, the traditional Jewish notion of the *eshet chayil* (woman of valor) was transformed, in a time of war, into defender of the people Israel. In this regard, *Hadassah Newsletter* mirrored the discourse in women's columns in Israeli newspapers at the time, as contributors "depicted food, clothes, and comfort-giving as strategies central to defending the country," as Shira Klein has argued.[58]

This subject—Jewish wife and mother as defender of Israel—formed the basis of a regular column in *Hadassah Newsletter*, "Diary of a Jerusalem Housewife," written by Molly Lyons Bar-David. The column, which first appeared during the siege of Jerusalem in 1947–48, provided readers a firsthand account of Israel's struggles and triumphs from the perspective of a latter-day pioneer.[59] As eyewitness to the War of Independence and the birth of Israel, Bar-David was performing a function much like that of the American journalists who spent time in Israel during this momentous period and then wrote about it for American audiences. Considering the substantial notice given to journalistic books about Israel by *Hadassah Newsletter*, readers of Bar-David's column knew of these books and, presumably, read some of them as well. Bar-David, however, offered a fresh perspective to her readers: that of an erstwhile American housewife in Israel, whose experience of historical events was shaped by her status as *olah* (immigrant) and homemaker. (While technically a former Canadian rather than United States citizen, Bar-David wrote in English for a largely American audience, both for *Hadassah Newsletter* and for the *Jerusalem Post*, where she was a food columnist.)[60]

Presenting herself as a genial matron whose everyday concerns as wife and mother matched those of her readers, Bar-David offered American Zionist women an even more intimate version of contemporary history than accounts by journalists such as Ruth Gruber and Robert St. John. For Bar-David, her fervent love of and devotion to her family informed her love and devotion to Israel, and vice versa. The author's status as American and as housewife made her a kind of surrogate for her readers, who were invited, implicitly, to imagine themselves in her place—in spite of the fact (or perhaps because of the fact) that they were personally unlikely to ever emigrate to Israel or witness historic events there firsthand.

In 1952, G. P. Putnam's Sons published Bar-David's first book, *My Promised Land*, culled from her *Hadassah Newsletter* column. Bar-David knew her audience well. She wrote with the assumption that readers of her column and book were, like her, unabashed supporters of Israel at the very least, if not also lifelong, dyed-in-the-wool Zionists. There was certainly a relatively large audience for her memoir: According to Bar-David's own estimate, more than 250,000 women (the number of Hadassah members nationwide) were regular readers of her "Diary," and supportive fan mail spoke to its popularity.[61]

Central to Bar-David's narrative was the notion that the responsibilities of a housewife were completely compatible with those of pioneer, fighter, and, ultimately, Israeli citizen. Bar-David's American Jewish readers were doubly removed from the war in Israel: safe in America, to be sure, but also more or less confined, as women and homemakers, to observe rather than participate in the front lines of history, as their experience on the home front in World War II had illustrated. Bar-David's project was, in a sense, to both dramatize *and* humanize the exigencies of the Zionist cause to American Jewish women.

In *My Promised Land*, Bar-David coolly juxtaposed domestic life as a mother of young daughters with the mounting violence in Palestine during 1947 and the outbreak of war with the surrounding Arab nations in 1948. Bar-David told of a transformation in her own and her children's lives as the fighting moved closer and closer to home:

> We had an inner room, tiny and windowless . . . where we sat when the battles were on. Our Airedale, Peter, would shiver with every crack of a bullet against our walls, and look at me with his huge eyes, pleading for mercy. But the children took it well. Baby learned to say "Shooting, shooting," before she knew a dozen words. Geila played hand grenade, mortar, rifle or revolver, and when she once picked up a grapefruit and shouted, "Bomb," Varda took it from her smartly and reminded her that although there were many bombs in Jerusalem there were now few grapefruits. But seven-year-old Varda would get bored and complained bitterly that she wanted to go into her room for her crayons or dolls. Sometimes, to quiet her, I would crawl on my hands and knees to fetch the things she wanted. (139)

She described the outward signs of the onslaught, too. Their house became a besieged fortress, according to the author, with bullet dents on the front door, bullets in the front room wall, bullet holes in the curtains. Readers of her book surely could not help but notice the contrast between Bar-David's home and their own homes in peaceful, postwar American suburbs. Bar-David was also explicit about her willingness to fight:

> I wanted to use [my] gun. I went up on the roof when the shooting got hot and asked just to take one crack. . . . [S]omething savage in me wanted to take just one pot at a legionnaire. I was trigger happy, but so was every Arab bootblack. Or is it that my gun reinforced my elemental right to live, to save my babies and defend my home? Out on the prairies in Canada and the States, the women were familiar with weapons too. They would not have been prevented at a stockade from mowing down scalping Iroquois. Is this much different? (139)

In explicitly conjuring the heroic frontier women of the American past, Bar-David alerted her readers to a congruence between the Israeli and American experiences. According to this parallel, just as the women of the American frontier had mustered outsize courage to defend their families, so Israel's brave mothers had embraced their roles as defenders of the soil, adopting violence as an appropriate response to impossible circumstances.

Largely, however, Bar-David focused her narrative on the more typical concerns of a housewife in time of war and its aftermath. A subject that she returned to repeatedly throughout the memoir was that of food, and especially food-related deprivations brought about by the war. This was yet another area of everyday life under siege that required the especial resourcefulness of a confident housewife. Bar-David catalogued the lengths to which Jerusalem's women had to go to procure food in the spring of 1948, with Passover approaching and after strict rationing had been introduced. News of the occasional, unexpected appearance of dried fish or macaroni noodles "spread like wildfire," as Bar-David recounted, "and women waited hours for a handful of beans" (160). Bar-David, like her relatives, friends and neighbors, was left hungry and frustrated:

> The streets were full of shoppers dangling empty string bags. Aunt Jeanette and I went again and again in search of food; we scoured the city. In the Oriental market we found three tins of fish paste; in another market we were able to get some stale candy. When we got home we were so tired we were ready to cry with fatigue. There had been a surfeit of expensive tinned fruit, but . . . now even that vanished. There was still corn flour and we bought a lot of that, though we had no milk or sugar to make anything of it. Vinegar and vinegar and vinegar was available everywhere. (160)

Water rationing, too, presented a challenge, one that Bar-David and others had to manage with acuity. "We learned to make every drop of water do triple duty and more," she wrote, delineating exactly how the five to ten quarts of the daily water ration were stretched to cover consumption, bathing, and laundry (159). Stateside homemakers accustomed to run-of-the-mill kitchen tips in women's magazines must have been impressed with Bar-David's description of her domestic acumen in a time of extreme crisis.

Bar-David depicted the period of austerity after the war had ended as almost as difficult as the war years had been for household managers. Hopes of sugar in time for the Jewish New Year were dashed when the Israeli government couldn't spare the money to bring that kitchen staple into the country in time for the holiday. Fresh milk continued to be rationed; so were nylon stockings and shoe leather. "Coffee" consisted of roasted barley. Cooking, too, was a travail: Bar-David's electric stove was useless without electricity; the gas stove lay empty of fuel; the kerosene stove lacked a wick, with no replacement forthcoming; and with nothing but cheap matches available, even the old primus stove, the very symbol of kibbutz-style asceticism, was nearly impossible to light. But Bar-David and her fellow Israelis persevered, often with the help of the black market—a necessary evil, Bar-David admitted—and black humor. If food supplies were scant, dark jokes regarding the minister of supply, at least, abounded (265). Yet Bar-David conveyed that Israelis had been through worse. Children were fed, one way or another, during the austerity years; it was even possible to do a little entertaining.

Many reviewers of My *Promised Land* wrote of the book as a fresh and intimate glimpse of a larger-than-life topic. "While the warmth and sincerity of the writer gives value to her story," wrote one critic, "its greater appeal seems to be in her ability to bring home to the reader an intimate picture of the difficulties under which these consecrated men and women have worked and suffered while building the Jewish state."[62] (That the reviewer described Jewish Israelis as "consecrated men and women," suggested the sympathy with which Bar-David's intended readership viewed Israel.) Though others had recently written about the same time and place in history, Bar-David told her own story in her own fashion, "call[ing] no names and rarely rais[ing] her voice," as a review in the *San Francisco Chronicle* noted, an approach that exemplified Bar-David's maternal persona.[63] What's more, as another reviewer pointed out, My *Promised Land* was sure to be "welcome to . . . all women who have had desires and ambitions which they [strive] to fulfill."[64] Like Golda Meir in the *Good Housekeeping* profile, Bar-David presented readers a vision of womanly competence, benevolence, and grit in the face of personal and communal trials; both Bar-David and Meir were also, each in her own way, participants in thrilling historical events. The American provenance of each made for a shared context with readers. It was their experiences as newly minted Israelis, however, that made their stories unusually compelling.

Bar-David was not the only "American housewife" writing books about Israel in these years. In 1958, for example, Mary Clawson, a native Californian with a doctorate in economics, published *Letters from Jerusalem*, an account of the first year of a two-year sojourn in Jerusalem in the early 1950s with her husband and two young sons. Clawson's Jerusalem, like Bar-David's, tested the mettle of the individual American housewife. Like Bar-David, Clawson portrayed the challenges of shopping, cooking, and entertaining, as well as raising children, in a city and country living under austerity measures. Indeed, Clawson's story can be seen as a kind of conversion narrative, in which she transforms herself, with pluck and good cheer, from academic to home economist. "If I had no other reason for remembering Jerusalem," Clawson mused, "I should always remember it as the place I learned to bake" (109). Far from the bosom of American affluence, where modern gadgets and Betty Crocker mixes had simplified the housewife's task, Clawson described finding her true self in 1950s Jerusalem.

Clawson, unlike Bar-David, was not Jewish, and her perspective as an outsider shaped the book's tone. Israel was not California. Clawson had to acclimate not only to making do with much less, but also with the linguistic, social, and religious differences between her and her neighbors. The author's eagerness to learn about a society and culture so different from her own, as an American Gentile, made her an appealing proxy for the curious postwar American woman, sharing and seeking knowledge about the wider world in general, and about developing nations in particular.

Yet for Clawson, too, as for many other authors of "Israel books," Israel's significance exceeded its status as simply another developing nation in the postwar world. While Clawson's perspective within the book is that of a nonreligious, ecumenically minded individual, she acknowledged her Quaker background. The table of contents in *Letters from Jerusalem* was interspersed with apt biblical quotations about Jerusalem and the land of Israel. (Similarly, each chapter of James McDonald's *My Mission in Israel* opened with a passage from the Bible, divided between the Old and New Testaments.)[65] Indeed, the dust jacket blurb of *Letters* opened with a well-known quotation from the Book of Psalms, a classic statement of yearning for Jerusalem: "If I do not remember thee, let my tongue cleave to the roof of my mouth; if I prefer not Jerusalem above my chief joy."[66] The book's warm introduction by Eleanor Roosevelt, one of the most prominent of Israel's non-Jewish American supporters, signaled to the reader that this would be a book sympathetic to the Jewish state. Roosevelt wrote that she hoped the book that followed would "make many people understand better the life and the people and the spirit of Israel."[67] (The subtitle of *Letters from Jerusalem*—"A non-Jewish woman's love affair with Israel"—also left no doubt about Clawson's inclinations.)[68] By the book's conclusion, however, Clawson was not only infatuated but also militantly partisan, proclaiming that she would eschew her pacifist inclinations and fight to the death for Jerusalem if necessary. "These may not be my people and this may not be my land," Clawson explained, "[b]ut I feel they are and it is."[69] Like Bar-David, then, Clawson presented a persona both maternal and unapologetically combative.

The Citadel Press published its entry into the subgenre—entitled simply *An American Housewife in Israel*—in 1962. Author Shula Hirsch, an American Jew, spent the summer of 1961 in Tel Aviv with her children and wrote a slim account of her exploits there, including her witnessing a portion of the Eichmann trial. At this time, too, American publishers published the first cookbooks on Israeli cuisine, presumably for a female readership: Lillian Cornfeld's *Israeli Cookery* in 1962 and Molly Lyons Bar-David's *The Israeli Cook Book* in 1964. (Meanwhile, Israeli publisher Sadan brought out an English-language version of Naomi and Shimon Tzabar's *Yemenite and Sabra Cookery* in 1963, distributed by Bloch Publishing in the United States.) Using a familiar strategy, Americans writing about Israeli cooking highlighted elements of Israeli cuisine that American readers would find exotic while simultaneously stressing commonalities between American and Israeli food. "Almost anything you could desire, from a lowly hot dog to a char-coal-broiled steak, can be had in Israel," insisted Norma Mayron in the pages of *Women's League Outlook*. Sharing recipes for hummus, falafel, and pita, she encouraged her readers, women members of Conservative congrega-

Figure 2.1. The cover of Shula Hirsch's *An American Housewife in Israel*, published by the Citadel Press in 1962. Like other examples of the women's interest subgenre of non-fiction about Israel, Hirsch's book toggled between the personal, quotidian aspects of life in the Jewish state and events of historical interest. Collection of the author.

tions in postwar America, not to be afraid "to improvise . . . [and] to make them more palatable for your taste."[70] Similarly, food columnist Willetta Bar-Illan portrayed contemporary Israeli cuisine to American readers as a gastronomical melting pot that juxtaposed (in theory) rustic *kebabs* and *puris* with such elegant Western imports as *soufflé au Grand Marnier*.[71]

Dorothy Rossyn, reviewing a recent spate of Jewish cookbooks in *Hadassah Magazine*, homed in on the larger significance of such publications. Cookbooks were "becoming increasingly cultural," she wrote, drawing upon a wide range of expertise and imparting knowledge beyond simple recipes. In writing *The Israeli Cook Book*, for example, the reviewer noted that Bar-David availed herself of experts in "gastronomy, the arts, professions, literature, [and] political leadership," as well as consulting "travelers, just cooks and, above all, the Bible and the Talmud." The book industry, according to Rossyn, was capitalizing on the genre's newfound appeal and status, purveying "all kinds of cookbooks . . . of all countries and all climes," which publishers ensured were "pouring off the presses."[72]

In this light, one can speculate that cookbooks about Israel, like books on Israel more generally, addressed a perceived desire among American Jews to augment their cultural storehouse. Whether depicting American fighters in Israel or the denizens of cosmopolitan Tel Aviv, describing the art of keeping house under austerity or sharing the perfect hummus recipe, American writers and publishers assumed that American readers, and Jewish readers in particular, thirsted for knowledge of Israel. Just as important, writers and publishers of Israel books counted on the cultural aspirations and capacities of their intended readership. Following the news was one thing; buying a book, however, was a cultural investment as well as a quest for information.

"ANOTHER NEW BOOK" ON ISRAEL: ASSESSING NUMBERS AND SIGNIFICANCE

As the number of visitors to Israel increased in the course of the postwar period, so did the number of books written about Israel. "Practically every visitor who has stopped in Tel Aviv long enough to sip a glass of Richon wine on the terrace of the Kaete Dan Hotel seems to feel a strong compulsion to write about the new land called Israel," wrote one commentator in 1950, claiming that there had been "more books and magazine articles published on Israel these past two years than have been published on canasta."[73] Nearly one hundred more American books about Israel, fiction and nonfiction, had appeared by the mid-1960s, penned by amateur and professional writers, American Jews and non-Jews. Subjects now encompassed satires of Israeli life and customs, children's literature, Israeli cuisine, and new accounts of the Arab-Israeli War of 1948, among other topics.[74]

For the majority of American Jews who did not visit Israel, the works of a number of American writers offered vicarious access to the young Jewish state. For all the authors considered in this chapter, and many more, writing about Israel served as a key means of familiarizing American readers with the contemporary Jewish state. Yet writing about Israel was, of course, an act of translation. In shaping images of Israel for American audiences, writers Robert St. John, Ruth Gruber, and Molly Lyons Bar-David, among others, developed several common themes that foregrounded Israel's apparent kinship with the United States. These writers focused upon Israel as heir to, and fulfillment of, the Judeo-Christian tradition; upon the shared experiences, in Israel and America, of hardscrabble pioneer subsistence and frontier bravery; and upon a mutual American and Israeli love of—and willingness to fight for—independence. (Ruth Gruber presented another congruence between America and Israel—the increasing ubiquity of American mass-produced commodities—in *Israel Without Tears*.) Authors often made these parallels explicit, either in their own words or by means of proxies, as with the Irish American fighters featured by Robert St. John in *Shalom Means Peace*. All of the nonfiction works considered in this chapter presented Israel from an American point of view, whether that of the globe-trotting journalist or intrepid housewife.

The composite image of Israel that emerged in the works of journalists and memoirists was an overwhelmingly positive one. St. John, Gruber, and Bar-David, among others, wrote of Israel and its people in largely admiring terms. This was characteristic of the vast majority of "Israel books" published in the course of the 1950s and early 1960s. Books on Israel for American readers continued to "delineate the positive and lasting achievements of a martyr [*sic*] people whose heroic remnants have reestablished statehood in the land of their fathers," according to Solomon Kerstein, who surveyed the landscape of Israel books for the Jewish Book Council's *Jewish Book Annual* in the mid-to-late 1950s.[75] Kerstein's fully partisan comment, too, suggests the American Jewish predisposition to books that portrayed Israel in such a manner.

The relationship between book, author, and audience is not always straightforward. Certainly, a number of "Israel book" authors were admired figures, and even minor celebrities, in the American Jewish community in this period. Mordkhe Rudavsky, writing in the Yiddish-language *Jewish American* in July 1948, provides a window onto the Jewish community's reception of one of these figures, James Grover McDonald—three years before his book, *My Mission in Israel*, hit the market. "I have often gone to hear [McDonald] at large assemblies as well as at more intimate gatherings," Rudavsky wrote, "and every time the impression . . . was unforgettable. You feel the depth of his earnestness in his speeches, the warmth of his heart . . . one feels that he is a real mensch."[76] Rudavsky credited McDonald, who had been a member of the Anglo-American Committee of Inquiry on Palestine, with helping to win public opinion in the United States for Israel. McDonald and many other authors of Israel books had ready-made Jewish audiences, sometimes before their "Israel books" were published.

Molly Lyons Bar-David, too, was a known quantity before publishing *My Promised Land* in 1953. She had a huge readership as a *Hadassah Newsletter* columnist and toured America on Hadassah's behalf in the early 1950s to spread the word about austerity and the ongoing need for American aid for such programs as Youth Aliyah. In a visit to Los Angeles in January 1952, Bar-David reached audiences of approximately 1,600 Hadassah women over the course of two days.[77] Ruth Gruber, who followed *Israel Without Tears* with an updated account, *Israel Today*, in 1958, was a "popular lecturer" on the American Jewish speaker circuit.[78] She regularly appeared before sizable Jewish audiences at such events as United Jewish Welfare Fund fundraisers and Hadassah conferences.[79] (On a smaller scale, Mary Clawson, back in Washington, D.C., did the book group circuit for local women's organizations, appearing, for example, at a "dessert book review" at Temple Emanuel in Kensington, Maryland, and a luncheon for the Book Group of the University Park Woman's Club and speaking before the Ladies Auxiliary of the Silver Spring chapter of the Jewish War Veterans of America.)[80]

It is difficult to quantify the response of American Jews to the parade of Israel books, especially in the case of books that were not spectacular successes in the literary marketplace. And hard numbers, even when available, tell only a partial story. In the early postwar years, the publishing industry was grappling with the problem of accurately assessing book sales and analyzing the available data appropriately. In an editorial published in *Publishers' Weekly* in the wake of a broad government call for better statistics, for example, editor Frederic G. Melcher noted the American Book Publishers Council's recent efforts to tally numbers and wrote that "[s]tatistics that can be used on a comparable basis are not as easy to put together for books as for pig iron and automobiles."[81] The collecting of empirical evidence was bedeviled by a diversity of book formats and market venues (such as book clubs and mail order catalogs), discrepancies between the claims of publishers and booksellers, and the subjective and erratic methods the mainstream media used to report on book sales.[82] Some publishers simply refused to release information about sales.[83] Debates on how best to gather and interpret data—on how to gauge which books were really "best-sellers," for example—flared up in *The Saturday Review of Literature* and *Publishers' Weekly*, the latter of which noted in 1949 that the publishing industry was "conspicuously lacking adequate statistics."[84]

Even so, there does appear to be an incongruity between the popularity of "Israel book" authors as public personalities and the numbers of books that the authors actually sold. Critic Harold Ribalow argued this point in an article on "Zion in the Book Stores" in 1952. According to Ribalow's own survey of publishers and authors, Robert St. John's *Shalom Means Peace* had sold a "respectable" 22,425 copies till then, while Ruth Gruber's *Israel Without Tears* had sold a paltry six thousand. In many cases, he surmised, book sales fell short of expectations in terms of the authors' celebrity as speakers in the American Jewish community.[85]

Publishers of "Israel books" were clearly banking, to some extent, on the earlier successes of the authors under consideration and, one can infer, on the prominence of those authors in the public sphere. Doublebday & Co., which by the end of the 1940s was one of the leaders of the book industry, had published St. John's bestselling *From the Land of the Silent People* seven years before publishing *Shalom Means Peace*.[86] Doubleday must have considered St. John a worthwhile investment; indeed, the company published almost every one of the nearly two dozen books he authored—the majority of them, including several more books about Israel, appearing after *Shalom Means Peace*. A. A. Wyn had published Ruth Gruber's *Destination Palestine* in 1948, and published her book *Israel Without Tears* two years later. Wyn's Current Books had entered the book publishing industry only in 1945—Wyn was already well established as a successful publisher of comics and magazines—and one can assume that he considered Gruber a safe bet when he decided to publish a second title by the author.[87] (The earlier book had sold 9,500 copies, and was a Jewish Book Club selection.)[88]

In contrast, Molly Lyons Bar-David had never worked with Putnam's Sons before publishing *My Promised Land* in 1953. The publisher appeared to do little to promote the book, especially in comparison with (and perhaps because of) the prominent advertising campaigns undertaken for several of Putnam's other titles to appear in fall 1953.[89] Yet Bar-David was hardly an untried author, as a regular contributor to *Hadassah Newsletter* and other publications and as a public speaker, as noted above. Putnam's likely assumed that Bar-David's established popularity would ensure interest in the book among Jewish readers.[90]

Though publishers and some critics were no doubt disappointed in the performance of even the most popular nonfiction "Israel books," the fact remains that scores of thousands of Americans did purchase these books. (Of course, no one knows how many readers borrowed *Shalom Means Peace* or *My Promised Land* from libraries or from friends, or bought them second-hand.) The question remains: How did American Jews view contemporaneous attempts by writers to translate Israel for mainstream audiences? A report published in the May 1949 bulletin of the Los Angeles chapter of Hadassah gives an indication of how some American Jews greeted the appearance of such books. In the bulletin, Mrs. Samuel Fox, librarian for the Los Angeles chapter of the popular Zionist organization, alerted fellow members to the publication of Robert St. John's *Shalom Means Peace:*

> Another new book on Palestine has just been added to our collection of recent publications. . . .
>
> Having read Stone's "This Is Israel," Granados' "The Birth of Israel," Ruth Gruber's "Destination Palestine," and "Hate, Hope and High Explosives," by George Fielding Eliot, you will find "Shalom Means Peace" original and void of duplication of anything that has been written before.
>
> Robert St. John, famous correspondent . . . has indeed brought us the great human story being lived by an unforgettable people in Palestine!
>
> When you read "Shalom Means Peace," you will find peace in your heart![91]

Fox went on to cite the "great demand" among chapter members for Stone's *This Is Israel,* which was, like St. John's book, a journalistic account of the newborn Jewish state. According to this and other bulletin entries, Fox felt that reading was not only an educational imperative and one of life's great pleasures, but also part of Hadassah's propaganda work on behalf of the Jewish state. Upon the publication of Jorge Garcia-Granados's *The Birth of Israel,* for example, members were exhorted to order advance copies of the book, thereby "practically assur[ing] [it] a place on the best-seller list." It was hoped that such a strategy would bring the book "a wide American audience, thus helping immeasurably to spread the story of Israel among all sectors of U.S. opinion."[92] Though it was a bold claim, Fox had good reason to be confident in Hadassah's role in popularizing books. In a 1960 issue of *Congress Bi-Weekly* on Jewish books, writer David Boroff echoed this early prognosis, insisting that Jewish women were "responsible for that much-remarked phenomenon—the Jewish best-seller." The Jewish book circuit, he explained, was women's territory, and "[i]f a book achieves even a modest vogue in the Jewish circuit, it has it made," for, once on the best-seller list, "non-Jewish readers will pick up the cue and accelerate its success."[93]

The overwhelming success of Leon Uris's *Exodus,* one of the most popular American novels of the postwar period, provided the boldest evidence yet of a hunger for Israel among American readers. *Exodus* was the top-selling novel of 1959, with four hundred thousand copies sold in hardcover.[94] A paean to fighting Jews and the birth of Israel in the shadow of the Holocaust, *Exodus* was instrumental in disseminating an image of Israel as unapologetically strong and heroic to a wide swath of American readers, as a number of historians and literary scholars have argued.[95] By dint of its sheer popularity, Uris's novel—and the 1960 film adaptation of the book, which grossed millions of dollars—was critically important in shaping mainstream Americans' opinions of Israel. The Israel of *Exodus* called to mind, for many, the American revolutionary and frontier sagas of rugged freedom fighters and righteous conquest.[96] In fact, as this chapter illustrates, early nonfiction works about Israel introduced many of the themes that appeared again later in Uris's fictionalized account.

For many American Jews, books that portrayed Israel sympathetically were a welcome addition to the American cultural scene. The Sioux City matron who defended *Exodus* against its critics in the pages of *Hadassah Newsletter* no doubt spoke for many American Jews when she addressed the broader significance of such a book. "Do you know the effect this book is having on the people who read it?" she asked, and responded:

> I speak for my friends and acquaintances, the people out here in the very middle of our country, as far from the strong cultural and Zionist centers as can be. Most of them have been only mildly interested in Israel, most have been apologetic Jews without realizing it, some have even been opposed to Zionism; one had almost forsaken Judaism. This book has been like a bombshell among them.[97]

So, too, did the cumulative force of two decades worth of American nonfiction about Israel leave its mark on the American Jewish psyche. For many American Jewish readers in the postwar period, Israel had become the ultimate protagonist.

THREE

HORA HOOTENANNIES AND YEMENITE HOEDOWNS

Israeli Folk Dance in America

In May 1942, nearly six years to the day before the establishment of Israel, a large group of young people gathered at Constitution Hall in Washington, D.C., for the ninth annual National Folk Dance Festival. Among them were some forty young American Jews, a dance group calling themselves the Palestine Jewish Pioneers. The announcement of the group's participation had met resistance from a local rabbi, who insisted that Jews, as a religious group only, had no business on a program with dance troupes representing the nations of the world. Undeterred, the youngsters had marched onto the stage in their blue and white and khaki, singing and dancing the hora "to the thunderous applause of several thousand persons in the audience," according to journalist Carl Alpert—who was also the adult director of the dance group.[1]

Alpert noted that his Pioneers, hailing from diverse local Zionist youth groups, had heretofore "always existed in worlds apart from each other."[2] At least for the purposes of the festival, these young American Zionists had buried their ideological differences to perform the dances of Jewish Palestine together. Beholding the appeal of the hora for these young American Jews, Alpert envisioned a golden future for Palestinian folk dance in America. He prophesied that, "this summer, at their Zionist youth camp, they will teach that dance to others, it will catch on quickly, and will be taken back by the campers to a score or more of cities and introduced as the 'latest Palestinian dance.'"[3]

After the performance, the dancers from different troupes joined together for a spontaneous American barn dance. Alpert depicted the dance as a vision of harmonious diversity, as "two Scotch Highlanders . . . a Ukrainian, two Lithuanians, a Colorado cowboy, and two blue-skirted *halutzot* [pioneers]," as well as uniformed American soldiers, joined hands and danced together. He mulled the significance of this occurrence:

> Many of my forty protégés probably never heard of the phrase "cultural pluralism," yet they had discovered for themselves a "unity in diversity," in which their Zionism, their Jewish identity, needed no apology and was accepted on face value.
>
> There was an open wholesomeness about the gathering which is difficult to describe. There was none of the strained or exaggerated effect which is apparent at good will meetings. Jews were neither being "tolerated," nor absurdly praised for their "contributions." They were accepted as equals as a matter of course, nor was their right to be different challenged, for the philosophy of the entire affair was based on such differences.[4]

In retrospect, the experience of Alpert's dancing Pioneers at that wartime festival can be seen as a harbinger of things to come. With its imputed power to educate, to impart pride, and to provide enjoyment, Israeli folk dance became an increasingly compelling pastime to American Jews of the postwar era. For dance educators such as Dvora Lapson and Fred Berk, to name two influential examples, Israeli folk dance, more than traditional classroom learning, presented an unparalleled means of granting American Jewish youth access to Jewish culture and instilling loyalty to the Jewish people. These were key desiderata of postwar American Jewish education: Lapson noted that while "in former generations the cultural life of Jewry was maintained through the existence of a Jewish milieu with its traditional folkways on the one hand, and the perpetuation of Jewish study on the other, today our problem is altogether different."[5] She and others argued that dance provided a uniquely effective means for shaping Jewish culture and loyalties at a time when the Jewish population was increasingly dispersed geographically and Jewish life (in all its facets) was occupying proportionally less time. According to this line of thought, learning the content and studying the origins of Israeli folk dance would link young people to their Jewish heritage and raise their awareness of contemporary Israel. By emphasizing the idea of a Jewish dance canon that belonged to all Jews everywhere, Lapson and her fellow educators could reinforce the notion of a Jewish people with a shared national legacy. Equally important, Israeli folk dance was an inherently collective activity that embodied group identification in a concrete physical act.

It was not only dance educators that found in Israeli folk dance a powerful antidote to what apparently ailed American Jewry. In the post-1948 years, the leaders of American Zionist youth groups, like their adult counterparts, perceived that organized American Zionism faced increasing irrelevance as a political and cultural force. Their political goals had been fulfilled with the establishment of the Jewish state, and the Israeli government simply bypassed American Zionist organizations in order to solicit funds directly from the American Jewish masses. While movement ideology remained a dividing line among the various movements (left, right, and center), Israeli folk dance—a mainstay of Zionist culture in the new Jewish state—seemed to provide a matchless instrument for generating enthusiasm for Zionism and for Israel among a spectrum of Jewish youth, as this chapter will show. Just as Alpert had predicted in 1942, American Zionist youth had an important role to play in disseminating Israeli folk dance throughout the country, teaching and performing such dances within Zionist circles, within the larger American Jewish populace, and in the wider public sphere.

The Israeli folk dance phenomenon did meet some skepticism among young Zionist ideologues, who expressed concern that the increasing centrality of cultural programming was diluting the true aim of the Zionist youth movement (i.e., preparation for *aliyah*, or immigration to Israel). In truth, this contest between "hardliners" and cultural Zionists was less a battle over the role of Israeli folk dance per se than it was a struggle to define the purpose and agenda of American Zionism after 1948. Should preparation for *aliyah* take precedence, they asked, or should educational initiatives come first? For many members of Zionist youth groups, however, as I argue, Israeli folk dance came to seem an unqualified boon to American Zionism.

But this is only part of the story. For in the immediate postwar decades, Israeli folk dance also emerged as a popular genre within the flourishing folk dance movement in the United States. Writing on the phenomenon in the 1940s and 1950s, dance critic John Martin dated the growing interest in folk dance among the American populace from the World War II years. "Today," he wrote in 1941, "folk-dancing is enjoying what can only be described as a boom. All over the country groups of solid citizens of both sexes, all ages and virtually every nationality under the sun, gather periodically in school and town hall, on village green or in farmhouse dooryard" to learn and perform folk dances.[6] For those who articulated the goals of the movement, which first arose in the early twentieth century, folk dance embodied and reinforced the values of American cultural pluralism, among other physical and social benefits. Indeed, according to Carl Alpert's account, this seemed to be the prevailing spirit of the National Folk Dance Festival in 1942, in which the (American) Jewish Palestine Pioneers participated. As dance studies scholar Anthony Shay has written, the "concept and the prominent civic presence" of such international folk dance festivals have served liberal-minded Americans as a means to demonstrate "inclusiveness . . . and tolerance, and simultaneously to satisfy the quest of ethnic and immigrant communities for recognition by mainstream society."[7]

For Martin, learning others' ethnic national dance repertoires during the war years served as a "heartening symbol of international amity in . . . tumultuous times," an illustration that "it is not peoples but governments that make wars."[8] The cautious postwar peace of the 1950s and 1960s gave this notion a new urgency. In the context of the Cold War, proponents of the folk dance movement argued that its efficacy in bridging differences and softening rivalries was more important than ever. So, too, did folk dance aficionados continue to argue that celebrating ethnic difference while dancing together strengthened the fabric of American life.

Proponents of a cultural liberalism that posited the arts as a bridge between disparate groups, folk dance teachers and practitioners appeared to believe earnestly in the power of dance to defuse interethnic tensions at home and to mitigate political antagonisms abroad. The folk dance community thus drafted the Israeli folk dance repertoire into service as a link between non-Jews and Jews, Americans and other national groups. Learning Israeli folk dances provided exactly the same benefits to folk dance devotees as did learning the dances of other ethnic and national groups. In this light, the popularity of Israeli folk dance in the postwar years did not necessarily stem from interest in Israel per se among practitioners. This provides a bold contrast to the context in which Jewish dance educators and Zionist youth adopted Israeli folk dance; for them, Israeli folk dance mattered, above all, because it helped young American Jews explore their Jewish identity.

If different groups ascribed diverse meanings to the genre, enthusiasts of all stripes appeared to find Israeli folk dance an entirely positive manifestation in postwar American life. As encountered in dance classes and at youth group meetings, in local and national festivals, and on popular television programs, Israeli folk dance became an increasingly familiar feature of the American cultural landscape. The hora, it seems, was here to stay.

ISRAELI FOLK DANCE IN AMERICAN JEWISH CULTURE:
FORMULATING A CULTURAL AND EDUCATIONAL RATIONALE

In the summer of 1944, as World War II raged in Europe, a group of professional dancers in the Yishuv (Jewish settlement in Palestine) came together for the first time to teach, learn, and perform international and nascent

"Israeli" folk dances. Held at Kibbutz Dalia in the mountains surrounding Haifa, the Dalia folk dance festival lured the brightest lights of the Israeli dance world—among them, the festival's originator, Gurit Kadman (a specialist in ethnic dance), the modern dance choreographer Gertrud Kraus, and folk dance innovators Baruch Agadati and Rivka Sturman—whose larger mission was to create and showcase an indigenous folk dance corpus on Palestinian soil.

The first and subsequent Dalia festivals were supported primarily by the Histadrut (the central organization of the Zionist Labor Federation) and were understood from the beginning to be of great importance to the nation-building effort. Organizers and observers perceived the festivals as prime laboratories for the creation of the new Hebrew body, muscular, proud, and free—everything the cringing, stunted Diaspora Jewish body was not, according to the classic Zionist assessment.[9] Participants in the festivals as well as cultural commentators understood Israeli folk dance to be a key component in building a new national community with a store of shared symbols and experiences. The presence of massive audiences—twenty-five thousand at the second Dalia festival in 1947, for example, some 5 percent of the population—assured that Israeli folk dance was, indeed, a collective enterprise.[10]

Israeli dance necessarily functioned very differently in American Jewish culture than it did in Israel in these same years. For one, Israeli dance was a highly centralized operation in Israel, with a core committee responsible for teacher training, vetting and approving new folk dances, and preparing national festivals. Under the auspices of the Histadrut in the early 1950s, this folk dance committee created Israel's first national dance company and extended its educational reach into the new immigrant development towns.[11] In the context of American society, Jewish dance was not a centralized national prerogative but the cultural pursuit of a small ethno-religious minority. Rather, American Jewish dance educators viewed Israeli folk dance—and Jewish dance generally—as, at most, an educational and cultural opportunity and a social outlet. American Jews, in contrast to their Israeli counterparts, wished to contextualize Israeli folk dance in a manner that did not repudiate the worth of Diaspora existence.

The first formal attempts to introduce Israeli folk dance to American Jews date from the late 1930s, when Jewish thinkers and educators fully articulated the project of an enriched Jewish culture in America—then a novel and somewhat revolutionary concept, considering European Jewry's longstanding cultural dominance. Foremost among these thinkers was Mordecai Kaplan, on faculty at the Jewish Theological Seminary in New York. In *Judaism as a Civilization*, his major work (published in 1934), Kaplan declared art to be a critical component of Jewish survival in the Diaspora, writing that, "[a] civilization cannot endure on a high plane without the preservation and cultivation of its arts."[12] Kaplan advocated a renaissance of Jewish arts, from music and theater to domestic objects and synagogue worship, and inspired a young generation of American Jewish educators and artists to take up the cause as their own.[13]

Corinne Chochem, a Jewish dance specialist who had trained with Martha Graham, was among the first to teach the new folk dances emerging from the Yishuv. In the interwar period, Chochem had been active with Hanoar Haivri ("the Hebrew Youth"), a Hebraist youth movement, whose founder, Moshe Davis, advocated for a creative, Hebraist-Zionist culture in America that would nurture the *adam shalem* (whole person) and the whole community. Davis himself was a protégé of Mordecai Kaplan, and, like Kaplan, insisted that the nurturing of Jewish art forms was critical to American Jewry's survival as a distinct and vital community. Davis criticized the limited relevance and impact of the Hebraist movement in the United States as it then stood, which, in his estimation, had reinforced a bifurcation between the majority of the Jewish population and the Hebrew-literate elites of the Jewish world: rabbis and Hebrew teachers. He argued that there was no better, more effective way of rooting Hebrew culture and Judaism in the hearts of American Jews than through the arts, through which the "strongest of human bonds may be established, the bond of mutual emotional experience."[14] To this end, Davis instituted a Hebrew Arts Committee in 1942, a project that was originally intended to bring Hebraist culture to the masses.

Chochem headed Hanoar Haivri's dance division, choreographing dances and performing with fellow youth group members at local events and in annual arts festivals. Beginning in 1942, she served as director of Rikkud Ami ("Dance of My People"), the dance group of the Hebrew Arts Committee, a related project instituted by Davis. Chochem also published an instructional book on the subject of Israeli folk dance, *Palestine Dances!*, in 1941. The book, a compendium of detailed instructions, musical scores, and lyrics for seventeen folk dances, proved popular, leading to a series of "Folk Art evenings" at the Jewish Theological Seminary. Here was proof, Chochem felt, that "Jewish youth was . . . eager to experience its culture" firsthand, rather than simply learning about it in lectures or stale classroom exercises.[15]

Like Chochem, Dvora Lapson was a choreographer and performer who applied her talents to the nascent field of Israeli folk dance in America. Lapson had studied ballet and modern dance as a young woman, and was the first to incorporate Jewish themes into the field of concert dance, deriving inspiration from the Bible, Hasidic tradition, Jewish mystical texts, and Zionism.[16] While performing her dances in America and abroad, Lapson also devoted much of her attention to the role of dance in Jewish education. She was associated with a circle of progressive educators then active and influential in Jewish communal life in New York, known collectively as the "Benderly Boys" after their mentor, Samson Benderly.[17] Progressive pedagogy taught that "learning by doing," rather than the transmission and mastery of a body of specific, text-based information, was a key to sound educational development in young people. Benderly and Mordecai Kaplan, both of whom were influenced by philosopher of progressive education John Dewey, provided the intellectual foundations for this approach in the Jewish educational

Figure 3.1. Dvora Lapson, one of the chief interpreters of Israeli dance within the American Jewish educational sphere, published several books about the genre and oversaw the production of musical recordings for dancers. The cover of her *Dances of the Jewish People*, published in 1954 by the Jewish Education Committee of New York, showcases dancers with a variety of ethnic and religious identities; for Lapson, exposing young American Jews to Israeli folk dance taught them that the Jewish people, while diverse, shared a national legacy. Collection of University Library, California State University, Long Beach.

sphere. Dance, in this context, was an important element of experiential education, and Lapson became a major proponent of the educational value of Jewish dance. As director of the Dance Education Department of the New York City Jewish Education Committee (the successor to Benderly's Jewish Bureau of Education), Lapson oversaw a staff of specialists who integrated Jewish dance into Jewish educational curricula in New York City.[18]

It was in her capacity as teacher that Lapson articulated a role for Jewish folk dance in American Jewish life. For Lapson, Jewish dance had a crucial role to play in the development of a rich Jewish cultural life within the larger non-Jewish society. It also served as a means of connecting the Jewish youth of America to Jewish life throughout the world. As she wrote:

> In this country, without . . . a complete Jewish group life . . . Jewish education is called upon to do more than has been its share in the past in the shaping of Jewish communal group life and cultural practices. If Jewish education is to perform this great role successfully . . . [i]t must also summon to its aid the arts, and utilize them as instruments to help create a Jewish atmosphere. . . . In this respect the dance has much to contribute. The discovery by the child of certain Jewish values by means of a pleasurable physical and emotional experience through dance produces attitudes of a deep and positive nature. In such an atmosphere the educator can capture what may seem to be a fleeting emotional expression and build it into the permanent fabric of Jewish cultural existence.[19]

Lapson, like other proponents of progressive Jewish education, insisted that the most effective learning happened outside of the formal classroom environment. The cultural sphere, in Lapson's estimation, was a critically important arena for creating an indelible Jewish sensibility and environment in America.

Lapson perceived that Israeli dance could offer unique contributions to this effort. She argued that Israeli folk dances provided students a glimpse of contemporary life in Israel, particularly the diverse ethnic groups making up Israeli society by the early 1950s. Studying the "colorful dances of the Bukharian Jews, and the subtle and spiritualized gestures of the Yemenites" alongside the hora would instill in American Jewish children "the joy and enthusiasm which the new Jewish homeland has stirred up in the heart of every Jew."[20] Other contemporary Israeli folk dances taught by Lapson hearkened back to ancient biblical rituals and festivals, providing a means of connecting ancient and modern Israel in the minds—and bodies—of dancers. According to Lapson, the popular dance "Mayim, Mayim" ("Water,

Water"), for instance, which incorporated movements of water drawing and the singing of a relevant passage from the Book of Isaiah, served to remind children "of the importance of water in an arid country," to help them imagine life in biblical times, and to connect these images with the Jewish textual and religious tradition.

The dancer to have perhaps the greatest influence on the development of Israeli folk dance in America was Fred Berk, born Friedrich (Fritz) Berger in Vienna in 1911. In 1931, Berk joined Gertrud Kraus's professional dance company in Vienna. Having recently toured in Palestine, Kraus brought her experiences of the place into her studio, where Berk first encountered the movements and style of Yemenite Jewish dance, among other forms. Berk credited his exposure to Jewish dance in Kraus's studio with awakening his Jewish identity and his desire to explore that identity through the medium of dance.[21] Berk's career in Europe ended with Hitler's invasion of Austria in March 1938, and he emigrated to the United States in 1940. He ultimately settled in New York, where he began working with an old friend and fellow European refugee, Katya Delakova, to whom he was married in the 1940s and early 1950s.

Beginning in the 1940s, Berk and Delakova performed their Jewish dance programs in concert halls, synagogues, resorts, camps, and Jewish community centers, for Zionist youth groups and on college campuses, throughout the country. With the support and encouragement of the Jewish Welfare Board, Berk and Delakova published books and cut records on Jewish and Israeli folk dance. As did Corinne Chochem, the two also worked with the Hebrew Arts Committee, performing at festivals and teaching classes at the Jewish Theological Seminary, where they established a Jewish Dance Guild. On staff at the 92nd Street Y, the duo taught various courses, including one on Palestinian and Jewish folk dance. While Berk was not religiously observant and had limited Jewish literacy—he barely knew any Hebrew at this time, by his own admission—he felt that Jewish folk dance was his particular forte.[22] Indeed, Berk's "conversion" to Jewish folk dance underscores the accessibility of the medium for individuals with little formal Jewish education, a benefit in the contemporaneous American Jewish scene.

Berk saw himself as an educator and, much like Dvora Lapson, he argued that Jewish dance was an incomparable tool for inspiring youth to learn about, and commune with, the Jewish legacy, past and present. He insisted that Israeli folk dance served as a stimulus to further Jewish learning:

> It has happened many times that young people are introduced to Israeli folk dancing who never before participated in any Jewish activity and who know hardly anything of their own background, but they love to dance and get more and more involved. . . . Now,

they start to ask questions about themselves; who they are, where
they come from; and why they feel this type of dancing is part
of themselves. These young tyros sometimes start to read books
on Jewish topics, the history and religion of the Jewish people,
even going to the Bible. . . . [They] might join a group for a
visit to Israel, not only to join in the dance activities but to get
to know the country and its people.[23]

Berk treasured folk dance, too, for its recreational, therapeutic, and theatrical qualities. Yet its chief value for the Jewish community was clearly its
efficacy (Berk claimed) as an educational medium. "Dance is an exciting
key with which to unlock the heritage and culture of the Jewish people," he
wrote, "their habits, customs, traditions, language and philosophy of life."[24]
    Berk first traveled to Israel in 1949, and during this and subsequent
visits he selected new dances to bring back to teach in America. Because
of his preeminent position in the Jewish folk dance world in the United
States, prominent Israeli folk dance choreographers came to see Berk as a
kind of ambassador of Israeli folk dance in America, through whom they
might disseminate new developments in the field.[25] At the regional level,
meanwhile, American Jewish dance specialists such as Miriam Lidster and
Florence Freehof (both based in California) taught Israeli dances as well.
Another way in which dance educators disseminated Israeli folk dance in
the 1950s and 1960s was through publications: like Corinne Chochem
before them, Berk, Delakova, Lapson, Lidster, and Freehof all published
instructional books on Israeli dance, as did the Jewish National Fund and
local Zionist bodies.[26] While American-based Jewish dance educators clearly
played an important role in the transmission of dances, Israeli folk dance
specialists from Israel also extended their influence in the United States
by teaching and performing in America with increasing frequency in the
1950s and 1960s. These included Rivka Sturman, Gurit Kadman, Dani
Dassa, Danny Uziel, Moshiko, and Ayalah Goren (Kadman's daughter),
among others.[27]
    Lapson, Berk, and many other Jewish educators expressed abiding faith
in the educational benefits of Israeli folk dance for young American Jews.
Inculcating "Jewishness," broadly speaking, was central to their goals; so
was introducing American Jewish youth to Israel and encouraging young
people to feel connected to the Jewish state. Proponents of Israeli folk
dance insisted that the medium created just this affective bond. Ben Zion
Schreiber, writing of the importance of Israeli folk dance for young participants at the Brandeis Camp Institute in greater Los Angeles, expressed
exactly this notion. As he put it:

> The average young American is an avid dancer. Dancing is the
> core of his social life. But how could it be given a specifically
> Jewish character [at camp]? It was felt that it would be worth-
> while to experiment with folk dancing of the type that prevailed
> in Israel. . . . It was sufficient that the camper was reminded of
> Israel, something that he had come to recognize as positive and
> creative in character. He saw . . . an answer to the questions
> that had so badgered him. Were the Jews a parasitic people?
> No, look at Israel. Were they cowardly? No, look at Israel. Were
> they enterprising? Of course, look at Israel. . . . Folk dancing
> became the norm. . . . By relating Jewish symbols . . . to a
> dynamic Jewish culture, the opportunity was presented to invest
> the Jewish youth with new meaning.[28]

Instilling positive feelings about the Jewish state through the medium of
dance, Schreiber implied, was even more important than granting campers
deep knowledge of contemporary Israel. This attitude cohered with that of
other progressive Jewish educators, for whom dance, like "[t]rips, clubs, arts,
[and] crafts," shaped young Jews, including their attachments to Israel, more
meaningfully than did the transmission of intellectual content. Whether or
not this proved correct is an open question.[29]

Lapson, Berk, and others targeted Jewish youth as the key constituency for Israeli folk dance and the population that would accrue the greatest
benefits from it. Yet one may ask: did American Jewish youth agree? More
specifically, how did young people themselves think and feel about Israeli
folk dance?

ISRAELI FOLK DANCE AND AMERICAN ZIONIST YOUTH

As important as the Israeli folk dance educators and performers were in
presenting and disseminating Israeli folk dances to Americans, the contribution of American Zionist youth in this regard was crucial. As was true
of dance educators Dvora Lapson and Fred Berk, some members of Zionist
youth movements emphasized the importance of cultural work in capturing the imaginations of Jewish youth and in binding them to the global
Jewish community. For them, focusing on accessible and inclusive cultural
and educational programming (including folk dance) rather than on *aliyah*
would provide American Zionism its raison d'être after 1948.

Beginning in the late 1940s and continuing through the mid-1960s,
members of Zionist youth organizations debated the best means of remaining
relevant in the wake of Israel's establishment and in light of American Jewry's

rapid upward mobility. It was in this context that Zionist ideologues within various movements grappled with the role of dance and related cultural activities in the lives of their members. Throughout the 1950s and 1960s, leaders and commentators from the *aliyah*-centered movements—which stressed preparation for settlement in Israel as a primary goal—maintained a degree of discomfort with Zionist cultural programming. They lamented a core precept of American-style cultural Zionism: that Israel should serve primarily as a crucial stimulus to Jewish life *in America*. "Hardliners" in the Zionist youth movements argued, to the contrary, that Jewish group survival hinged irrefutably on settlement in the Jewish state, and not on wide-ranging cultural work in the Diaspora.[30]

Yet the times had changed. *Halutziut* ideology—with its emphasis on the heroic self-reliance of the Jewish pioneers as they established cooperative agricultural settlements in Palestine—had peaked during the 1930s, a period of relative anxiety for American Jewry. In the postwar period, antisemitism was in retreat, and most American Jews were no longer interested in exploring utopian solutions to society's ills, particularly if it meant emigrating from the United States.[31] "As we see it, the entire frame of reference in which the Zionist youth movement must work has changed drastically" since the founding of Israel, wrote the editors of *Furrows*, a journal for the socialist-Zionist youth group Habonim, in a symposium on the future of the Zionist youth movement in America. "This has been said many times," the editors continued, "yet we still feel that the failure to *really* grapple with this fact and to develop and execute a program which takes fully into account the new situation," had left American Zionist youth on the sidelines.[32]

For some, an inclusive, cultural Zionism offered a compelling alternative to the ideological fractiousness and marginality of the Zionist youth movements as they presently stood. Only a cultural Zionism, focused on building knowledge of Jewish history and strengthening attachments to the Jewish people, rather than an ideological Zionism embroiled in party politics, would ensure "the preservation of the Jews as a viable entity in and outside of Israel," in the words of one proponent.[33] "The only way to instill in the Diaspora Jew a taste for Jewish life and a sense of meaning," argued another, "is to imbue him with the content and values of Jewish culture and Jewish spirit—Jewishness."[34] Emigration to Israel was not essential to this project of imbuing youth with "Jewishness," according to this line of reasoning; cultural work was.

Movement leaders also understood that, in order to survive, American Zionism had to take seriously the social and cultural needs of postwar teenagers and college-aged youth. An article in *Ohalenu*, the newsletter of religious Zionist youth group Hashomer Hadati (later B'nei Akiva), addressed this dilemma, concluding that a broadened cultural emphasis was the only solution to the problem of low retention in the movement. Navigating between the Scylla of worldly American social norms and the Charybdis of yeshiva-bred "asceticism," the author assessed the situation in stark terms, arguing that, "*hachshara* [preparation for life in Israel] and kibbutz become unattractive if the group is not suitable for one's self-expression."[35]

Israeli folk dance appeared to be one of the most appealing, accessible forms of self-expression available to Jewish youth. In an evaluation of their movement on the occasion of the twenty-fifth anniversary of Hashomer Hatzair ("the Young Guard") in 1949, leaders of that organization—generally considered to be the most ideologically rigorous branch of the Labor Zionist movement in America—grappled with "the needs of the adolescent and the means employed by Hashomer Hatzair to satisfy" them.[36] This assessment of the strengths and weaknesses of the educational system for the pre-teenage and teenage cohorts illustrated a pragmatic, if grudging, acceptance of the role of folk dance in the movement in the absence of widespread ideological maturity. The program for younger members, which was meant to develop "an awareness of Jewish values in the vast American desert," was something of a lost cause, intellectually speaking, according to the report. In practice, the program tended to "combine a vague smattering of *tzofeh* [scouting] practices with the whole Hebrew-Zionist environment provided by the *shirim* [songs], *rikudim* [dances], holidays and special celebrations" in social halls and camps. If the youngster in the movement failed to develop a coherent ideological system at this age, however, he was "at least able to associate a good time with Hashomer Hatzair," ensuring that "the youngster stays in the movement and builds the beginnings of group life." Indeed, a leader-training manual produced by the movement claimed that it was Israeli folk dance "more than anything else" that initially attracted people to the group.[37]

Folk dance constituted a resonant symbolic act that spoke more eloquently of movement idealism than did the simple recital of ideological principles. Indeed, for some (and probably many) members, hard-line Zionist ideology was almost beside the point. Israeli folk dance was the clearest embodiment of the particular aesthetic sensibilities and psychological modes that characterized the Zionist youth movement as a whole, aspects that appeared to be more essential to members of the movement than were Zionist political commitments. Turning to a number of personal reminiscences by former members of Habonim which appear in the edited collection *Builders and Dreamers: Habonim Labor Zionist Youth in North America*, it becomes clear that the Zionist youth movement was appealing, to some degree, in that it was "cool." Israeli folk dance comprised an important component of a Zionist subculture, along with other special modes of expression (including specific forms of dress and music and the use of a rhetoric of nonconformism).

Writer and communal activist Leonard Fein shared in his reminiscences that, even for the most committed Habonim members, "it is probably a mistake to say that the ends of the movement were more important, or even as important, as its means. . . . My impression is that our ideological intensity was principally a device for rationalizing, justifying, extending the core experience, which was psychological rather than political." Folk song and dance, in this context, woven together with a leftist political idiom, formed a quasi-countercultural American Jewish sensibility:

> We sang the Spanish Civil War songs without knowing much about the Spanish Civil War . . . we marched with the NAACP . . . we eagerly debated with the Marxists . . . on the corruption of the revolution, and went home to sing folk songs that the Weavers were later to make famous. We knew that Adlai Stevenson was Jewish and Dwight Eisenhower was white bread . . . and that folk dancing was more honest than cheek-to-cheek stuff and a hundred other things that no one else knew, or so we believed.[38]

The Zionist youth subculture that Fein describes shared much with the nascent American counterculture, with its topical discussion sessions and folk song hootenannies that "wink[ed] in the direction of revolutionary ideas," as David Hadju has written.[39]

The political scientist Daniel Elazar, who had joined Habonim in 1949, recalled similarly that the movement, as he experienced it, hovered "on the fringes of radicalism" in Detroit of the late 1940s and early 1950s. The group fraternized with various politically radical groups then active in the city. Members of Detroit Habonim, like Fein's comrades, "sang the right labor songs" and were "at the vanguard of the folk song revival." Elazar was religiously observant, devoted to Hebrew studies, and a lonely newcomer to his Detroit high school; in Habonim, which "was looked at as a little bit wild," Elazar found a thrilling social outlet in which group members "[chose] the way we dressed and stay[ed] out all hours of the night."[40]

Fiction writer Mordecai Richler echoes these same themes in his recollections of Habonim in the late 1940s. He joined the group—and remained a member through four years of high school—at the invitation of a hip friend who, with his "rakishly pegged trousers and . . . condoms in his billfold" embodied "everything [Richler] admired." The group provided Richler and his friends a platform for mild cultural and political defiance in postwar Montreal. Richler recounts his group's response to the UN's approval of the partition of Palestine in November 1947: he and his fellow Habonimniks "marched downtown . . . waving Israeli flags, flaunting our songs in Anglo-Saxon neighborhoods, until we reached the heart of the city where . . . we faltered briefly, embarrassed, self-conscious—before we put a stop to traffic by forming defiant circles and dancing the hora in the middle of the street."[41]

Marion Magid, a regular contributor to *Midstream* magazine in the 1950s and 1960s, described the Habonim sensibility in similar terms. Why did she join the organization as a teenager? "The reason," she explained, "was that it appealed to my sense of the heroic." It was a heroic affect, rather than any particular deeds or political commitments, that seemed to matter most to the author and her fellow members. "Neither I nor the people I knew then had a particular gift for dialectics," she recalled; "the main thing was the energy," an earnest Zionism expressed through grand romantic gestures.[42] Expressive idioms such as dress were particularly alluring to Magid. The boys in Habonim, she recalled, "wore white shirts, open at the neck . . . like scions of a noble house." Describing the moment when, in the wake of the UN partition vote on Palestine, all the Zionist youth movements gathered to dance the hora en masse on the streets of midtown Manhattan, Magid remembered that "Hashomer Hatza'ir members had snappy dark blue shirts with red strings at the neck—they made a better showing than we [Habonim] did."[43]

The movement satisfied Magid's bohemian proclivities at the time; for her, Habonim provided a cultural awakening. It was through regular Habonim meetings at a townhouse on the Upper East Side, for example, that the author became acquainted with Manhattan for the first time, a watershed in her transformation from Bronx girl to New York sophisticate. At a leadership training camp in Vermont, Magid and her comrades learned "to cook shish kebab Israeli style, to roll cigarettes out of Bull Durham tobacco with one hand, to spring to our feet in case of ambush." There, she absorbed the knowledge that "Socialist-Zionism was a metaphor for every kind of gallantry. On Shabbat we carried around Borochov, Achad Ha'am, A. D. Gordon, but we read Kafka, Thomas Wolfe, Dos Passos."[44] Habonim was, for Magid, a gateway to a wider world of culture and ideas.

It is not surprising that, as denizens of postwar America, members of Zionist youth groups partook of cultural forms—whether dance, music, or literature—that had little to do with Zionism per se. What is more interesting is that Zionist youth consumed these forms in the context of the Zionist youth organizations. For older cohorts, "Pete Seeger and the Weavers were number one," according to Elazar;[45] likewise, a former member of religious-Zionist B'nei Akiva recalled that "Pete Seeger was a god."[46] For younger members, Western square dancing appeared to be a favorite. In 1951, for example, a Habonim chapter in Minneapolis began the year with a "real live western style barn dance," while, the following season, their counterparts in Chicago considered its barn dance, for which they hired a professional square dance caller, "the social event of the year." It appears that Western-themed movies, musicals, and dance were a significant pop culture influence on younger Zionists through the early 1950s.[47] As these examples and the recollections of former Habonim members suggest, American Zionist youth embraced both popular and highbrow forms of American culture and integrated them into Zionist programs and activities.

However much they consumed and enjoyed "American" rather than explicitly "Jewish" cultural forms, though, Zionist youth seemed to treasure Israeli folk dance (and song) above other genres. All evidence suggests that Israeli folk dance was ubiquitous in Zionist youth programming in the 1950s and 1960s, something that was not true of other genres of dance such as square dancing. According to publications from the postwar decades, Habonim's *chugei rikkud* [dance groups] throughout the country, for example, would practice Israeli folk dances regularly and perform often on their chapters' behalf at group events.[48] As one former member of Los Angeles Habonim recalls, "Israeli singing and dancing were always present," at the region's annual Neshef (festival) in the 1950s and 1960s.[49] Meetings and special events alike often began or ended with entire Habonim chapters singing and dancing together. This was characteristic, too, of Young Judaea, the centrist, non-*aliyah*-centered movement sponsored by Hadassah, the Women's Zionist Organization of America. In this period, *Young Judaean*, the magazine for younger members of the movement, was filled with news of folk dance activities occurring across the nation—not only in New York and California, but also in places such as Chattanooga, Tennessee and Waco, Texas.[50]

Even in religiously oriented B'nei Akiva, where mixed dancing between men and women violated traditional religious norms, Israeli folk dance was a central activity.[51] According to former members of the movement, young men and women would dance Israeli folk dances together in many local chapters, but would refrain from doing so at larger regional or national gatherings.[52] Israeli folk dance and song, as formal performances and informal activities, were listed prominently among the offerings in an undated brochure for B'nei Akiva's Camp Moshava—along with scouting, Hebrew lessons, arts and crafts, baseball, Ping-Pong, and volleyball.[53] A former member recalls that, in his chapter, each meeting would start with the hora, which served as the backdrop for a call-and-response exercise in which participants would test their knowledge of everything from the weekly Torah portion to the geographic locations of kibbutzim in Israel.[54]

Examples abound, too, of Zionist youth bringing Israeli folk dance to audiences beyond their local chapters. Members of Young Judaea, for example, arranged performances in hospitals and homes for the elderly as well as at local festivals to raise awareness of Israel and garner funds for Young Judaea causes.[55] Likewise, Habonim chapters from Vancouver to Cleveland to Providence performed Israeli folk dances in community-wide festivals in these years.[56] The national Habonim dance group even appeared on prime time television, performing on *The Steve Allen Show* in October 1956.

In 1963, *Young Judaean* published an interview with the movement's dance director, Irene Friedman, who taught every summer at Young Judaea's Camp Tel Yehudah in Barryville, New York. While exhorting readers to learn new dances and host "Hora Hootenanies" in their own chapters, Friedman also discussed the larger significance of Israeli folk dance for Young Judaea members. For them, she argued, Israeli folk dance offered important lessons in a unique medium. As she explained it,

> Dance brings that special feeling of *ruach*—the spirit of well-being in doing things together. While Judaeans learn about many things through books, discussions, making things, etc., they can learn a great deal about Jewish life by learning Israeli dance. Knowledge of the Bible is brought in thru [sic] dances such as the Miriam Dance. . . . Knowledge of other peoples in Israel . . . are shown through the different Israeli folk dances. The dances teach us about the Israeli *army*, about the *geography*, about . . . the *work* of past and present pioneers. Even some of the *problems* of Israel have been sung and danced to—like "Mayim" [water]. . . . Israel is a dancing country from which we can learn how to rejoice.[57]

Friedman's understanding of the function of Israeli dance within Young Judaea cohered with the ideas of dance educators Dvora Lapson and Fred Berk regarding the role of Israeli folk dance in the American context more generally. For all three, and many others, it was precisely through the cultural medium of dance that young American Jews might strengthen their ties to Jewish life—and to each other.

This notion achieved full fruition in the form of the Israel Folk Dance Festival, held annually in New York beginning in 1952. The festival, which brought together the best dancers from the various youth movements in a one-day performance program, was meant to underscore and enhance the unifying function of Israeli folk dance within Zionist youth subculture. After the first year, the American Zionist Youth Council (later, the American Zionist Youth Foundation) selected Fred Berk as the festival's director.

Both participants and audience members were apparently swept up in the spirit of the event each year. Starting in 1957, the festival program even requested that, in deference to neighbors, "the audience . . . refrain from dancing in the street at the conclusion of the program."[58] (The statement seemed to do little good: at the 1963 festival, at Carnegie Hall, the audience "unintentionally blocked traffic on . . . 57th Street as they joined in circles dancing the Hora," according to one partisan observer.)[59] Between 1952 and the mid-1960s, the numbers of participating dancers nearly doubled in size. Close to two hundred dancers were taking part in the festival by the mid-1960s, and they spanned the full spectrum of Zionist life—from right-wing, Revisionist-Zionist Betar to leftist stalwarts Habonim and Hashomer Hatzair and religious Zionists B'nei Akiva and Mizrachi Hatzair, along with nonideological groups Young Judaea and Junior Hadassah. In addition, "non-Zionist" groups—that is, youth groups not affiliated formally with the American Zionist Youth Foundation—were now participating, including dance troupes from the Orthodox, Conservative, and Reform movements.[60]

A report on Habonim's Twenty-fifth Anniversary Convention, held in Washington, D.C., in December 1959, serves as yet another illustration of the sanctioned—and beloved—role that dance played for Zionist youth. To be sure, the convention's guest speakers had harsh words for contemporary America. Judd Teller, for example, a Yiddish poet and frequent contributor to the American Jewish press who served on the editorial board at *Midstream*, condemned American Jewry as a "Marjorie Morningstar society," reflecting the movement's avowed discomfort with mainstream American culture. The author of the report, Frances Zynstein, had little to say about the lectures, however. She saved her praise for the mass dancing and singing that followed. Leaving "the kingdom of important words" for the "universal kingdom of music and dance," Zynstein wrote, participants embraced folk song and folk dance as the "greatest outlet for expression." Every evening, "large winding horas accompanied the sounds of stamping feet and singing voices." Song and dance spoke "far better than words," she testified, of the Zionist ardor and support for "Jewish unity" that Habonim wished to inculcate in members.[61]

WIDENING AUDIENCES, DIVERSIFYING MEANINGS

Though the medium embodied the specific sensibilities of Zionist youth culture in the first postwar decades, Israeli folk dance proved accessible enough to become a popular medium within the American Jewish populace more broadly. As demonstrated above, Zionist youth groups had made Israeli dance a staple of festivals and fundraisers within the wider American Jewish community. The results of this endeavor could be seen in places such as Philadelphia and Boston, to name two examples, where Israeli folk dance activities had spread to local synagogues, campus Hillels, and even the public school system (in the case of Philadelphia) as well as being featured

in community-wide Israel folk dance festivals.[62] The increasing diversity of
Jewish contexts in which Israeli folk dance occurred suggests the flexibility
of the medium as a marker of Jewish identity and as an educational tool.
By the early 1960s, for example, young Reform Jews in that movement's
national youth group and its summer camps had adopted Israeli folk dance
as a pervasive activity. In this context, Israeli folk dance furthered the
Reform movement's larger goals at the time: invigorating youth education
and building affective ties to Israel and to the Jewish people as a whole.[63]
Israeli folk dance was now thoroughly ensconced in the American Jewish
denominational wing that, historically, had been most hostile to Zionism.

Israeli dance did not remain the sole purview of the American Jewish
community, however; in these years, participants in the burgeoning folk
dance movement in the postwar United States adopted Israeli folk dance
as an essential part of their repertoire, too. Folk dance activities and performances were taking place across the United States in the postwar years
in diverse settings: YMCAs, museums, rural campgrounds, churches, public
recreation facilities, and on the concert stage. Schools were also primary
venues for folk dance activities: By one estimate, 80 to 90 percent of schools
and colleges canvassed in a contemporaneous national survey claimed to
offer folk dance courses to their students.[64] According to a leader of the
folk dance movement, Vyts Beliajus, Israeli folk dance was "an overall favorite among all folk dancers," regardless of ethnic or religious background.[65]
Though Beliajus's statement is subjective and difficult to verify, a wealth of
evidence points to the pervasive presence of Israeli folk dance among folk
dance practitioners across the country.

At the influential Pacific Folk Dance Camp in Stockton, California,
for example, Dvora Lapson, Rivka Sturman, and others taught Israeli dances
to diverse audiences: participants hailed from all over the United States
and Canada, and about a quarter of the participants each year were school-
teachers who brought the dances (including, of course, Israeli folk dances)
back to their elementary and high school classes.[66] Examples abound of folk
dance groups, composed exclusively or mostly of non-Jews, performing Israeli
dances in these years, from Tacoma, Washington, to Norwalk, Connecticut,
at events such as United Nations Week Festivals, folk dance showcases, and
holiday celebrations.[67] One commentator, noting the popularity of Israeli
folk dance in America among non-Jews, shared an anecdote about a folk
dancer who "had learned the 'Hora' from a [presumably Christian] YMCA
leader, 'Im Hoopalnu' from a Chinese instructor, and the 'Hora Aggadati'
from a Swedish-American boy whose activities in the field were, until
recently, confined to western-style square dance calling."[68]

General folk dance groups integrated Israeli folk dances into a broader
repertoire, learning and performing Israeli horas as well as Czech polkas and

Yugoslavian kolos (to name a few). In this context, a group's adoption of Israeli folk dance did not signal that the performers were Zionists or even Jews. This interethnic "borrowing" appears to have been a general phenomenon. A writer for *Dance Magazine* reported in the mid-1950s, for example, that while it was "not unusual to see costumes of nearly every nation" on display at folk dance festivals, with increasing frequency, ethnic costumes did not "correspond to the wearer's actual nationality." As she wrote,

> Native Austrians seeing the Schuplattler [*sic*] danced by a group dressed in the traditional leather pants have been amazed to discover that not one of the group was Austrian in descent! Many were Irish! On one occasion a group of dancers . . . presented a Peruvian dance. After the dance was finished a man rushed out on the floor and was literally speechless when he discovered that the group did not speak Spanish, were not Peruvian, and, as a matter of fact, none had ever visited Peru.[69]

This phenomenon points to questions about the uses of Israeli folk dance in postwar American life. How did leaders and followers of the folk dance movement—the majority of whom were, presumably, not Jewish—explain their desire to learn and perform the dances of other groups? Did the impetus for learning Israeli folk dance, in this context, differ from folk dance aficionados' appropriations of the dances of other ethnic or national groups? And how did the desires and expectations of non-Jews converge with or diverge from those of Jews in this field?

To answer the first question, it's necessary to uncover the roots of the folk dance phenomenon. The folk dance movement arose in the context of Progressive urban reform during the era of mass immigration in the early twentieth century; at the time, leaders of the newly founded Playground Association of America (PAA) sought to develop recreational spaces and programs in urban areas in which immigrants could congregate and enjoy themselves while absorbing ideas about good citizenship. Luther Gulick and Elizabeth Burchenal of the PAA found folk dancing to be an ideal vehicle in this regard. They valued folk dance as a medium that foregrounded ethnic pride and educated other Americans about the heritage of newcomers while also "subordinat[ing] the individual to the greater whole, promot[ing] team play and stress[ing] unity and interaction rather than division," as Patricia Mooney Melvin has argued.[70] At the behest of Gulick, director of New York City's physical education programs, Burchenal (a folk dance specialist) introduced folk dance into the city's schools. Burchenal in particular stressed the medium's educational value in a pluralistic society: folk dance, "vivid, human and universally comprehensible" was uniquely well suited to teach Americans to appreciate differences among themselves while literally embodying the benefits of mutual cooperation.[71]

Folk dance teachers in the post–World War II era provided similar rationales for the importance of the movement. Dance educator Esther Brown, for example, devoted an article in *Dance Magazine* in 1954 to the subject of "ethnic dance" as an educational medium. Airing fears shared by many in the field of progressive education, Brown noted that educators were continually searching for tools to ameliorate the "vitiating effects of imitation [and] the mechanical aspects of technical drill, and the increasing fear of creativity" among students. The author proposed an antidote to rote classroom learning: dance, and "ethnic" dance in particular. "For those of us who are primarily concerned with dance as an educative process," she argued, "[ethnic dance] provides rich potentialities. As a source of fresh vitality . . . and greater awareness of the total personality; as a means to a deeper understanding of others, these ancient ethnic dance forms can be used in a most valuable way in education." Brown was particularly interested in connecting ethnic minorities to their own heritage through the medium of folk dance. This, she insisted, was a crucial means of fostering the full psychological and social development of the individual. By reconstructing and mastering the dances of their ancestors, Brown claimed, Hawaiian or American Indian students might recover "some forgotten part of themselves," releasing "a dormant deep-seated energy and emotional vitality of which they had never before been aware."[72] Vyts Beliajus, too, understood his own promotion of folk dance, as a teacher and publisher, in this context. "Yes . . . we must all be good Americans," he wrote in *Viltis*, the folk dance magazine that he edited and published, "but let us also cherish and not be ashamed of the heritage of our parents." An "ethnic awakening," as he called it, was underway, and folk dance provided the key instrument for that awakening.[73]

Rank-and-file practitioners, too, appeared to value folk dance as an educational medium, broadly speaking. In an article for *Dance Magazine* published in 1955, Lisa Lekis, a folk dance specialist, asked some of the participants of a major California folk dance festival in 1954 to explain why they participated in this "mass movement." She found that many participants were teachers in elementary schools, high schools, and universities, and that many mastered the medium at the request of school administrators who wished to integrate folk dance into the educational curriculum. Lekis conveyed some of these teachers' reflections on the value of folk dance: they reported anecdotally that children exposed to the medium did better academically and exhibited more appropriate classroom behavior. One participant stressed the progressive, democratic character of folk dance education and its affect on the social adjustment of young people, claiming that "[f]olk dance is essentially a 'dance of the people' and general participation is more important than individual skill. I use folk dance to teach children how to work and play together." Another informant emphasized that folk dance taught children "about other ways of life through the international language of dance and music."[74] None of the sources in Lekis's piece mentioned Israeli folk dance specifically. Yet one can assume that the folk dance enthusiasts interviewed for the article contextualized Israeli folk dance within this same framework, just as they did the other common national and ethnic dances in the folk dance repertoire.

It appears that the Cold War provided a further impetus for the folk dance movement. In the first postwar decades, the U.S. government (and the State Department in particular) was seeking to extend its cultural influence abroad as a "soft" alternative to aggressive political propaganda and overt military maneuvers. To this end, in the course of the 1950s, the United States government sent a production of *Porgy and Bess* to Yugoslavia, opera singer Marian Anderson to India, and the Martha Graham Dance Company to Indonesia. Government officials hoped that such cultural exports would win America new admirers.[75] Folk dance, too, had a role to play here. In the 1950s, the State Department sent recognized folk dance specialists Mary Ann and Michael Herman to Japan to teach European and regional American dances, presumably for the same reasons that the American government sent opera and modern dance stars abroad.[76] Rhetoric in support of folk dance and music in this period tended to stress the medium's role in furthering peace and amity among nations. Meeting in Oslo for its annual conference in 1955, for example, the International Folk Music Council delineated three chief reasons for preserving and promoting folk dance and music; promoting world peace was one of them. (According to the council, folk traditions formed "a bond of union between the people of all countries at all levels of culture.")[77]

On the home front, meanwhile, American audiences were treated to "goodwill tours" by such institutions as the Moscow-based Moiseyev Dance Company, the Yugoslav National Folk Ballet, the Polish dance company Mazowsze, the Ukrainian Dance Company, the Filipino export Bayanihan, and the Ximenez-Vargas Ballet Español. The Cold War period was the golden age for such state-sponsored dance ensembles. Moiseyev, for example, attracted audiences in the hundreds of thousands during its first U.S. tour in 1958, and many millions also witnessed the ensemble's appearance on *The Ed Sullivan Show* during its American sojourn.[78]

One can interpret the significance of Inbal's appearance in 1950s America in this context. Inbal, the National Dance Theatre of Israel, was a beneficiary of the America-Israel Cultural Foundation; the foundation organized tours of Inbal and other Israeli cultural institutions, in part, in an effort to portray Israel as a natural cultural—and political—ally of the United States during the Cold War. Inbal made its debut in the United States in January 1958, appearing in concert halls as well as performing and teaching at Zionist youth events.[79] (Winthrop Sargent, writing in the *New Yorker* about the "colorful and lively" program by Inbal that he attended, dubbed the event a "Yemenite Hoedown"—yet another indication of the pervasive influence of the "cowboy" idiom in 1950s culture.)[80]

Indeed, *Dance Magazine* publisher Rudolf Orthwine gave Inbal special notice as an ambassador of good will in a 1958 editorial in that magazine. Orthwine contended that, in the age of the atom bomb, new responsibilities had fallen to artists the world over. As he wrote:

> Right now, mankind has reached a solemn time of decision. The man-made satellite and the arms race have forced us to a choice between self-destruction and boundless achievement. . . . [T]here must be a new awareness of the reasons for human behavior. . . . The feeling of fellowship, of mutual respect and cooperation, is all too alien in many areas of human endeavor. But it does permeate the world of art. The artist speaks a language that has not yet been mastered by science and politics. When foreign performers—an Emil Gilels, a Shanta Rao, an Inbal— come to this country, a new bond of understanding is forged. And when a Jan Peerce goes to Russia or a Ballet Theatre to Brussels, the feeling is reciprocated.[81]

Dance Magazine, Orthwine pledged, would continue to play an important role in "fostering the image of understanding and of keeping that image bright and constant."[82]

It is important to note that this type of rhetoric is absent from the writings of Jewish dance educators such as Corinne Chochem, Dvora Lapson, and Fred Berk. Their views of the educational importance of Israeli folk dance more nearly match those of Esther Brown and Vyts Beliajus (quoted above), who stressed the medium's role in fostering interest, pride, and further commitment to one's particular heritage. To be sure, many Israeli and Jewish dance specialists of the postwar period taught dances to Jews and non-Jews alike. Yet Chochem, Lapson, and Berk did not articulate a role for folk dance generally in teaching Jewish children to appreciate the backgrounds of other Americans, for example, or in fostering world peace. Their focus was upon the benefits that Israeli folk dance *in particular* provided to American Jews *specifically*.

Likewise, practitioners of Israeli folk dance among Zionist youth— especially within the designated dance units of the various movements—

devoted themselves exclusively to Israeli dance and did not appear interested in exploring other types of folk dance. Examples of occasional square dance activities among the youngest cohorts of Zionist youth movements provide the sole exception. Square dance activities, however, appear to have been purely recreational; in other words, when Zionist youth performed folk dances in formal programs and festivals, those dances were Israeli folk dances. Interestingly, the first Israel Folk Dance Festival, held in New York in 1952, featured a square dance performance by the aptly named American Square Dance Group. After Fred Berk became director the following year, however, the festival presented only Israeli folk dances. Neither square dances nor any other type of regional, ethnic, or national folk dance appeared on the festival program again.[83]

In this light, Israeli folk dance served very different symbolic functions for American Jews and among members of the folk dance community, respectively. Folk dance leaders and enthusiasts tended to emphasize the importance of learning the dances of others (including Jews) as a means of bridging differences in anxious times. The example of the Los Angeles International Folk Dance Festival, established in 1947, provides a case in point: the festival was meant to encourage understanding between peoples and combat prejudice, offering reassurance that, despite a fascinating diversity of folk expressions, "man is the same the world over."[84]

American Jewish educators and aficionados of Israeli folk dance, in contrast, promoted Israeli folk dance as a means of strengthening Jewish group identity. Teaching and learning Israeli folk dances, in this context, demanded at least some sort of commitment to the preservation and furtherance of Jewish culture. Florence Freehof, in her *Guide for Israeli-Jewish Folk Dancers*, decried the " 'mishmash' of dances paraded under the title, 'Israeli.' " She wrote that, "When one represents any culture relating to a country, with it should come a feeling of responsibility to that culture."[85] For Fred Berk, authenticity did not arise from slavish devotion to accurate execution, but to knowledge of the culture that produced the dance. He noted that

> [w]atching an evening of international folk dancing . . . it becomes obvious that, in spite of "authentic" teaching, the dances all seem to look much alike. In order to execute a folk dance in a truly authentic way, it is hardly enough to teach the steps and formations of the dance. . . . The key that eventually leads to authenticity is the knowledge and understanding of peoples, their religion, philosophy, habits and customs—in short, their complete way of life.[86]

As his career and his writings make clear, Berk encouraged young American Jews to approach Israeli and Jewish folk dance in this spirit.

Considering their overwhelmingly liberal political profile, most American Jews at the time would certainly have agreed with liberal folk dance enthusiasts that it was important to fight prejudice and encourage harmony among America's citizens and among the nations of the world. Israeli folk dance, however, appears to be one area in which American Jews were eager to emphasize Jewish particularism—albeit in a medium that did not demand especial Jewish literacy or ask participants to draw deep and abiding distinctions between themselves and non-Jews.

There were circumstances, of course, in which American Jews did use Israeli folk dance in order to cultivate good relations with other groups. The participation of Jewish groups in informal exchanges, international folk dance festivals, and training programs can be considered implicit endorsements of this approach. The dance group of the Israel-American Club at the University of Minnesota, for example, provides a glimpse of how some American Jews (and Israelis) used Israeli folk dance as a means of outreach to others. The dance group, established in 1953 by Israeli students studying at the Minneapolis campus, began meeting with other folk dance circles and exchanging dances with them. Why? "[T]he dancers feel they are learning about cultures of other countries, and in turn can depict to others some aspects of life and feelings of the people of the state of Israel," one participant reported.[87]

For proponents of interfaith brotherhood, too, Israeli folk dance appears to have offered unique educational possibilities. Religiously motivated enthusiasts of Israeli folk dance came from different branches of Christianity, including Lutherans, Catholics, and Mormons (to name a few). A report on Israeli folk dance activities in the United States in *Dance* magazine noted, for example, that a group of nuns from Pittsburgh had learned Israeli folk dances with the intent to teach them to students at their parochial school. The author of the article offered no rationale for the particular appeal of Israeli folk dance for Catholic nuns, as if no explanation was necessary. Generally speaking, she attributed the interest of non-Jews in Israeli folk dance to the "contagious joy" of the hora, on the one hand, and the "tremendous interest in folk dancing" of all varieties in the United States, on the other.[88] Perhaps this explains the appeal of Israeli folk dance for the Pacific Lutheran University Folk Dancers, a troupe that performed Israeli dances alongside German, Lithuanian, and Polish numbers, according to a folk dance program roundup in *Viltis* magazine.[89]

Some Christian groups undoubtedly turned to folk dance in general in this period as part of a broader impulse to integrate the arts into religious life. At the time, some leaders of American Christianity sought to strengthen the role of the arts in the life of the church as an expression of the nobility of the human endeavor and as a spur to the spiritual imagination and to religious devotion.[90] Dance, in this regard, was an appropriate means of spiritual connection to one's own faith as well as to humanity at large in the wake of a devastating world war and the existential challenges that postwar life presented.[91] As was true in progressive Jewish education circles, some Christian educators also stressed the unique efficacy of informal education, including dance, in bringing youth into the fold. "If a child is denied creative participation, he becomes inoculated with the feeling that what is 'told' to him in religious education has little to do with his own life as individual," argued religious dance specialist Margaret Fisk Taylor, in a special symposium on religion and dance published in the journal *Religious Education* in 1958. "Gradually," she continued, "[the child] comes to consider 'religion' as 'a philosophy to discuss' rather than 'the way one meets life.' "[92] Encountering religious narratives and feelings through the medium of dance, in contrast, appeared to grant young people agency as religious actors and to weave religion into their own experiential world. (Similarly, Moshe Davis, rabbi and architect of the Hebrew Arts Committee, wrote in 1957 of the critical role of dance education in "unfolding the personality and helping the individual to discover his relationship to God and to the world he lives in.")[93]

Just as, according to folk dance practitioners, learning Israeli dances might foster harmony among ethnic and national groups, so too might it bridge religious divides. It was in the context of ecumenical relations that Miriam and Saul Teplitz taught Israeli folk dances to a group of Protestant Christians in the summer of 1957. Writing in *Women's League Outlook*, Teplitz described how she and her husband, a Conservative rabbi in Long Island, along with their young son, had spent two weeks on staff at a camp in upstate New York sponsored by the Evangelical and Reformed Church. They had been invited to the camp to "acquaint our Christian friends with the history and development of Judaism as a religion, through its rituals, its customs and ceremonies," so that participants might better appreciate the Jewish "roots of Christianity." The Jewish couple was also the resident resource on the state of Israel, about which, Teplitz noted, participants had many questions. Along with showing a film (*Israel, Land of the Bible*), facilitating a discussion, and leading a Hebrew songfest, the Teplitzes taught the hora to the two hundred Christian lay families at the camp, to the accompaniment of "popular Israeli hit tunes." "Long after the camp had quieted down," recalled Teplitz, "the telling notes of our Jewish music hung in the atmosphere as though to whisper, 'Behold how good and how pleasant it is for brethren to dwell together.' "[94]

Teplitz seems to have understood Israeli folk dance as one important vehicle for conveying quintessential "Jewishness" to non-Jews and, at the same time, of creating common ground with Christians through the shared experience of dance. In her essay, Teplitz held both notions—of the value of differences *and* commonalities—in tension. On the one hand, Teplitz noted with approval that "[w]e [Jews] were, in their sight, brothers, created by one God, with differences . . . which became modulated as understanding increased."[95] On the other hand, Teplitz stressed the admiration that her Christian audience expressed for distinctly Jewish practices, such as kashrut. For Teplitz, people of diverse religions formed bonds of mutual understanding only through appreciation of real differences among them. According to this reasoning, Israeli folk dance could be taught to and enjoyed by all, but it also provided a means of showing how Jews—their religion, their heritage, their culture—were special.

For the "Yovail Dancers," a group of young Mormons in Pasadena, California, Israeli folk dance constituted their entire dance repertoire. In broad terms, interest in Israeli folk dancing accorded well with the Church of Latter Day Saints' commitment to dance, and the arts more generally, as an important component of individual and group development for young people. Beginning in 1910, the Mormon Church had begun hosting mass dance festivals for its youth, encompassing speech, drama, music and dance. According to one source, by the late 1950s the church oversaw some eighteen thousand dance events a year; thousands of dancers participated in the church's annual dance festival in Salt Lake City, which garnered some thirty thousand audience members. The Mutual Improvement Association (MIA), the church's youth movement, vetted appropriate dances and musical genres carefully: the waltz, fox trot, and tango were acceptable; jazz music and the jitterbug were not. In the early 1940s, folk dance became a sanctioned component of the festival program.[96]

The Yovail Dancers developed a repertoire of thirty Israeli folk dances under the guidance of Dani Dassa, an Israeli choreographer and instructor active in the western United States. They also studied Hebrew and the history and geography of Israel. Fifty members strong, the troupe performed before large audiences at festivals, civic centers, and Jewish community centers in California as well as on television, and even toured Israel in the summer of 1964. When asked about the purpose of such a dance group, founder Mildred Handy responded, "If these young people will have added to their knowledge the treasure of Solomon—understanding—our efforts will have been worthwhile."[97]

Perhaps Handy meant that the group studied Israeli dance to further ecumenical relations; her statement is vague enough to be interpreted this way. Theological considerations probably had much to do with the young dancers' quest for greater understanding of Israel through folk dance, however. Mormons trace their origins to the biblical Israelites; founder Joseph Smith believed that descendants of Joseph had sailed to America in ancient times and that contemporary Mormons were their spiritual heirs. Mormon eschatology assigns a significant role to the land of Israel, too. Mormons began making pilgrimages to Palestine after the Civil War to visit the biblical sites and to contemplate the Second Coming of Christ, to take place in Jerusalem and in America simultaneously.[98] One can speculate that, considering the significance of Israel in the Mormon imagination, the Yovail Dancers understood the learning and performing of Israeli folk dances as an extension of their religious education as Mormons.

In retrospect, non-Jewish perceptions of Israeli folk dance betray a blend of sincerity and solipsism, combining a genuine yearning for greater cultural and religious awareness with limited knowledge of (or even interest in) the specific historical or cultural contexts out of which Jewish and Israeli folk dance grew. A particularly illuminating example of this can be found in a feature article in *Viltis*, appearing in May 1962, reporting on Fred Berk's Israeli folk dance workshop at Camp Blue Star in North Carolina. The article drew particular attention to the Annual Mountain Dance and Folk Festival in Asheville, North Carolina, where, for the second year, Camp Blue Star dancers were slated to perform Israeli dances for an audience of bluegrass and clogging fans.

A description of the previous year's festival, published in *The Asheville Citizen* and quoted in *Viltis*, unwittingly reveals a notable gulf in understanding between American Jewish practitioners of Israeli folk dance and participants and observers from the surrounding (non-Jewish) community. The reporter for the *Asheville Citizen*, Lewis Green, described watching "a dance team with music strange to these mountains," who contributed "Jewish and Israeli traditional dances which were old when Moses was young." In the dances' rhythms, the reporter continued, one detected an "echo from afar" of "ancient Hebraic sorrows and joys and tales of a race lost to wandering." That the Blue Star campers were presenting dances of contemporary Israel seemed not to register; Jews were, for the reporter, an exotic remnant from ancient times.[99] One wonders if Green's fellow audience members would also have contextualized Israeli folk dances (and the Jews presenting them) primarily as relics of the biblical past. To be sure, many Israeli folk dances did draw explicitly upon biblical phrases, stories, and images as crucial source material. It is also true that American Jewish educators such as Dvora Lapson emphasized this aspect of the dances in connecting young Jews to their religious heritage. Yet, for Berk's dancers as for many American Jewish practitioners, Israeli folk dance symbolized and bolstered a dynamic, vibrant Jewish culture in the present. The reporter's description of the program suggests that, for him and perhaps for others with little knowledge of Jews, an Israeli folk dance performance actually conveyed little of the contemporary context in which the medium had arisen.

On the other hand, as the author of the *Viltis* article insisted, it was possible that the event provided mountain folk "long familiar [with] the skirl of fiddles and the plinking of banjos" an opportunity to sample "the dramatic history and cultural diversity found in the Holy Land today."[100] In any case, however Israeli folk dance was perceived by "outsiders," the critical component of such folk festivals appears to have been the cooperative spirit in which all folk dances were performed. Functioning as an indispensable element of the international folk dance repertoire in America, Israeli folk dance ultimately served as one star in a larger folk dance constellation. In the final analysis, non-Jewish practitioners in the folk dance movement seemed to treasure Israeli dance more for the cultural diversity that it helped provide than for the culture it represented in and of itself.

"THE VITALITY AND EXALTATION OF BEING FREE": ISRAELI DANCE IN THE LIMELIGHT

By the mid-1960s, expressions of Israel's new "folk" culture were garnering ever broader audiences. Earlier in the postwar period, several small, specialized record labels had begun producing Israeli folk dance music for the folk dancing community under the supervision of acknowledged specialists;[101] now, major record companies such as Elektra, RCA, and CBS began producing albums of Israeli folk music, too.[102] Elektra, for example, produced its first Israeli folk music album, Theo Bikel's *Folksongs of Israel,* in 1955. In the next several years, this was joined by four records by the Israeli folk-pop group Oranim Zabar, as well as albums by Israeli performing acts Hillel and Aviva, Ron and Nama, the Dudaim, and the Maccabee Singers.[103] (Bikel, for his part, recorded a second album on the theme, *Harvest of Israeli Folksongs,* in 1961, in addition to recording an album of international folk songs with Geula Gill, of Oranim Zabar, in 1958.)[104] So popular were such acts becoming that an Israeli Artists Bureau was established in 1958 "to serve Jewish organizations, community centers and all others interested in Israeli culture."[105]

In addition, polished Israeli folk-pop professionals such as Gill, Shoshana Damari, and Yaffa Yarkoni began appearing in urban nightclubs and on American television in these years, even as they continued to participate in American Jewish communal programming, from Israel Bond events to the Israel Folk Dance Festival.[106] Gill's career, in particular, highlights the crossover appeal of Israeli folk dance and music in America at the time.

By the early 1960s, Gill had performed in concert halls and clubs in New York, Boston, Philadelphia, Chicago, St. Louis, and Los Angeles, among other places; at the 1960 Newport Folk Festival; and at community centers and colleges across the country (including campuses in Indiana, Texas, Ohio, and Oregon) as well as touring with comedian Jackie Mason and appearing on popular American television programs such as Johnny Carson's *Tonight Show*, *The Steve Allen Show*, and *The Ed Sullivan Show*.[107]

Israeli folk dance, too, took on a measure of show-business luster in the postwar years. This is evident from a television broadcast, on July 5, 1959, of the weekly folk dance program *Rhapsody*, a production of the CBC.[108] During that evening's half-hour program, as the camera panned and zoomed from one elaborate set to the next, viewers were treated to a miniature tour of an ersatz, contemporary Israel. Geula Gill, arrayed in a succession of chic ensembles, provided the musical entertainment, while a team of lithe, bright-eyed dancers presented a succession of Israeli folk dances for the television audience. For the finale, the entire ensemble performed a lively barefoot hora, the studio orchestra joined by the pounding rhythm of hand drums and dancing feet. The program was Canadian, the musicians were Israeli, but most of the dancers were American—among them, members of the Fred Berk Folk Dancers, one of the choreographer's several folk dance troupes active in the postwar period. Some of the dancers, such as Gila Melandoff and Teme Kernerman, were products of Zionist youth movements who went on to teach and perform Israeli folk dances in the broader community; one dancer, Mary Carrigan, wasn't Jewish.[109]

With the appearance of the musical *Milk and Honey* on Broadway two years later, Israeli folk dance truly found its place in the limelight. At the request of a producer who wanted a musical set in contemporary Israel, the show's composer, Jerry Herman, and the writer of its book, Don Appell, crafted a tale of middle-aged American Jewish widows touring Israel in hopes of finding love.[110] It was to be Herman's first Broadway show (he is still best known for his later musicals, *Hello, Dolly!* and *La Cage aux Folles*), and he won accolades for his songs, including a Tony nomination for Best Score. Contemporaneous reviews devoted particular attention, however, to the role of dance in the musical—according to one, there was "more dancing in *Milk and Honey* than any show since *West Side Story*."[111]

Critics waxed rhapsodic about the dance numbers, including examples of Israeli folk dance. Indeed, several critics singled out the musical's "Independence Day Hora," which appears early in the musical, as a centerpiece of the show; for such critics, Israeli folk dance, "vigorous and rousing," helped lend the musical its "ethnic freshness and vitality" and gave it the flavor of "a joyous folk festival."[112] Choreographer Donald Saddler, who traveled to the Jewish state to observe Israeli folk dance in situ, wished for his interpretation of the hora to convey "the vitality and exaltation of being free after centuries of persecution and wandering."[113] For Saddler, then, Israeli folk dance served as the chief expression of the Zionist dream come true, telegraphing an earthy and romantic vision of Jewish dignity to Broadway audiences. And audiences appeared to bask in the musical's good spirits and its Zionist-friendly élan: Herman, at least, recalled audiences "stomping their feet to the music" of the Independence Day Hora and "laugh[ing] and cry[ing] and clapp[ing] their hands in rhythm with the songs."[114] Herman hadn't intended to make a "patriotic pro-Israeli show," yet the musical turned out to be, in his own estimation (and despite his deliberate inclusion of an Israeli character who grumbled about the hardships of kibbutz life), a "valentine" to the Jewish state.[115]

From one perspective, the *Rhapsody* program and especially *Milk and Honey* seem a far cry from the spontaneous, all-night dance sessions of American Zionist youth. Herman's aim in *Milk and Honey* was to deliver a taste of Israel to American palates: he described composing a score that drew upon "the kind of music Americans think of as Israeli."[116] A Broadway stage set was not a campfire at a Zionist training farm in rural Vermont, and Israeli folk dance, in each context, conveyed a distinct sensibility: slick Broadway hijinks versus leftist, bohemian romance. Habonim, too, brought Israeli folk dance popular attention by appearing on *The Steve Allen Show* in 1956. Reflecting on their television debut, however, Habonim's central committee considered their appearance on the variety show "harmful" to their goals; they felt that "the show itself gave an inaccurate picture of Israel and generally detracted from the purpose for which [the folk dance] was presented."[117] Though the committee did not specify the precise source of their discomfort, one can surmise that its members felt that the primary purpose of Israeli folk dance was not the audience's entertainment. For television and Broadway producers, in contrast, this was exactly the point.

Nevertheless, members of American Zionist youth movements also used Israeli folk dance to their own ends. They danced the hora and sang boisterous Hebrew folk songs much in the same spirit as they listened to American folk revivalists such as Pete Seeger sing "Where Have All the Flowers Gone?" and "If I Had a Hammer."[118] Doing Israeli folk dance distinguished Zionist youth from their non-Zionist, non-Jewish counterparts, on the one hand, while serving as a means of participating in broader currents in American culture, on the other.

These examples illustrate the unusual position of Israeli folk dancing in American culture in the postwar years, where it straddled the border between Zionist subculture and popular entertainment, amateur pursuit and professional artistry. Jewish dance educators felt that Israeli folk dance forged affective ties between Jewish youth, their Jewish heritage, and the state of

Israel. They claimed that participation in Israeli folk dance led to greater interest in Jewish subject matter, but that the medium of dance also provided an entrée to Jewish life that book learning could never do. Zionist youth, for their part, adopted Israeli folk dance as an essential component of an American Zionist sensibility. True, some tension existed between proponents of a hard-line Zionist ideology and those who privileged an inclusive, cultural program in making Zionism relevant to American Jews. Yet Israeli folk dance fulfilled a central function for Zionist youth: it drew young people to the movement with its energy and with the qualities it seemed to embody. Participating in Israeli folk dance expressed commitment to the Zionist project, but it also conjured romance, cultural confidence, and bohemian cachet.

What *did* Israeli folk dance represent, beyond the specialized circles of Jewish dance educators and Zionist youth? At the very least, Israeli folk dance provided American participants and observers of various stripes a taste of Jewish ethnic pride without challenging the limits of American cultural pluralism. For devotees in the American Jewish community at large, Israeli folk dance buttressed Jewish dignity; for non-Jewish aficionados, it served primarily as a link between Jews and non-Jews, Americans and other groups. Seemingly offering something for everyone, Israeli folk dance became both a socially sanctioned cultural pastime and the vehicle for a forthright public attachment to the Jewish state at a time of relative political diffidence among American Jews.

FOUR

A CONSUMING PASSION

Israeli Goods in American Jewish Culture

Readers browsing through *Hadassah Magazine* in November 1965 would have encountered, on page eleven, a full-page advertisement for the Israel Gift of the Month Club. It was an idea that anyone familiar with the popular Book-of-the-Month Club would have immediately comprehended.[1] Following the Book-of-the-Month Club format, the Israel Gift of the Month Club promised to send subscribers "uniquely designed giftware," direct from Israel, once a month. Only in this case, customers would not know in advance what they would be receiving, injecting an element of surprise into the exchange. In the absence of photographs or illustrations of the wares to be delivered to subscribers' doors, the advertising copy tantalized readers with descriptions of the purported treasures that awaited them at ten dollars a month:

> It may be a brilliantly-colored ceramic plate, ideal for your living room or china display . . . or a wooden musical cigarette box with a mosaic lid . . . or a handsome oil and vinegar set with a native olive wood stopper and holder . . . or wrought-iron candlesticks with a strikingly modern design . . . or a Phoenician glass vase bound to be a conversation piece on a bookshelf or coffee table in your home.[2]

These items, and others like them, were made by Israeli "craftsmen and designers, using Israeli material, Israeli know-how and Israeli skills," and each came with a brochure providing detailed information about the object and its designer. Thus armed with information, subscribers would be ready to

81

answer any questions that might arise when "admiring friends want to know where you got it, how it was made, what materials were used in creating it and how the designer got his idea."[3]

While the advertisement tempted readers with the promise of beautiful *objets* for the home, one thing it did not do was explain why someone would want such objects from Israel in the first place. The promoters of the Israel Gift of the Month Club seemed to assume that potential subscribers needed no further explanation; the company was merely satisfying a demonstrated demand for objects from Israel. Indeed, as this chapter illustrates, by the mid-1960s Americans were consuming a variety of imports from Israel, from modern cigarette boxes and brass menorahs to bathing suits and evening gowns. (Considering that a majority of the American Jewish population had never actually traveled to Israel—a phenomenon that has not changed to this day[4]—most American Jews who desired such wares purchased them as imports.) What was novel about the Israel Gift of the Month Club was simply the company's marketing strategy—that is, having the club's authorities, rather than consumers themselves, regularly choose what Israeli objects Americans would display in their living rooms.

American Jews were well primed to become avid consumers of Israeli objects, following patterns that were already in place by 1948. Earlier in the century, participation in mass consumption had served American Jews as a primary means of both acculturating to American norms and of crafting a particular American Jewish identity and culture. Jewish immigrants and their children reinterpreted the Jewish calendar, Jewish rituals, and the Jewish home as venues for confident consumption, announcing American Jews' successful adoption of a middle-class American standard of living; at the same time, Jewish entrepreneurs and consumers reshaped American markets, from foodstuffs to the nascent film industry, drawing on their growing professional expertise as marketers and attuned to their community's particular ethnic and religious needs.[5] As consumers of kosher and religious goods, American Jews shaped a thriving ethno-religious submarket in the first decades of the twentieth century, made up of networks of specialty purveyors, advertisers, and venues. Anyone wishing to bring Israeli products to American Jewish shoppers could draw and expand upon these networks. In addition, well before 1948, American Jews had developed a brand of Zionist philanthropy-cum-consumerism, marketing Palestinian goods (especially agricultural products) in polished, American-style advertisements, as a means of aiding the Yishuv.[6]

As a highly educated, increasingly affluent population in the postwar period, American Jews were full-fledged participants in what historian Lizabeth Cohen has termed the postwar "Consumer's Republic." In the years immediately following World War II through the 1950s, Cohen has argued, politicians, economists, business interests, and many everyday Americans concurred that mass consumption powered the American economy and that providing consumers full access to the mass market would ensure an equitable society. This consensus was premised upon the idea of America as a capitalist democracy centered upon "the purchaser as citizen who simultaneously fulfilled personal desire and civic obligation by consuming."[7]

American Jews, as this chapter will show, appear to have internalized this discourse. As their rhetoric and behavior make clear, they understood their promotion and consumption of Israeli goods, in part, as a means of participating in the predominant American civic ritual of mass consumption. Buying goods was assumed to be an absolute good. Yet this point underscores a paradox in the thoughts and actions of American Jews. Those American Jews who promoted investment in and consumption of Israeli products often argued that an American economic partnership with Israel would provide a model for, and access to, markets in the developing world, an American desideratum. The U.S. government saw the exporting of American goods as an opportunity to capture new markets for American business and to win steadfast admirers of the "American way."[8] This was not the first time, of course, that the exporting of goods had figured significantly in America's understanding of its political "mission" in the wider world. Beginning in the late nineteenth century, American economists and policymakers proposed increasing exports to foreign markets as a response to the perceived problem of overproduction in the American economy; this economic drive to capture new markets dovetailed with national ambitions to remake sectors of the developing world in America's image, including through the conquering of territory and intervention in other nations' governance (as in the Philippines, for example).[9]

What useful role, though, did the *importing* of goods from other nations play in the postwar era? Any stable modern economy depends upon healthy trade with other nations, of course. Yet, in light of the predominant national discourses of the day—winning the Cold War, in political terms, and fueling mass consumption of American goods, in economic terms—the act of championing imports from another nation did not, on the face of it, satisfy a perceived need. The American Jews who promoted and consumed Israeli goods labored to show that their behavior did, in fact, further America's political and economic interests. One senses that the American Jews under investigation here often saw the equation of American and Israeli concerns as self-evident; at other times, however, as when arguing for the economic interests of Israelis and against the economic interests of Arab nations, the case had to be made more strenuously that "buying Israel" was good for America.

Certainly, the appearance of Israeli-made objects in the postwar United States reflected a concerted effort by the Israeli government to tap into the world market. Trade fairs constituted one particularly visible indication of this effort. In 1954, for example, Israel participated in eight international exhibitions spanning the globe from New York to Milan, and Johannesburg to Izmir, Turkey. By 1957, the numbers of visitors to Israel exhibits at international fairs had exceeded eleven million.[10] This foray into the global marketplace reflected an urgent necessity: Israel needed foreign money to survive in the period of economic development and immigrant absorption after 1948, and the government embarked on a program of both domestic austerity and liberalized trade with foreign nations in the early 1950s.[11] The Israeli leadership developed a three-part approach to procuring funds from America: increasing trade with the United States, requesting large aid packages from the American government, and soliciting direct contributions from the American Jewish community by appealing to Zionists and non-Zionists alike.[12] With the first sale of Israel Bonds in 1951, for example, the Israeli government sought to harness the largesse of American Jews by pointing supporters of Israel away from previous charity-based fundraising practices. Israel Bonds, in contrast, offered American Jews an opportunity for direct investment in Israel.[13]

While Israel Bonds became an important focus of American Jewish support for the Jewish state in the first postwar decades, Israeli-made objects in particular came to occupy a special position in everyday American Jewish culture. For one thing—and in contrast to Israel Bonds—many of the available Israeli goods, by their very nature, invited integration into the fabric of American Jews' day-to-day lives. Touted as beautifully made objects (as exemplified by the Israel Gift of the Month Club advertisement), such goods were meant to inhabit the homes and adorn the bodies of upwardly mobile, middle-class Americans. At the same time, highlighting the unusual or exotic qualities of Israeli goods made such objects stand out from the warp and woof of American material culture. In other words, American promoters and purchasers of Israeli goods understood such imports as complements to American middle-class wares, on the one hand, and as novel conversation pieces, on the other. In this light, an Israeli-made "gift of the month," procured in an American context, emblematized the new Jewish state while granting its purchasers an enhanced cultural cachet. Like Israel Bonds, the purchase of Israeli goods provided a channel through which American Jews might aid Israel directly, but there was more to it than this. Supporting Israel in the marketplace, I argue, could also fuel American Jews' cultural aspirations.

In the same years that vendors—Jewish and non-Jewish—began introducing Israeli goods in the broader American marketplace, American Jews also worked to promote Israeli objects within their local communities. This phenomenon occurred largely within the associational arenas that characterized postwar American Jewish life. The synagogue, now the central address for Jewish communal activity in the suburban era, offered a distinct approach to the promotion of Israeli goods within American Jewish culture. As one might expect, synagogue affiliates involved in the promotion of Israeli goods did so under the rubric of religious life. They assessed Israeli objects as potential transmitters of Judaism and of a distinctively Jewish ethos, particularly within the family domain. Members of Conservative and Reform synagogue sisterhoods were particularly important to this enterprise; as recognized arbiters of the domestic sphere, these American Jewish women decisively shaped the place of Israeli goods in the postwar American Jewish home.

Hadassah, the Women's Zionist Organization of America, provided an alternate model. In contrast to the synagogue, Hadassah conceived of its promotional efforts on behalf of Israeli goods as an eminently public endeavor. The organization placed public relations high on its agenda, working to acquaint Americans with its humanitarian projects in Israel while raising funds for these projects in the United States. By the postwar period, Hadassah was a mainstay of organized American Jewish life, and counted roughly one out of every ten American Jewish women as a member. In the context of suburban life in particular, Hadassah also functioned as a cultural outlet for its members, hosting reading and discussion groups among its calendar of social and fundraising activities.[14] The promotion of Israeli goods—exemplified, as I argue, by local productions of the annual Hadassah Fashion Show, beginning in 1949—must be seen as part of Hadassah's cultural agenda in the postwar United States, furthering the organization's philanthropic work in Israel while crystallizing the cultural aspirations and identifications of its members.

To fully understand the process by which American Jews domesticated Israeli goods, however, one must turn also to the work of the America-Israel Chamber of Commerce and Industry (AICCI). The AICCI, established in the early 1950s by American Jewish businessmen, sought to strengthen ties between business entrepreneurs in both countries and the U.S. and Israeli governments. The organization's journal, *American-Israel Economic Horizons* (successor to the Jewish Agency's *Israel Economic Horizons*), documented its advocacy for the Jewish state in the economic realm and published news of Israel's industries and exports, as well as highlighting opportunities for Americans to invest in Israel. As with Hadassah and the synagogue sisterhoods, the AICCI also promoted Israeli goods extensively in the American marketplace. Much like Hadassah, too, the AICCI premised this work on a belief in the congruence of American and Israeli societies and culture. While the rhetoric and strategies of the AICCI, Hadassah, and synagogue auxiliaries necessarily reflected the highly gendered frameworks in which they functioned—the world of international business versus that of philanthropic voluntarism and domestic religious life—these organizations shared a basic assumption that American Jews, as supporters, distributors, and consumers of Israeli goods, could further America's loftiest cultural, economic, and political goals.

Whether bearing overt Zionist iconography, showcasing sleek modern design, or simply displaying a "Made in Israel" label, imports from Israel proved popular indeed, capturing a share of the American Jewish imagination as well as the American Jewish wallet. Contemporaneous observers in the Jewish community saw that American Jews were fast becoming avid consumers of Israeli goods and they analyzed the significance of this phenomenon. While pro-Israel business elites (such as those affiliated with the AICCI) trumpeted American consumption of Israeli goods as a boon to both nations, and members of Hadassah and the synagogue sisterhoods hoped that such consumption encouraged stronger philanthropic and spiritual ties to Israel, some cultural commentators in the American Jewish community were less sanguine. They questioned the primacy of consumption in American Jews' relationship with Israel, arguing that purchasing Israeli objects demanded very little commitment or thought of any kind on the part of American Jews. Regardless, in their roles as entrepreneurs, marketers, and shoppers, American Jews transformed Israel-focused consumption into a chief means of expressing Jewish identity in both the private and public spheres and even of amassing political capital. They positioned such imports as a significant means of conceptualizing and aiding the Jewish state—and of literally bringing Zion home.

CONSUMING ISRAEL: THE MARKET FOR ISRAELI GOODS IN POSTWAR AMERICA

As Jeffrey Shandler and Beth S. Wenger have shown, consumption of goods was one important way in which American Jews supported the Yishuv in the pre-1948 period. "Beginning in the 1920s," they write, "advertisers promoted consumerism as a form of Zionist advocacy, urging the readers of American Zionist periodicals to buy wine, almonds, olive oil, oranges, honey," and other products grown and made in Palestine.[15] Such goods served an important symbolic function for American Zionists, whose spending served the Zionist cause while bringing home a whiff of the faraway Holy Land.

In the post-1948 period, however, as the state of Israel increasingly turned its attention to industrial rather than small-scale agricultural development, the bulk of Israeli exports to America had a decidedly more prosaic profile. Industrial materials were among the top Israeli exports by the early

1950s, for example, hardly the stuff of romantic advertising campaigns.[16] Nonetheless, burgeoning new Israeli industries such as the apparel and crafts sectors served much the same function for the American Jewish community as had Palestinian oranges and honey in the 1920s. Like them, the new Israeli apparel and crafts symbolized the Jewish state for its supporters while offering a practical means of aiding the struggling Israeli economy. Thus, many Israeli objects were designed to be readily perceivable as "Israeli" in terms of iconography, design, or both. Bezalel, first established in 1906 and reconfigured as the New Bezalel School in 1935, was the pioneer in this regard, though, according to historian Jenna Weissman Joselit, it had made little impact on the American market in the first part of the twentieth century.[17] In the postwar period, Bezalel continued to turn out souvenir-like objects bearing familiar images of sacred Jewish sites of the Holy Land as well as producing sleek, Bauhaus-influenced ceremonial objects. Several other craft manufacturers established reputations in the post-1948 period by introducing new types of affordable, mass-produced decorative objects. Partnering with American Jewish distributors such as Israel Creations, Israeli Arts and Crafts, the Israeli Gift Shop Service, Imports from Israel, and the Israeli Art-Craft Importing Company, among others, these manufacturers were able to reach consumers well beyond Israel's borders on an unprecedented scale.[18]

American proponents were eager to point out, too, that these new industries appealed to the tastes and spending habits of postwar, middle-class Americans. In truth, though, products did not even need to be distinctively "Israeli," in a visually apparent way, for retailers and customers to frame consumption of those products as a means of expressing support for Israel. Wares as seemingly quotidian as raincoats and shoes were freighted with special significance when they were made in Israel. In the pages of *Israel Economic Horizons*, Spencer Witty, the vice president of Witty Brothers department store, testified that the company had initially bought Israeli-made raincoats because "they were good value and we wanted to help Israel's economy." He added that "sales have been so surprisingly good because . . . our customers buy the raincoats with their heads as well as their hearts."[19] Even in a statement to the contrary in the same article, Leo Feigenbaum, a buyer for Namm-Loeser's, suggested that emotionally motivated consumption was assumed to be a factor for shoppers. He insisted that customers were buying Israeli shoes "on the basis of quality rather than sentimentality," a comment that complimented Israeli industry as well as American hard-headedness, but which also revealed the symbolic context in which consumption of Israeli goods was presumed to take place.[20]

To capitalize on this phenomenon, advocates for Israeli imports took care to broadcast the provenance of Israeli goods, including information about the artisans who crafted the products. Announcements of new Israeli imports in publications such as *Israel Economic Horizons* and *Hadassah Newsletter* often conveyed this type of information. The American debut, in 1954, of apparel crafted in Israel from locally grown flax was heralded in just this manner. The bounty, which included espadrille-like cloth shoes as well as blouses, handbags, aprons, and table linens, had been embroidered by "Israel women working under the auspices of WIZO [Women's International Zionist Organization] Home Industries," as *Israel Economic Horizons* publicized.[21] Later that year, the journal informed readers that B. Altman's Department Store in New York would soon begin selling Israeli hand-woven rugs crafted by "two former cave dwellers from Tripolitania," who had recently presented Mamie Eisenhower with one of their rugs during a visit to Washington, D.C., for a trade exhibition.[22]

Retailers could, and did, provide this sort of information on placards within their shops and in window displays. Sometimes they telegraphed the provenance of Israeli goods boldly through the showcasing of the Israeli flag, as an extant photograph of a window display at McCurdy's department store in Rochester, New York, attests.[23] (The store was selling Israeli-made raincoats.) Retailers also created themed events that placed Israeli goods firmly in the spotlight. Such was the case at Jordan Marsh Department Store—one of the largest and oldest department stores in the country—in May 1951, in honor of Israel's third birthday and the store's one hundredth anniversary. There, shoppers found a full range of Israeli products—from ceremonial objects to ceramics to food—in "almost every department" of the grand store in downtown Boston.[24] These products were accompanied by special exhibits, including a model of Solomon's Temple, Israeli paintings, and synagogue paraphernalia, and a set of dioramas illustrating Jewish history, comprising a kind of museum within the halls of commerce. The Jewish Agency, the organization that oversaw immigration to Israel, had a hand in the proceedings, too. It contributed a display on the history of immigration to Israel and presented a stamp collection "tracing Jewish history for the last hundred years."[25] This spectacle suggests that, in the realm of Israel-focused consumption, the line between commerce and culture was fluid.

The example of Israel Creations, a distribution company established in 1949 by Israel Wolsky and based in New York, illustrates the growing demand for Israeli wares among American consumers. In 1954, Israel Creations was reportedly distributing Israeli goods to more than 1,400 venues in the United States; by 1962, the number of retailers stocking Israel Creations imports had climbed to roughly six thousand. In addition to showcasing wares twice a year at the major gift shows in New York, Los Angeles, and Chicago, the company had two showrooms in New York, permanent displays on view in Chicago and Dallas, and had begun establishing a presence in Toronto and Montreal.[26] Meanwhile, the first retail store in New York devoted entirely to products from Israel opened in 1960. (In fact, New York was not the first city to support such a venture; an all-Israel shop had opened in Detroit in the spring of 1952.)[27]

Mainstream retailers appraised and marketed Israeli goods for their commercial strengths *and* their edifying substance and emotional relevance, a move that accorded such goods a special status in the marketplace. This strategy apparently resonated with shoppers, as retailers' successes in selling Israeli goods suggests. In the hands of American vendors, Israeli commodities served as vehicles for supporting and celebrating Israel. By the same token, interpreting Israeli goods as cultural receptacles spurred sales. As we will see, this blend of entrepreneurship and cultural ambition characterized such transactions in the American Jewish organizational sphere as well.

DOMESTICATING ISRAEL: THE SYNAGOGUE, ISRAELI GOODS, AND PRIVATE JEWISH SPACE

The rising prominence of Israeli goods within private Jewish space—particularly the home—is inextricable from a related trend: the advent of the postwar synagogue as a cultural arbiter within American Jewish life. Both the Reform and Conservative movements, home to the vast majority of affiliated Jews in the postwar period, endeavored in these years to grow and diversify as communal institutions while deepening their influence in the lives of members.[28] Both movements sought to enrich the synagogue's relationship with the arts as part of this wide-ranging project. The Reform wing appears to have been particularly ambitious in this arena: early in the postwar period, for example, Reform leaders positioned the movement as an authoritative resource on synagogue design by convening conferences on the subject, assembling an architectural advisory board and list of affiliated artists, and creating a special library devoted to synagogue art and design for use by constituent congregations.[29] *American Judaism*, the Reform movement's magazine, published regularly on synagogue art and design and, by the early 1960s, also featured a "Living Arts" section with reviews of Jewish books, films, music, and theater by professional critics. And in the fall of 1965, the Reform movement announced the launching of a nationwide arts program encompassing drama, art, music, and dance, with plans to open a Religious Arts Center in New York.[30] The Conservative movement, too, developed cultural resources and embarked on new cultural ventures in the postwar period, including a Book and Art Service (to encourage the purchase of ceremonial objects and books), the Zamir Chorale (a young people's singing group with an all-Hebrew repertoire), and a Jewish repertory theater.[31] Conservative and Reform congregations across the country hosted arts festivals and musical performances in these years.[32]

Such efforts to place the American Jewish religious movements "in the vanguard of cultural expression," as UAHC president Maurice N. Eisendrath put it,[33] were surely meant to elevate the cultural standing of American Judaism in the eyes of constituents, potential affiliates, and non-Jewish observers. At root, however, synagogue-sponsored cultural programs at the national and local level were understood as bids to enhance and elevate the quality of postwar Jewish life. "The rapprochement of religion and the arts has deep social and philosophical significance," proclaimed W. Gunther Plaut, a prominent Reform rabbi, in that it would foster "an appreciation of all that makes man whole." To Plaut, "To bring the arts, all the arts, into the confines of the temple is to me to take up the biblical ideal of Bazalel [*sic*]," the craftsman credited with building the Tabernacle, according to the Hebrew Bible.[34] Cultural programs would also serve an educative function, by "confront[ing] American audiences with Jewish ideas and Jewish history," as one proponent noted, and by "utiliz[ing] art for the teaching of Judaism," in the words of another.[35]

This mission emanated from the synagogue, but also focused explicitly upon the home—the other primary axis of Jewish religious life in the suburban age. Women members of Reform and Conservative synagogues were key players in this regard, for while (male) rabbis certainly viewed the Jewish hearth as a critically important sphere of activity, the two movements' women's divisions placed greatest emphasis upon the Jewish domestic scene. To be sure, efforts to elevate Jewish culture within the home grew from an ongoing campaign, in both movements, to increase Jewish ceremonial observance in private life.[36] For its advocates, the creation of a Jewish home was not simply a matter of following religious precepts, however, but of shaping Jewish domestic space in a broader sense—of honing "the fine art of living" in a Jewish idiom.[37]

If, in part, the synagogue sisterhood was meant to serve as a "vehicle for cultural and intellectual self-improvement," as Mrs. Harry Jacobson, a retiring vice president of the Reform movement's National Federation of Temple Sisterhoods (NFTS), argued, the Jewish home provided an appropriate setting for such cultural growth.[38] It was this impulse that had fueled the Jewish Home Beautiful movement, a popular pageant dating from the interwar years—and still successful in the first postwar decades—in which local Conservative sisterhoods staged a series of domestic Jewish holiday scenes that were both impeccably appointed and religiously sound.[39] The pageant embodied the notion that "to live as a Jewess, a woman . . . must have an appreciation for beautiful things and a desire to create those beautiful things herself," in the words of the production's co-creator, Betty Greenberg.[40]

In *Across the Threshold: A Guide for the Jewish Homemaker*, written by and for Conservative women, authors Shonie Levi and Sylvia Kaplan insisted that even those housewives on a modest budget could (and should) furnish their homes with the fruits of the Jewish cultural marketplace. A well-appointed Jewish home enshrined the necessary ceremonial objects, to be sure, but also encompassed Jewish music, books, art, and other accoutrements—including, crucially, works of Israeli provenance. "The ingathering in Israel of Jews of many lands has resulted in a variety of creative artistic expressions which are meeting with great favor in the American market," wrote the authors. "In the craft field, there is no limit to the imagination of contemporary Jewish artisans—working with dolls, small tapestries, embroidered pictures . . . decorated tiles, modern and exotic costume jewelry . . . [and] beautiful wood carvings and ceramics." Levi and Kaplan noted that contemporary crafts designers offered interpretations of Israeli subjects such as the halutzim (Zionist pioneers in the land of Israel) and Yemenite dancers, in addition to traditional religious themes.[41]

Levi and Kaplan's enthusiasm for Israeli products as building blocks of the artfully outfitted, contemporary Jewish home was echoed elsewhere in the Conservative movement. Earlier in the decade, this notion had been amply illustrated through the "model Jewish home" showcase at the 1952 National Convention of the Women's League for Conservative Judaism. Within a tableau representing the living room of an "average modern home"—replete with such details as "modern blond wood" and a "modern upholstered living room set"—the exhibit's organizers set out an array of objects that they felt "set this room apart as a Jewish home."[42] Alongside the traditional implements of Jewish observance such as the hanukkiah, seder plate, kiddush cup, and etrog box were a number of Israeli imports: a decorative platter, candy dish, ash trays, picture frames, and autograph and picture albums. The fact that these patently secular items helped mark the model living room as "Jewish," in the eyes of the exhibit's organizers, suggests the exalted position occupied by objects of Israeli provenance, whatever their function, within the American Jewish domestic sphere.

A distinctive arsenal of forms, materials, and iconography distinguished Israeli *objets* from both traditional Jewish religious articles and American-made household durables alike. Prominent Israeli design firms such as Pal-Bell, Dayagi Brothers, Oppenheim, and Tamar labored to adapt the forms of postwar European design to objects that forthrightly announced their Israeli genesis. For example, designer Maurice Ascalon of Pal-Bell, in order to underscore the ancient provenance of many of the company's mass-produced, modern forms, introduced an antique patina finish to his bronze and brass repertoire. This green patina became a standard feature of Israeli metalwork in the 1950s and distinguished such objects as Israeli in the global marketplace. Reuven Dayagi, another prominent designer, marked objects as Israeli by decorating them with stones from Eilat, a resort town at the southern tip of Israel. Israeli Hanukkah menorahs produced by the major metal factories were also among the most distinctive forms available to American consumers; in contrast to the traditional "bench" style of oil lamp, with its long, low base and back plate, Israeli hanukkiot often took the shape of symmetrical, branched candelabras, a reference to the menorahs of the ancient Temple in Jerusalem. The major firms also cultivated a common set of thematic images that they felt represented the spirit of modern Israel to consumers, including maps of Israel and Israeli folk dancers.[43] These firms understood that utilitarian function of Israeli objects, as bookends or ashtrays, was nearly irrelevant. What's more, their elevated status as markers of Jewishness did not derive only or even primarily from their essential function in Jewish ritual life. What mattered was that they emblematized Israel in some readily perceivable way.

The closer one looks at American Jews' promotion and consumption of these goods, the more one is struck by a potent and untidy intermingling of the secular and the sacred, the commercial and the philanthropic, the cultural and the political. American Jews were not alone in this regard; one can compare their flexible approach toward Israeli objects to the uses of material goods and artifacts among other religious, ethnic, and racial groups in American life.[44] In light of scholarship on Christian material religion, for example, it appears that, in important ways, postwar Jewish actors engaged with Israeli objects in the American Jewish home much as American Christians have done with objects of Christian devotion.

David Morgan and Colleen McDannell, for example, have analyzed visual and material objects as the media through which Christianity has been woven into the daily lives of Catholics and Protestants, often in ways that aren't "religious" in theologically orthodox terms. In his book *Visual Piety*, Morgan frames the home, so central to American conceptions of happiness and success, as the mediating site for American Christianity as it is actually practiced; he argues that, for an object such as a portrait of Jesus, the object's sacredness arises from its perceived talismanic function (protecting inhabitants from harm), its role as a vehicle for intergenerational continuity (as heirloom or repository for family memories), or its significance as a social conduit (as a gift from a person or community marking a religious or social milestone) as much as from its officially sanctioned purpose as an object of prayerful devotion or as a tool for proselytization. That an object is mass produced and mass marketed presents no barrier to meaningfulness, in these regards. What's more, practitioners don't simply "read" such objects as conveyors of ideas, according to Morgan, but actively place and use devotional objects within the choreography of their lives, where the objects serve as agents of corporeal, sensory knowledge.[45] McDannell, for her part, has written of the "scrambling of the sacred and the profane" as a hallmark of material Christianity, an indication of the malleable and dynamic nature of religion in everyday life.[46]

To be sure, Jewish ceremonial objects traditionally perform different functions in Jewish ritual life than do Christian appurtenances in the lives of Christians. A domestic Jewish object such as a Hanukkah lamp or an image of Jerusalem is not devotional—that is, an object of veneration—in the sense that a portrait of Jesus is for Christians. Jewish objects, as sanctioned by Jewish law, are tools for the performance of proscribed rituals (i.e., kindling the Hanukkah lights; praying toward Jerusalem) and not objects of religious contemplation or worship, though they are meant to be aesthetically pleasing (a commandment known as *hiddur mitzvah*). What's more, many of the Israeli objects purchased by American Jews and displayed in the American Jewish home were not ceremonial objects in any traditional, halakhic sense.

And yet, as essential props in the performance of both everyday life and domestic Jewish ritual, one can see Israeli objects as serving many of the same functions as those Morgan has ascribed to Christian visuals. So, too, might an Israel-made or Israel-themed object have served its owners as a talisman, repository of memories, or manifestation of communal ties. Israeli objects, like the stuff of material Christianity, straddled the border between the secular and the sacred. Indeed, for American Jewish purveyors and purchasers, Israeli *objets* seem to have been coded at the time as "explicitly Jewish objects," in the manner that anthropologist Vanessa L. Ochs has defined it. Ochs has written that explicitly Jewish objects are "articulate, revelatory, self-evident, and unambiguous"; they serve as "*signs* that clearly say, 'a Jew inhabits this space,' *props* that say, 'This object is needed in Jewish life,' and *catalysts* that say, 'The presence of this object creates and maintains Judaism.' "[47]

The case of the postwar synagogue gift shop provides further evidence that Israeli wares were becoming increasingly important features of a Jewish home, where they accrued a kind of sanctified status heretofore reserved for traditional ceremonial objects. In the postwar period, Jewish residents of the newly settled suburbs across the country, removed from the social and economic nodes of urban Jewish life that hosted traditional religious-goods shops, sought local retailers to serve their needs as Jewish consumers. The synagogue gift shop filled this void by providing a primary venue for promoting and procuring the "stuff" of Jewish domestic life in postwar America. Run primarily by Reform and Conservative sisterhoods (Orthodox synagogues did not, in the main, offer similar venues),[48] such shops were stocked with a spectrum of ceremonial objects for daily use and holidays and appropriate gifts for life-cycle events such as bar mitzvahs and weddings. At its best, one proponent argued, the synagogue gift shop was not only a marketplace, but also a means of cultivating the sisterhood as a "patron of the arts" and of injecting the "glamorous atmosphere of culture" into the realm of Jewish life.[49]

In her history of the synagogue gift shop, Joellyn Wallen Zollman has found that, while Conservative sisterhoods promoted Israeli wares more consistently than their Reform counterparts, Conservative and Reform shops stocked similar Israeli objects and incorporated Israeli goods into their inventories "almost without exception."[50] Synagogue sisterhood leaders advised their members to set up an "Israeli corner" in their shops. There, consumers could choose from an array of Israeli objects—brass Hanukkah lamps, postal stamps, chocolate, and jewelry made from Israeli coins, among many other offerings—to mark a special occasion or to serve as the perfect hostess gift.[51]

Spanning secular and religious functions, Israeli goods constituted a special niche within the synagogue gift shop. The Conservative sisterhood's *Guide for the Judaica Shop Committee* put the matter bluntly, advising that, "sisterhood shops should only sell such non-religious items as are Israeli or have Jewish significance."[52] In this light, Israeli objects appeared to constitute a significant means of expressing Jewishness, one that did not depend upon the objects' recognizable utility in Jewish religious observance. In fact, according to Marshall Sklare and Joseph Greenblum's classic study of postwar suburban Jewry, American Jews were just as likely or even *more* likely to have Israeli objects in the home as they were to have basic Jewish ceremonial objects.[53] It was precisely the "Israeliness" of Israeli objects that secured them all—ceremonial objects and knickknacks alike—a quasi-sacred place in the contemporary Jewish home.

"All things from Israel have artistic beauty," proclaimed Esther Fink, the national chairman of the National Women's League Gift Shop division, underscoring the intrinsic value of such objects, whether secular or religious in nature.[54] Fink insisted, however, that Israeli imports were valuable not simply because of their visual qualities as purveyors of "Israeliness." The owner of an Israeli-made "*menorah, mezzuza,* wine bottle, *sedar* [*sic*] plate or . . . a pipeholder, ash-tray or hand-painted scarf" would enjoy such objects for their artistry but also be satisfied "knowing that the industry of the New State is being aided."[55] Altruism, from this perspective, mattered as much as aesthetics. Indeed, this philanthropic and economic rationale loomed large for both Conservative and Reform women. For example, at a presentation at the NFTS Biennial in 1948, Miriam Jackson, director of the Palestine Galleries for Arts and Crafts in New York, appealed directly to her audience's philanthropic instincts. She shared the stories of two recent immigrants to Israel, refugees from Europe, who "with the help of Palestine Galleries [had] become useful members of a new state."[56] Jackson urged her audience—that is, Reform Jewish women—to support the work of such struggling, skilled immigrants by selling Israeli crafts in their synagogue gift shops.[57] This rationale—that the selling and buying of Israeli goods was a form of enlightened consumption, a targeted intervention to buttress Israel's economy—appealed to Jewish women within and beyond the postwar synagogue.[58]

EMBODYING ISRAEL: HADASSAH, ISRAELI GOODS, AND THE PUBLIC SPHERE

As the largest American Zionist organization of the postwar years, with local chapters "in every major city and in thousands of towns and hamlets from one end of America to the other," and an immense philanthropic program in Israel, Hadassah was, like the synagogue sisterhoods, advantageously positioned to usher Israeli products into American Jewish life.[59] In contrast to the Reform and Conservative sisterhoods, however, Hadassah did not understand this project in religious terms, as part of a mission to Judaize the private sphere. Rather, Hadassah's promotion of Israeli goods accorded with its self-understanding as a social welfare organization.

Established in 1911, the organization had been intimately involved in the upbuilding of the Yishuv, applying American know-how to such projects as the development of a state of the art health care system. Above all, Hadassah promoted Israeli crafts as part of its larger commitment to "human rehabilitation"—that is, caring for and educating disadvantaged and underserved Israeli populations, particularly women and youth.[60] Hadassah turned its attention to the crafts sector in Israel as a means of transforming refugees and immigrants into productive citizens of the Jewish state—an urgent task for the Israeli government after 1948. Yet, as a mass-membership organization thoroughly ensconced in American Jewish life, Hadassah focused Israeli goods through a specifically American lens. The organization's leaders, eager to enlarge its membership in the era of suburbanization, emphasized the domestic prowess and stylish sensibilities of current and potential members and presented Hadassah as a natural fit for postwar, middle-class Americans. Hadassah's promotion of Israeli goods and of the organization's own vocational programs that produced such goods must be seen in this light.

Articles, announcements, and advertisements in *Hadassah Newsletter* (later *Hadassah Magazine*), the organization's mass publication, alerted its American Jewish readers to the availability and quality of Israeli goods. Under the headline "Gifts from Israel for Americans," for example, the September 1948 issue prominently featured photographs of four "beautiful examples of Israeli craftsmanship" (including Maurice Ascalon's "olive branch" Hanukkah lamp). The caption noted that the Palestine Galleries for Arts and Crafts, purveyor of these wares, constituted "a non-profit organization sponsored by official Zionist bodies." This designation set the depicted wares apart from the usual goods and services—Mah-Jongg sets, plastic "Handi-Bags" for leftovers, and kosher restaurants, for example—advertised profusely in every issue of the magazine.[61] At the same time, branding these crafts clearly as gifts placed them firmly in the realm of consumption. As one contributor to *Hadassah Newsletter*—and champion of Israeli goods—put it,

> An up-to-the-minute fashion picture of what milady will wear could include shoes, gloves, blouse and coat from Tel Aviv, knitwear from B'nai Brak, and diamonds cut in Natanya. Should the sky become cloudy, she could don the latest model Israel-made raincoat. Her costume jewelry and her leather handbag could derive from the Holy Land. She could tell time by an Israel-made watch with exquisite Hebrew lettering. Even so intimate an object as her bra could be "Totzeret Haaretz" ("Made in Israel").[62]

In this scenario, to wear Israeli apparel was to dress and act like any other middle-class American. Quotidian Israeli fashions and accouterments, according to *Hadassah Newsletter*, fit squarely within the parameters of postwar American consumption and aesthetics.

The editors of *Hadassah Newsletter* also insisted that shopping could and should be an enlightened pursuit. To support Israeli goods, in other words, was to further social, economic, and cultural progress. In an article published in 1952, for example, Molly Lyons Bar-David (author of the regular "Diary of a Jerusalem Housewife" column in the *Newsletter* and the book *My Promised Land*) contextualized the subject by presenting an overview of the ongoing development of the Israeli crafts industry and explaining to her readers why such an endeavor mattered at all. Bar-David emphasized the pioneering work of WIZO (Women's International Zionist Organization), Hadassah's counterpart outside the United States, in protecting and strengthening the craft traditions of new immigrants to Israel. This work of cultural maintenance, Bar-David argued, was part and parcel of a progressive social welfare agenda. Accompanied by photographs of North African filigree jewelry, a "primitive loom" used by Libyan immigrants, and a European-influenced silver tea set, among other objects, the article highlighted the importance of preserving the ancient craft traditions of Jewish immigrants from Yemen and North Africa as well as the design skills brought by European Jewish refugees. The key, Bar-David argued, was to stoke and satisfy increased demand for crafts without sacrificing the quality of traditional handiwork.[63] In another issue of the magazine, Mordecai Ardon-Bronstein, a prominent Israeli artist and director of art in the Israeli Ministry of Education and Culture, agreed that training Israelis in craftwork and commercial art would aid in the social and economic development of the country. He apprised American readers of a further imperative: cultural harmony. Culture, he wrote, "is the connecting link between new and old citizens," a critical means of recognizing the worth of immigrant traditions while integrating new immigrants into Israeli society.[64]

Hadassah members learned that support for Israeli goods started at home and that Israeli wares belonged in the American marketplace. This was the message that Sylvia Satten Banin, editor of the *Israel Export and Trade Journal*, conveyed to readers of *Hadassah Newsletter* in a 1957 article entitled "Israel Makes It America Buys It." Cataloging the most successful exports from Israel to America—not only diamonds, cement, and steel pipes, but chocolate, raincoats, knitwear, and collectible postage stamps—Banin also encouraged further consumption of smaller-scale Israeli crafts, including ceramics, "character dolls," and Yemenite jewelry and embroidery. She framed the consumption of Israeli goods as a thoroughly American endeavor. The United States "buys a great many commodities from abroad to meet the insatiable demands of her vast and exacting public," Banin wrote. "[A]lthough [the U.S.] makes most things better than other countries, the label 'imported' is, for many, synonymous with 'especially selected.' "[65] In this light, Israeli goods—particularly the more distinctive arts and crafts among them—offered American shoppers a novel, even exclusive, new arena for satisfying their consumer desires. Hadassah could help stoke this apparent craving for new and unique Israeli products. As Jennie C. Lowenthal, a Hadassah member from Chicago, wrote to the editors of the *Newsletter* in 1959: "I believe that it is incumbent upon all of us to . . . create a demand for Israel imports. Let us contact as many people as possible and inform them of the fine prospects of securing hundreds of items. Department and retail stores should be alerted and assured that we want Israel items and will buy them."[66]

Beginning in 1949, Hadassah provided members a particularly concrete means of promoting Israeli goods in postwar America. That year, Hadassah founded its Fashion and Design Institute in Jerusalem as a training program for talented graduates of the organization's Alice Seligsberg Vocational High School (established in 1943). Hadassah turned to vocational education in the 1940s as a natural extension of its longstanding rehabilitative focus, and the organization argued for the importance of vocational programs in the Israeli state-building project. As Julia Dushkin, chair of the Vocational Education Department, proclaimed, the heroic era of the settlement of the land and illegal immigration to Palestine was now over; vocational education in Israel provided the hard and worthy work ahead.[67] While synagogue affiliates championed Israeli crafts as a means of promoting Jewishness in the home, Hadassah's foray into the Israeli fashion industry grew from its declared mission to help mold Israel as a socially progressive, first-world country.

On the home front, however, Hadassah worked primarily to alert the public to the work of the Fashion and Design Institute in Israel in a manner that spoke to American women's tastes, sentiments, and consumer savvy. Leaders also wished, as always, to translate this consciousness into monetary support. The leadership of Hadassah's vocational education department developed a straightforward means of doing this: offering a public spectacle that would show Hadassah members, and the American public generally, exactly what the young women at the Fashion and Design Institute were designing and producing. The idea of hosting fashion shows of Israeli-made clothes in America took root in the spring and summer of 1949. The first fashion show, held by the New York chapter of Hadassah, was a success, leading Miriam Freund, now chair of Hadassah's National Vocational Education program, to consider expanding the program. (Indeed, the Philadelphia and Rochester, New York, chapters of Hadassah had inquired about the possibility by March 1949.) She suggested hosting a show of institute-made clothing at the upcoming national Hadassah convention, "and then perhaps sending it throughout the country for the purpose of fundraising."[68] Members of local Hadassah chapters would serve as the live models for the traveling fashion shows.

The fashion shows were conceived, from the beginning, as highly public events. Hadassah's preparatory guide promised that a fashion show would be "one of your best publicity-getters of the year, if you play your cards right" and offered specific suggestions for ensuring this outcome.[69] These suggestions included securing a "well-known fashion editor, writer, merchandiser or department store buyer," as the fashion-show commentator; sending out news releases (a sample was included in the guide); and arranging newspaper interviews. Local chapters were encouraged to organize preview showings for reporters, photographers, and television stations.[70]

According to Helen Kittner, the principal of the Seligsberg High School in Jerusalem, the Fashion and Design Institute was inspired by American vocational programs and modeled according to American principles—namely, to use the institute to train young women in the mass production of ready-to-wear clothing.[71] Thus, at least in part, the clothing on display needed to illustrate that the young Israeli designers training under Hadassah's tutelage were successfully following American industrial models. To this end, fashion show organizers attempted to demonstrate that Israeli-made fashions were not only au courant, but that they were virtually indistinguishable from the standards and styles familiar to American shoppers. Audience members, assumed by Hadassah to be avid consumers of tasteful, mass-produced goods, might then envision themselves bedecked in Israeli products from head to toe.

Figure 4.1. This photograph, dating from 1950, captures a window display at Gimbels department store in Philadelphia. The sign in the window alerted passersby that the mannequins were dressed in Israeli fashions produced by the Alice Seligsberg Trade School for Girls in Jerusalem, and that the Philadelphia Chapter of Hadassah would be presenting the clothing in a fashion show at the Broadwood Hotel. Courtesy of Hadassah, the Women's Zionist Organization of America, Inc.

This strategy emerges clearly in an extant script from December 1949, intended for use by narrators during local productions, which was packaged with Hadassah's preparatory guide for mounting a fashion show. In describing the suits, dresses, and evening gowns featured in the show, the script repeatedly emphasized the high standards and American-like qualities of Israeli fashions. The narrator cited the influence of American designers such as Claire McCardell, a pioneer of ready-to-wear fashion, alongside French couturiers. A particular dress on display was not only well designed and executed, the script trumpeted, but a "commercially right" take on the "crisp, smart little dresses that are turned out in such vast quantities by American manufacturers" and which, with American support, would also characterize the new Israeli fashion industry.[72] The commentator assured viewers that the Israeli fashions would "look right at home in the cocktail lounge" of any American hotel—narrators were to fill in the name of the appropriate local venue here—"or anywhere, in fact, where good taste and fine quality are recognized and appreciated."[73]

In this light, displaying American-like Israeli fashions presented an opportunity to render Israeli goods "invisible" in the context of everyday American culture. Through the medium of the fashion show, in other words, Hadassah suggested to potential consumers that one might support the development of Israeli industry without publicly distinguishing oneself as such a supporter in an immediately apparent way. If decorating the private home with identifiably Israeli objects designated that space as Jewish, as it apparently did for many American Jews, wearing Israeli-made fashions in the public realm was a more ambiguous act of identification with the Jewish state. Indeed, one could wear such Israeli-made clothes and pass as an avid middle-class consumer of presumably American goods. The information that such clothing was made in Israel would have to be provided by the wearer, if she wished.

At the same time, however, organizers of the fashion shows seemed eager to convey an additional, contrasting message: that Israeli fashions, drawing upon the unique skills of Israel's immigrant population, were indelibly, iconically Israeli. One dress featured in the 1949 fashion show, for example, was decorated with handmade Yemenite embroidery "handed down from one generation to another," as the scripted commentary announced.[74] Although the goal was ultimately to produce such embroidery with American-style efficiency, by machine, the fact that the dress "could only have come from Jerusalem" was seen as an asset.[75] To name another example, a particular copper-hued coat was dubbed the "Pekiin," after a village in Israel with a large Bukharian Jewish population; the 1949 script touted the coat's similarity to the caftans of Bukharian rabbis while noting its "fashionable shoulder line."[76] Likewise, a woven silver tunic that appeared at the end of the same show, while not "Israeli" per se, was meant to "charmingly [illustrate] the exotic East."[77] Historian Shirli Brautbar has noted that Hadassah's ensembles in these years included "veils, harem pants, tunic tops, and Middle Eastern motifs," expressive of "the complexity of Jewish ethnic identity in Israel and in the United States."[78]

Indeed, in the show's second year, its organizers decided to push farther in this direction by incorporating costumes representing Israel's various immigrant populations. At the Hadassah convention in 1950, the fashion show opened with a Yemenite dance featuring two young women wearing "Oriental costumes." This spectacle drew upon the popularity of Israeli dance among American audiences while directing attention toward a purported Eastern influence on Israeli fashion.[79] A publicity photograph from 1953 illustrates that Hadassah continued to showcase both "Western" couture and "Eastern" costumes in its traveling fashion shows. In the photograph, three smiling Hadassah models face the camera outfitted in apparel inspired by Indian Jewry, "modern Israeli women," and Yemenite Jewry, according to the caption.[80] Attired in a floor-length, strapless evening gown, the model designated as a "modern Israeli" would, in fact, have looked right at home at any American function requiring fancy dress. The ensembles of the other two women were strikingly different, however, than anything available to the average American consumer.[81] In the context of postwar American culture, such attire belonged to the world of international folk dance festivals and ethnic parades rather than to the realm of retail stores and glossy fashion magazines.

As public spectacles, the Hadassah fashion shows constituted a visible, public means of propounding two seemingly incompatible messages: that Israeli goods were cognates for mass-produced American products, on the one hand, and that Israeli crafts comprised a unique artistic genre redolent of the "exotic East," on the other. Thus, by extension, the shows conveyed a double vision of Israel as both soothingly familiar and strikingly dissimilar from postwar America. This approach, in fact, characterized the promotional efforts of synagogue sisterhoods as well, who exploited the "delicate balance between exotic and familiar," according to Joellyn Wallen Zollman, in marketing Israeli objects to their constituents.[82] Hadassah members who dressed up in Israeli-made apparel for public productions of the Hadassah fashion show physically embodied this balance for national and local audiences. Participants presented their own American Jewish bodies for public view in order to illustrate the character of the Jewish state as an amalgam of "old" and "new," of "East" and "West," of "similar to" and "different from" the postwar United States. In so doing, they visibly telegraphed a complex portrait of Jewish identity in American public space.

Though hardly a display of flagrant Jewish difference in postwar America, Hadassah's performance of Jewish womanhood as "familiar-meets-exotic" represents a new twist within a longstanding discourse about Jews and dress in the American public sphere. One of America's freedoms for Jews, from the beginning, was the freedom from the sartorial control of internal religious and external governmental authorities, both of which exercised this power for much of Jewish history in the Diaspora. The fashion choices of Jewish newcomers to the United States did not go unobserved, however. In American newspapers, literature, and theater in the nineteenth and early twentieth centuries, for example, American Jews were often depicted as flashy parvenus or luxuriant Orientals.[83] While fashion served American Jews as an expressive medium and a central vehicle of acculturation, thus, it was also a site of social anxiety and communal concern, often directed specifically at Jewish women.[84]

One has to look back to the late nineteenth century and mostly to male, rather than female, bodies to find a comparable example of Americans regularly dressing up together in "Eastern" garb. Men took up this practice in the costumed pageants of the Chautauqua Assembly—where visitors to that organization's Palestine Park imaginatively transported themselves to the Holy Land of Jesus's time—and in the rituals of fraternal orders such as the Masons, wherein participants dressed up as biblical patriarchs and High Priests (among other things). In this light, mid-century American Jewish women, as models in the Hadassah fashion shows, were partaking of a pedigreed American practice, though their purpose was not to imagine themselves as biblical avatars, but to conceptualize and embody contemporary Jewish ethnic diversity.[85]

The public nature of this display was very much the point, and the fashion show fulfilled its organizers' expectations as a publicity-generating event. In 1950, Paramount Newsreel photographed the Israeli clothing on professional models, and then showed the photographs on its nationwide news service.[86] Hadassah's 1951 annual report noted that the shows "took the Conventions of 1949 and 1950 by storm," and had been used to raise funds and "promote Hadassah" in 214 local chapters.[87] Likewise, a report presented to Hadassah's National Board in January 1952 proclaimed the fashion show "a tremendous success in carrying a visual message" of the organization's work for vocational education in Israel. The show was not only the "piece de resistance" for chapter membership drives, the report noted, but served "in every case . . . to stimulate good public relations," with the wider community."[88] Hadassah further spurred its efforts and visibility by co-sponsoring a gala fashion show in New York with the Israel Bond Drive in 1952. (Seizing upon a successful experiment, the women's division of the Israel Bond Drive began sponsoring its own fashion show in 1955.)[89] Television celebrities, who began appearing at the annual convention fashion shows in 1954, provided further publicity.[90]

Hadassah described its fashion show as a great success well into the late 1950s and early 1960s. A photograph and caption accompanying the 1958 convention report, for example, published in *Hadassah Newsletter*, proclaimed that the fashion show, "as always, [was] a highlight of the convention." Elsewhere in the report, the author described a "glowing" fashion show and asked, "What woman would not [like] to make a dramatic entrance at her next meeting clothed in such shining raiment?"[91] Reporting on the status of Israeli fashions in the United States in 1966, Ruth Gruber (now Ruth Gruber Michaels) described "2,000 women from all of America applaud[ing] the exciting Hadassah Fashion Show" at the most recent convention and asking where they might procure Israeli fashions for themselves.[92]

Though Hadassah certainly highlighted the show's success as a crowd-pleasing spectacle, the organization was equally eager to frame the event as a humanitarian cause, arguing that supporting Israeli fashion was a means of making the world a better place. By imparting new skills to young immigrant women and fostering the modernization of the Israeli fashion industry, Hadassah felt that it was playing an important role in "civilizing" the developing world. A report on the Institute of Fashion and Design written three years after the institute's founding articulated exactly this notion. The point was not merely "to turn out skilled designers and stylists," the report read, but to build "an unlimited market for Jerusalem fashions, not only [for] the ever expanding population of Israel, but [for] the awakening masses of people in the Middle East, India, [and] China . . . who are ever more exposed to Western influences and ever more interested in raising their standards of living."[93] By supporting the Institute of Fashion and Design, according to this logic, Hadassah members were doing their part to spread the American way of life in the developing world.

Though the organization's philanthropic work remained focused upon Israel, Hadassah made itself relevant to postwar American Jewish women by emphasizing the organization's role in helping members to be "good American citizens and Jews through advocacy, public policy, and education," as historian Rebecca Boim Wolf has shown.[94] To this end, Hadassah's leaders and members devoted themselves to furthering a liberal political agenda at home and abroad, including support for federal aid to education and international safeguards for human rights. Hadassah, from this angle, was not only a philanthropic and social outlet but also a gateway to the wider realm of postwar global politics. "[T]he Hadassah woman often receives her first indoctrination into world affairs through her local chapter," explained the authors of an article in *Hadassah Newsletter* seeking to describe the typical Hadassah member. They continued:

> The Jewish State, on behalf of which she is directly involved, serves as a "peephole" for her into the larger world picture. Through her American Affairs committee she may work toward better understanding of the United Nations, of the problems which America faces on the domestic scene; or, armed with printed information from the national office, [she may] give a public report on Dag Hammarskjold's latest Middle East mission. She typifies the vanguard of American men and women who are shaking off the ill-fitting jacket of isolationism to put on the mantle of international cooperation. . . . Today, the dream of a homeland realized, and with knowledge that work for Israel strengthens American efforts to spread the democratic ideal, our young woman . . . joins to keep up with the times.[95]

The authors' use here of the idiom of fashionability—"shaking off the ill-fitting jacket of isolationism to put on the mantle of international cooperation"—to characterize members' growing political awareness is characteristic of Hadassah's rhetoric in the postwar era. Hadassah's promotional brochures for potential members, for example, typically depicted "fashionably dressed American women, suitably bejeweled with pearls and gold earrings."[96] The message for middle-class American Jewish women was that being "in the know" was a matter of both style and substance, aesthetic taste and educational aspiration. Hadassah's postwar fashion shows exemplify this rhetorical approach and illustrate the intertwining of culture, education, philanthropy, and politics in the organization's activities and self-image.

In contrast to synagogue-based cultural arbiters, Hadassah's leaders did not explicitly articulate their organization's promotion of Israeli commodities as a Jewish cultural project per se. Yet Hadassah's fashion shows and the Israeli goods promoted therein surely inhabited the cultural realm. They were conceived of as theatrical events and as vehicles for shaping the aesthetic expectations and consumer habits of postwar Americans. In deploying "culture" as a means of furthering its institutional goals, then, Hadassah's rhetoric and actions mirrored those of the postwar synagogue in important ways. Though they framed and executed their actions differently, Hadassah members and synagogue affiliates shaped Israeli goods into powerful cultural markers whose significance extended into the private (domestic and religious) and public (economic and political) realms. For synagogue affiliates, Israeli goods helped shape and designate private Jewish space; for members of Hadassah, these goods helped articulate Jewish taste, behavior, and identity in the American public sphere. For both, however, purchasing and promoting Israeli wares served as a form of enlightened consumption, benefiting Israel, American Jews and, implicitly or explicitly, postwar America at large.

COMMODIFYING ISRAEL: THE AMERICA-ISRAEL CHAMBER OF COMMERCE AND INDUSTRY

In 1953, a group of businessmen headed by Nathan Straus III—scion of one of American Jewry's most important philanthropic families—joined together to form the America-Israel Chamber of Commerce and Industry (AICCI). The organization would serve, in Straus's words, as an "independent and responsible body" to coordinate between American and Israeli businessmen and the Israeli government and U.S. Department of Commerce.[97] Under the motto of "trade, not aid," to Israel, Straus and his fellow members sought to inspire confidence and spur investment in the Israeli economy among American businesses and corporations, turning away from the philanthropic model to one of mutually beneficial capitalist partnership. The organization viewed building a market for Israeli goods in America as part of this agenda.

The AICCI expounded its vision in terms that spoke to America's power—and its concomitant responsibilities—in the postwar world. The organization's first years corresponded with a time of relative tension between the United States and Israel, reaching a crescendo with a freeze on American economic aid to Israel during the Suez-Sinai War of 1956. This crisis provided the first real test of the durability of American and Israeli commercial relations, and the AICCI set out to make the case that such relations were in America's best interest. Like Hadassah, the organization argued that promoting Israeli goods (and, for the AICCI, investing in Israel more broadly) would benefit not only Israel, but also America *and* the developing world. As Straus explained,

> As larger numbers of foreigners realize profits on their business with Israel, greater amounts of capital will become available through normal private channels. It will originate from American entrepreneurs and others seeking to participate in the economy of dynamically growing Israel and, through Israel, in the whole awakening African continent. The profit motive has been one of the major forces responsible for the economic growth of the Free World, and Israel should have the full benefit of that same driving force.[98]

For the AICCI, Israel essentially served as a proxy for America, sharing core moral and, now, economic principles as that country moved away from socialism and toward private enterprise. Israel, the logic went, represented an intermediate stage in the march toward capitalism; by providing a model of gradual capitalist development for postcolonial nations, Israel would draw those nations into the Western orbit.[99]

Aside from the Suez-Sinai crisis, the comprehensive Arab economic boycott of Israel provided the most sustained challenge to the AICCI and its rhetoric about the congruence of American and Israeli economic and ideological interests. The boycott, which began in the late 1940s—first, as a boycott of Israeli goods, and then, beginning in 1952, including the blacklisting and boycotting of corporations trading with or investing in Israel—meant that American firms stood to lose vast markets in the Arab Middle East by establishing economic ties with Israel.[100] In the early 1960s, the AICCI mounted a serious challenge to the boycott, requesting that Congress introduce legislation opposing it on the grounds that it violated the Treaty of Friendship, Commerce and Navigation between the United States and Israel.[101] The Export Control Act, which passed in June 1965, included three such provisions prohibiting compliance with a foreign boycott against a friendly nation: a statement of opposition to "such practices as the Arab boycott of Israel"; a demand that requests for cooperation with the boycott be reported by American businesses to the Department of Commerce; and a proclamation of strong "encouragement and request" to American firms not to participate in the boycott.[102] With this campaign, the AICCI's consumer advocacy on behalf of Israel began to look very much like political lobbying.

The relationship between economics and politics became increasingly fraught for the AICCI over the course of the 1950s and early 1960s, as the organization's confrontation of the Arab boycott suggests. Despite the AICCI's confidence in the compatibility of American and Israeli interests, challenges to the equation seemed to demand a more robust public relations campaign on behalf of American-Israeli economic friendship. The AICCI's involvement in the New York World's Fair in 1964 through its new subsidiary, the American-Israel World's Fair Corporation, exemplifies this attempt to promote Israeli goods more vigorously in the public sphere and to argue for the larger cultural relevance of such imports. The organization's sponsorship of the "American-Israel Pavilion" at Flushing Meadows provided the AICCI an opportunity to celebrate Israel's achievements and to foreground America's role and stake in that success, all the while increasing public exposure to Israeli-made goods. (Harold Caplin, director of the effort, projected that the pavilion would single-handedly increase U.S. trade with Israel by 50 percent.)[103]

As was true of synagogue affiliates and Hadassah members, however, pavilion organizers connected to the AICCI stressed that Israeli goods were more than economic commodities. Nathan Straus insisted that the pavilion was "not simply a trade fair," a place to hawk products and services from Israel.[104] Like earlier Israel-focused exhibitions at American department stores and trade fairs, the pavilion was meant to provide cultural uplift and edification to visitors and, in a broader sense, to create an image of Israel as a fully American concern. The organizers stressed this notion in the dedication ceremony for the pavilion, for example, insisting that the exhibition would be a forum for educating visitors about Jewish civilization.[105]

The exhibition design embodied the organizers' cultural and educational ambitions. The main exhibition hall, designed by Israeli set designer Zvi Geyra, presented visitors a three-part journey through Jewish history focusing upon ancient Israel, the Diaspora, and modern Israel. In the first section, visitors encountered ancient stone and mud walls, architectural relics, and a model of Solomon's Temple; in the second, Geyra offered tableaux representing various world Jewish communities throughout history; the third section, entitled "The Land and Its Products," focused upon Israel's scientific and cultural achievements. Here, visitors encountered an assortment of Israeli wine, books, textiles, and jewelry, much of which would, by this time, be familiar to anyone who had ever wandered into a synagogue gift shop or witnessed a Hadassah fashion show.

Many of these very products awaited visitors just beyond the exhibition hall, in the indoor and outdoor shops. (Indeed, an extant copy of the *World's Fair Merchandise Sale Catalog* suggests that the organizers offered the very contents of the pavilion for sale, including textiles, photomurals, and archaeological relics.)[106] As pavilion officials expected, the shopping mall was commercially successful, introducing recent products to new consumers and providing shoppers with familiar favorites. As *American-Israel Economic Horizons* reported, "metal giftware, hand-crafted ceramics, chocolates and woven products retained their best-seller position" among shoppers.[107]

In this regard, the AICCI was capitalizing on a trend that was already well underway. Israeli exports to America had in fact risen rapidly in the course of the 1950s. By the close of the decade, trade between the United States and Israel had increased by 35 percent, making the United States the second-highest recipient of Israeli goods, after Great Britain.[108] Straus had noted in 1961 that, for the first time, "the flow of capital into Israel exceeded philanthropic contributions."[109] The AICCI was meeting its programmatic goals. The organization hoped that it's promotion of Israeli goods, whether in department stores, the New York World's Fair, or the halls of Congress, was influencing how Americans thought about Israel, too.[110]

"A GLOW OF GROUP FEELING AND IDENTIFICATION": FROM CONSUMPTION TO ADVOCACY

Cultural commentators responded to the newfound prominence of Israeli objects with a mix of fascination and apprehension. The success and abundance of Israeli wares was changing the material culture of American Jewry—that much was clear—but was this a change for the better? What, exactly, did the phenomenon signify? According to Ruth Glazer, a contemporaneous observer of postwar American Jewry, the change represented a partial victory in the cultural realm. She considered the spate of new Israeli objects now available to American consumers a welcome alternative to American-produced Jewish ceremonial objects. In an essay in *Commentary* in 1951, Glazer reported on the aesthetic offenses of the hanukkiot, matzah covers, and other ceremonial objects available to American Jews, now even at general department stores such as Macy's. American consumers, Glazer insisted, didn't have the wherewithal to notice the items' shoddy ugliness. For Glazer, the introduction of Israeli objects represented the dawning, at last, of a new aesthetic era. The author was impressed with the Israeli wares she saw in American stores, remarking that, "the bare simplicity that we have come to associate with 'modern' design, the emphasis on texture rather than decoration, seems to have conquered in Israel."[111]

The problem, for Glazer, was that American Jews seemed to be buying Israeli objects for the wrong reasons. Rather than being motivated by aesthetic good judgment, American Jewish consumers were using their dollars to cultivate "a glow of group feeling and identification"—that is, to express Jewish solidarity and pride.[112] Glazer concluded that an object's easy identification as "Israeli," rather than its modernist pedigree, was its most important quality for shoppers. This, for Glazer, signaled the continuing immaturity of American Jewish aesthetics and, by extension, American Jewish culture as a whole.

The critique lingered. In the spring of 1957, *Midstream* magazine published a piece about the advent of the "Jewish gift shop" and the preponderance of Israeli merchandise in this new venue. The writer, Sarah Schack, described the proliferation of such shops all over New York City. "[A]s recently as perhaps twenty-five years ago there were only a few such shops in New York," Schack explained, and they were found primarily on the Lower East Side, once the mecca of the immigrant religious-goods market.[113] The new breed of Jewish specialty stores, however, were located "in every predominantly Jewish neighborhood" in the city, where the broadened selection of items reflected "not only the affirmation by the American Jewish middle class of their religious faith but also their conscious, sometimes self-conscious, interest in Israel."[114]

Alongside prayer shawls and sacred books, holiday activity workbooks for children, and "Freilach in Hi-Fi" records, shoppers could find many objects from Israel—"the stores are full of them," Schack explained.[115] She continued:

> Just as the olive-wood inkstands and letter openers of forty and fifty years ago acquired a quasi-religious aura because they were made in the Holy Land, the present-day product is featured in the religious specialty shops. Now the choice is wider, ranging from ash trays and coaster sets to decanters and silent butlers; and the border line between secular and religious here becomes a border area through the decoration of these items with such motifs as the lion of Judah and the harp of David. One finds, too, candlesticks and candles, the Kiddush cup . . . and the nine-branched *chanukia*. These last are available in great variety: simple utility ones of brass; a new-fangled contraption which plays "Maoz Tzur" [a Hanukkah song] and "Hatikvah" [the Israeli national anthem], and imaginative free forms.[116]

The panoply of Israeli objects for sale reflected a new type of Jewish consumption, for "despite the full attention to the paraphernalia of holiday and Sabbath observance," Shack concluded, "the greater number of objects from Israel are intended for gifts." The author feared that the newfangled stores catered to the most superficial impulses of the American Jewish community. She surmised that purchasing an Israeli ashtray decorated with a biblical motif reassured shoppers that "they are Jews without asking them not to be Americans"—to be Jewish, but not too Jewish.[117]

This, in fact, was precisely the point for many American Jews. The postwar synagogue, as an institution, continually sought to calibrate the perfect balance between "American" and "Jewish" culture, an endeavor most visible to the public, perhaps, in postwar synagogue design. The postwar Jewish home, too, served as a key laboratory in the larger project to make Judaism and Jewish culture appealing and relevant to middle-class, upwardly mobile American Jews. Many of those joining synagogues in droves in the postwar years had little substantive Jewish literacy. Synagogue leaders and affiliates, and sisterhood organizations in particular, felt it a primary duty to tutor American Jewish women in the art of Jewish homemaking.

As these leaders claimed, ritual observance in the home was one important aspect of this project. The goal, more broadly, was to cultivate a modern Jewish cultural idiom in the domestic sphere. Exposing American Jews to Jewish arts and crafts "encourage[d] artistic expression of their religion and culture in their homes," as one proponent proclaimed in the pages of *American Judaism* magazine.[118] Synagogue sisterhoods promoted Israeli objects as essential to this campaign. These organizations insisted that contemporary Israeli crafts furthered the postwar synagogue's cultural mission in the domestic sphere: to introduce the aesthetics of contemporary Jewish design to American Jews while helping to make the American Jewish home more significantly Jewish. They argued that Israeli objects, whether secular or religious, belonged in suburban living rooms across the country.

Many American Jews appeared to agree. As sociologist Samuel Heilman has noted, "[The] accumulation of Judaica from Israel may be said to define a kind of sanctification of the profane. Indeed, for some Jews . . . these mementos of Israel, whether actually acquired there or gotten secondhand through a dealer or local shop, are often the great treasures of their Jewish life."[119] Postwar critics that viewed the mass consumption and display of (usually mass-produced) Israeli objects as aesthetically suspect and ideologically facile had little impact on the practices of everyday women and men. Colleen McDannell has written that significance of religious "kitsch" in the lives of religious actors demands that we "consider how religious meaning can be derived from objects or settings which are theologically trivial, aesthetically superficial, and frequently grossly commercial."[120] Rephrasing this supposition slightly to reflect the case at hand, one can argue that American Jews clearly have derived meaning from Israeli objects that may have been ideologically or aesthetically trivial, as well as forthrightly commercial.

It would be misleading, however, to focus exclusively upon the promotion and consumption of Israeli goods as expressions of Jewishness or as attempts to refine Jewish cultural sensibilities. As the example of Hadassah makes clear, promoters of Israeli goods also insisted that—as benefactors and shoppers—American Jews could simultaneously support Israel, effect long-term progress in the Middle East, and buttress the American way of life. It was precisely through such cultural engagements as the Hadassah fashion show that many American Jewish women entered into the contemporaneous political discourse about America's role in the postwar world and in the Middle East in particular.

The America-Israel Chamber of Commerce and Industry's role as promoter of Israeli goods provides another compelling example of the increasingly blurry lines between economic, cultural, and political advocacy on behalf of Israel. As "nonpolitical" groups such as Hadassah and the AICCI successfully domesticated Israel in American consumer and material culture, they also framed Israel as a global partner and an appropriate focus for increasing political activism.

FIVE

CULTURAL EMISSARIES AND THE CULTURE EXPLOSION

Introducing Israeli Art and Music

The signs of [the] [cultural] explosion are all about us—the mushrooming of city shops selling art supplies for amateur artists, the blooming of a generation of "hi-fi" addicts who build their own "tweeters" and "woofers" to get the ultimate expression out of fine music, a President who is not ashamed to admit that he paints (even if not very well), a mass market for fine reproductions of old masterpieces. . . . Qualitatively, it may or may not yet be great culture, but quantitatively there is an awful lot of it; with culture as with everything else they undertake, Americans have to have more of it than anybody else.[1]

Thus wrote the editors of *Life* magazine in the fall of 1954, in one of the first notices in the mainstream media of a startling new trend in American life. Since World War II, it seemed, increasing numbers of Americans were visiting museum exhibitions and attending theater, music, and dance performances, a phenomenon noted and debated in the public sphere. Cultural commentators spoke of a "culture boom," "culture explosion," and "culture fever," and weighed in on the apparent upswing in interest in the arts on the part of everyday Americans across the country.[2] Although no single national survey from the period exists to quantify the American hankering after culture, commentators gleaned evidence of the trend from institutions and individuals in major cities and heartland outposts alike. "Attendance and participation figures show that culture has blown up into a bigger thing than baseball, boating or even bowling," announced the editors at *Changing Times* magazine in an article examining the fiscal and artistic health of the newly robust cultural sphere in America. "The signs are erupting all over," they wrote, from chamber music festivals in Jackson, Wyoming, to traveling "Artmobiles" in Virginia.[3]

In his book *The Culture Consumers*, former *Fortune* magazine editor Alvin Toffler presented his own research on the phenomenon, citing millions of dollars spent on art museums, public libraries, symphony orchestras, books, and LPs; increasing audiences at such venues as the Metropolitan Opera; and a surge in participation in amateur music, theater, and art. Between 1950 and 1964, he wrote, the number of fine art galleries in New York doubled, from 150 to 300. This was not simply a big city phenomenon, Toffler insisted. In Phoenix, Arizona, for example, the number of galleries increased from two to fifteen between 1950 and 1960, while "nobody has been able to count up the hundreds [of art galleries] that have burgeoned in places like Flint, Michigan and Quincy, Illinois."[4] According to August Heckscher, John F. Kennedy's Special Consultant on the Arts, the United States was "in the midst of a vast quantitative expansion of its cultural life."[5]

As upwardly mobile, largely middle-class citizens, American Jews figured significantly in the purported upswing in cultural consumption. Toffler noted in *The Culture Consumers* that American Jews were responsible for a significant measure of the American cultural explosion. Interviews with arts administrators revealed disproportionately high Jewish attendance at galleries, orchestras, and other arts venues across the nation, a phenomenon Toffler argued was of recent vintage, at least outside of New York City. He pointed to evidence of Jewish overrepresentation in arts consumption—whether as audience members or as collectors and patrons—in such locations as Los Angeles, San Antonio, Dallas, and Detroit; this phenomenon, he felt, was a byproduct of American Jewish confidence as antisemitism dissipated and assimilation proceeded apace.

To be sure, Jews had long been producing and partaking of culture in America. Whether by commissioning a portrait in the colonial era or buying a piano for a tenement parlor at the turn of the twentieth century, American Jews were finely attuned to the centrality of culture in the process of acclimation to American life.[6] The postwar period offered American Jews extensive new opportunities to engage with culture. As Janice Radway has written, cultural consumption in twentieth-century America was "invested with symbolic significance by a generation of Americans desperately in need of markers to signal their accession to middle-class comfort and their command of middle-class refinement, achieved increasingly not by the accident of birth but by the rigorous process of institutional education and apprenticeship."[7] Exhibiting disproportionately high levels of educational and professional attainment after World War II, American Jews, as a group, were well positioned to hone their cultural savoir-faire and to enjoy the bounty of middle-class life at mid-century.

Toffler reported that some in the Jewish community expressed concern that high rates of Jewish consumption of general culture, undoubtedly good for the health of the arts in America, left fewer resources for Jewish communal needs.[8] Yet Jews were turning their attention to Jewish culture as well.[9] What's more, American Jews acted in these years not only as patrons and consumers of American art, music, and other forms of culture, but also as impresarios and enthusiasts of *Israeli* culture—in America. One organization in particular—the America-Israel Cultural Foundation (AICF)—exemplifies the phenomenon of American Jewish patronage of Israeli culture within the American cultural arena in this period. For the American Jewish impresarios and entrepreneurs affiliated with the AICF, Israeli high culture represented the best public face of Israel and served as a common denominator between Israel and America and between Jews and non-Jews. The AICF developed a range of activities in the postwar period meant to bolster the arts in Israel, including direct allocations to institutions, aid in building campaigns, a scholarship program for young artists and musicians, and support for festivals and educational programs. To this end, by the mid-1960s, the foundation had contributed more than $20 million to Israel's cultural institutions in the fields of dance, fine art, theater, and music.[10]

In the United States, importing Israeli cultural offerings into America's leading museums and concert halls was the AICF's chief strategy for raising public awareness of Israeli culture in general and the foundation's work in particular—and for securing funds for both. The AICF sponsored the appearances of several arts institutions in these years, including Israel's national theater and dance companies (Habimah and Inbal, respectively), as well as organizing a major archaeological exhibition, *From the Land of the Bible*, at the Metropolitan Museum of Art.[11] The organization's work in the fields of fine art and orchestral music, in particular, provide vivid examples of its successes on the public stage. As sponsor and co-organizer of two prominent group exhibitions of Israeli art—*Seven Painters of Israel* in 1953 and *Art Israel: 26 Painters and Sculptors* in 1964–65—the AICF undoubtedly raised the visibility and prestige of Israeli art among the cognoscenti. So, too, did the organization's sponsorship of two major tours by the Israel Philharmonic Orchestra, in 1951 and in 1960, grant audiences and critics access to one of Israel's most notable cultural achievements: the creation of a world-class symphony orchestra.

As was the case with American Jewish promotion and consumption of Israeli goods, American Jewish sponsorship and consumption of Israeli culture suited the national conversation about the appropriate relationship between American citizens and foreign nations in the postwar period. The AICF in particular emphasized that its efforts on behalf of Israeli culture furthered America's cultural *and* political goals in the Cold War, that it was natural and good that American citizens should support the cultural efforts of the Jewish state. It is worth remembering that, not long before, American Jews' transnational ties—largely to the Jewish communities of Europe—had been a source of tension and anxiety vis-à-vis the public sphere. In the 1930s, American Jews had observed the advent of Nazism with horror and hoped that the United States would intervene to defeat fascism in Europe. Until the Japanese attack on Pearl Harbor in December 1941 altered the national mood, however, most other Americans did not wish to embroil America in World War II. Moreover, many Americans harbored negative opinions of Jews at the time, and antisemitic demagogues and organizations had flourished in the years before World War II. American Jews were well aware of this and had modulated their public voices accordingly, even as they shipped off in disproportionate numbers to fight (in their view) the Nazi enemy.

Times had changed. As American Jews united in 1948 to support a foreign nation halfway around the world, they found themselves in step with an outward-looking America. The isolationism of the pre–War War II period had morphed into a "newfound internationalism" in the postwar era.[12] The U.S. government and American public were now investing heavily in both public diplomacy and cultural diplomacy. The government did this, in part, by sponsoring student exchanges, pen pal programs, and cultural congresses (among other programs), especially with European nations. The purpose of such public diplomacy efforts, according to historian Wendy Wall, was twofold: to fight communism by proxy, on the one hand, while allowing ethnic groups "to reconcile their religious and Old World allegiances with their new American identities and to incorporate themselves more fully into the American 'mainstream,'" on the other.[13] Meanwhile, by the mid-1950s, the United States Information Agency (USIA) and the CIA had taken up the field of cultural diplomacy as an alternative to the overt propagandizing and psychological warfare campaigns of the immediate postwar years. This was, in contrast to earlier interventions, an "evolutionary approach emphasizing straight news and information programs, cultural exhibitions, and East-West exchange programs," according to Walter L. Hixson.[14] The hope was that the gradual implanting of American culture into foreign societies (including Soviet society) would cause foreign populations to adopt the "symbols, lifestyles, consumerism, and core values" of the postwar United States, under the very nose of totalitarian regimes.[15]

The work of the AICF must be understood in this context. To be sure, the AICF's championing of Israeli culture in America did not, on the face of it, advance the government's anticommunist agenda in Europe, the focus of America's public and cultural diplomacy in the postwar period. Yet the foundation articulated its mission in a similar Cold War idiom and through comparable mechanisms. For the AICF, Israel's cultural accomplishments were more than artistic victories; the foundation viewed cultural philanthropy and diplomacy as a moral act with real political consequences for Israel and for the United States. By cultivating cultural institutions in Israel, on the one hand, and exposing American audiences to Israeli culture, on the other, the AICF hoped to help Israel achieve its cultural aspirations as a modern nation while encouraging an enduring partnership between two political states, America and Israel. AICF executive Leon Gildesgame once remarked, regarding the organization's role as impresario of Israeli culture, that "the propaganda value and goodwill for the state of Israel, for Jews generally and for the AICF directly, could not . . . [be] bought for a million dollars."[16] Yet this quotation is a rare statement by the AICF in regard to its role as a specifically Jewish organization with particular communal goals. In public statements, as we shall see, the foundation was more likely to emphasize the importance of its work in furthering America's Cold War strategies, by cementing cultural bonds with an ostensible American ally in the Middle East.

Though the AICF played a crucial role in shepherding Israeli art and music into the highest echelons of the American culture industry, there were, among the American Jewish populace, many other sponsors and organizers of Israeli cultural events in these years. Individuals and local communities also acted as "boosters" of Israeli culture, arranging exhibitions and concerts well beyond the major American museums and concert halls. They also approached Israeli art and music as consumers, buying increasing numbers of artworks and record albums. Even when American Jewish proponents of Israeli art and music acted in partnership with the professional arts establishment, as the AICF did, they appeared to be motivated by educative, philanthropic, and even political interests that were distinct from the overriding aesthetic concerns of arts professionals and critics. Indeed, the low priority of aesthetic issues among American Jewish impresarios of Israeli culture sometimes thwarted larger goals. This was true, for example, of the AICF's failed campaign in 1948–49 to entice the Museum of Modern Art to sponsor a group exhibition of Israeli art. In making the case for an Israeli art exhibition to MoMA officials, the foundation's executive director argued that such an exhibition would help strengthen bonds of friendship between America and Israel. This argument failed to persuade MoMA's staff, however, who judged the selected works according to aesthetic criteria alone and found them lacking.[17] No exhibition resulted at that time.

Yet professional critics, too, sometimes employed more than strictly aesthetic criteria in judging the value of Israeli culture. At times, American art and music critics apprehended Israeli offerings in light of recent history. Israel's cultural achievements provided proof, for them, that the Jewish state had transcended recent historical crises—the Holocaust as well as Israel's own tumultuous birth—to become a full participant in Western civilization. Other critics—particularly those active in American Jewish cultural circles—turned a gimlet eye toward American Jewish sponsorship and consumption of Israeli culture. Such critics expressed concern that American Jews were attracted only to the most debased and commercialized versions of Israeli culture and that average American Jews could not be trusted to make the distinction between art and trash.

In truth, it seems that American Jews, on the whole, had few qualms about their roles as champions of Israeli art and music. They viewed the stewardship of Israeli culture as the purview of the Jewish community. They supported Israeli art and music as crucial means of educating audiences about Israel, honoring the young nation's achievements before the public, and making the case for Israel's importance to America. Public exhibitions and private consumption served, too, as pragmatic means of raising funds for Israel and for other Jewish communal projects. And as impresarios of Israeli culture, American Jews also cast themselves as cultural ambassadors to their fellow Americans.

AMBASSADORS OF GOOD WILL:
THE AMERICA-ISRAEL CULTURAL FOUNDATION
AND "CULTURAL LEND-LEASE"

The AICF—known first as the American Fund for Palestinian Institutions, then as American Fund for Israel Institutions, and, after 1957, as the America-Israel Cultural Foundation—was established in 1939 by American Jewish businessman and philanthropist Edward A. Norman. The organization was originally created in order to centralize the scores of separate appeals for aid that were being brought before the American Jewish public every year by nonpartisan institutions unaffiliated with the World Zionist Organization.[18] While it had initially managed appeals and raised money for a spectrum of educational, cultural, and social welfare institutions in Palestine/Israel, by the late 1940s the mission of the organization had shifted to focus on the cultural sphere.

In recognition of its "pioneering program of cultural exchange," the AICF was one of a select group of philanthropic organizations approved by the Jewish Agency to raise funds independently in the United States on behalf of Israel.[19] While it found itself in the company of a diverse group of organizations—from the non-Zionist United Jewish Appeal to Zionist stalwarts Hadassah and the Zionist Organization of America, as well as several institution-specific groups such as the American Friends of the Hebrew University and the American Technion Society—the AICF carved a particular niche for itself as "the cultural intermediary between the United States and Israel."[20] With its unique and wide-ranging cultural approach, the foundation imagined its programs as appealing to Zionists and non-Zionists alike, as well as to non-Jews. Indeed, in light of its ostensibly broad appeal, the AICF considered itself to be a "non-political and non-partisan organization," clearly a selling point in the eyes of its leadership.[21]

A prospectus produced by the foundation in the early 1950s remains a key to understanding the organization's motives and mission as a major cultural philanthropy in the American Jewish community. In it, the organization's officers specified the tasks before them in the postwar period, including the launching of a full-scale public relations and informational campaign that would relate the work of the AICF to "the experience, interests and fundamental beliefs of the American community."[22] To this end, the authors of the prospectus delineated a number of strategic points that comprised the foundation's basic approach to fundraising. Among the eleven points on the list were the following directives: to underscore the consonance between American history and that of Israel, particularly shared traditions of pioneer settlement, fighting for independence, and providing refuge for the oppressed; to encourage the development of a robust culture in Israel that would be supportive of democracy and the "four freedoms" (freedom of speech and religion and freedom from economic deprivation and fear); and to remind Americans of Israel's "rich spiritual contribution of everlasting inspiration to all mankind."[23]

The authors of the prospectus spoke in broad terms, referring often to the beliefs and behavior of "Americans" and the "American community," but rarely to those of American Jews per se. Yet the foundation depended upon the Jewish welfare federations for its income, which was then augmented by funds from an annual campaign in New York City. This rhetorical approach remained a hallmark of the AICF throughout the period, as the foundation's core philosophy was articulated, time and again, in universalizing language that blurred the AICF's identity as an American Jewish philanthropy.

This can be seen, for example, in a 1951 essay on the AICF by Frank W. Buxton, former editor-in-chief of the *Boston Herald* and co-chairman of the Boston chapter of the AICF. (In 1946, Buxton had served on the

Anglo-American Committee of Inquiry, the body charged with gathering research on the feasibility of the partition of Palestine into Jewish and Arab states, and was one of the members to express admiration for the Yishuv during the committee's fact-finding mission there.)[24] As Buxton explained in the pages of *Israel Life and Letters*, the foundation's magazine, the AICF's programs were meant to foster a kind of "cultural lend lease" in which both Americans and Israelis might learn from one another and reinforce shared values. Listing founding fathers George Washington, Benjamin Franklin, John Adams, and John Quincy Adams as "posthumous champions of the ideals which the [AICF] is promoting," Buxton argued that Americans had "an unwritten moral commitment to the cultural movement" being culti-vated by the foundation.[25] To his mind, at least, the AICF's primary aims encompassed not only the cultural field, but the moral and, indeed, politi-cal realms as well: its practices would not only ensure Israeli democracy "a firmer foothold in the Middle East," but would make Israelis and Americans "aware of the benefits which will accrue to them and their nations by a moral alliance between the most vulnerable and the youngest, most experimental and most imperiled of democracies."[26] Even as the AICF accorded itself a unique role as a nonpolitical and nonpartisan American Jewish organization devoted to Israel's cultural development, statements such as these regarding its mission reveal a distinct political perspective, in which cultural patron-age served a significant role in the spread of American-style democracy in the postwar world.

Similarly, the AICF's president in the 1950s, Samuel Rubin, reasoned that a single-minded commitment to the cultural sphere was in the best interest of everyone—the organized American Jewish community, individual entrepreneurs and philanthropists, Israel, the United States, and, indeed, the world. Sustaining Israel through aid to its cultural development was more than mere philanthropy, he argued; it was an act that furthered the postwar imperative of international peace, albeit through the soft filter of cultural influence rather than the blunt force of government fiat. As Rubin explained in 1957,

> There can be no peace without understanding. And there can
> be no understanding without friendship among the nations and
> a brotherly interest in each other. The peoples of the world
> have only one common language. It is not the formal papers of
> the diplomats. It is the language of the arts—of music, paint-
> ing, the dance, philosophy, poetry, drama. . . . For only in their
> inter-cultural relations does the brotherhood of man become
> a reality for peoples separated by national borderlines and by

> linguistic, cultural and economic differences. If we in this, the
> richest country in the world, are to do our share in helping the
> less fortunate and the underdeveloped areas to take their rightful
> place in the civilization of the Twentieth Century [*sic*], then it
> follows that our own education, our own understanding of other
> peoples and their cultures, must be broadened, intensified, and
> enriched. Conversely, the American contributions to the arts
> and sciences can provide our country with innumerable ambas-
> sadors of good will.[27]

Through the act of cultural reciprocity, Rubin insisted, America and Israel would be strengthened. An enlightened America, the benevolent super-power, would fulfill its obligations to the world, while Israel would realize an equally lofty destiny as a source of "inspiration and guidance to the entire Middle East," in Rubin's words.[28]

Rubin's emphasis here on cultural exchange between the United States and Israel, with no acknowledgment of the special role of American Jewry in this endeavor, was typical of the AICF's public pronouncements regarding its work. This tendency to obscure the Jewish context of the organization's philanthropic mission suggests a careful consideration, among its leaders and allies, of how the AICF's work would be perceived in the public sphere. An essay in *Israel Life and Letters* by Horace Kallen, American Jewish philoso-pher, champion of cultural pluralism in America, and supporter of the AICF, exemplifies this guarded assertion of the organization's raison d'être. "Deeply sensitive about the basic condition of all civilizations," Kallen wrote, the American Jews who ran and supported the foundation were not simply directing their attention, as Jews, "toward the survival and growth of the spiritual heritage of the Jewish people in Israel." Rather, he continued, those involved with the AICF took up the cause of Israel's cultural well-being because, "as Americans dedicated to democracy, they look forward to a free trade in the spiritual values of the two countries, so that each may be enriched and strengthened by what it has not and the other can provide."[29] The message was clear: The AICF as a philanthropic institution transcended parochial loyalties, its mission being broadly American rather than specifi-cally American Jewish. In its campaign to promote Israeli fine art and con-cert music in the United States, the foundation stressed the universal value of Israeli culture—an approach that, in the AICF's estimation, would secure both the fiscal and ideological support of the American Jewish community while winning friends among the American public in general.

The philosophy and activities of the AICF were rooted in the general postwar climate of cultural expansion, at the nexus of corporate patronage—a significant factor in the new cultural developments in American life, according to Alvin Toffler—and American Jewish cultural consumption.[30] As the preeminent corporate impresario of Israeli culture, the foundation was instrumental in organizing the highest-profile Israeli cultural events in the American public sphere. Accordingly, the AICF articulated perhaps the most civic-minded rationale for sponsoring Israeli culture in America. As we will see, other American Jewish impresarios of Israeli art and music, however humble their efforts, had equally grand visions of the value of Israeli culture for American audiences.

INTRODUCING ISRAELI ART

American Jewish supporters of Israeli art set about presenting local, communally organized showcases of Israeli art soon after the emergence of the Jewish state. As organizers and observers of the first professional exhibitions of Israeli art in the years after Israel's founding, American curators and critics struggled to define Israeli art in categorical and qualitative terms.[31] American Jews outside the professional art world, in contrast, showed little interest in defining Israeli art as a national school, in judging its aesthetic contributions, or in securing a professional imprimatur for their own curatorial efforts. Rather, these amateur sponsors seemed more interested in exhibiting Israeli art in order to convey some sense of contemporary life in Israel and to publicly celebrate Israel's accomplishments.

In May 1949, for example, Los Angeles Jews hosted the first group show of Israeli art in that city since the establishment of the state of Israel in 1948. The exhibition, culled from the personal collection of Dr. Leon Kolb, a Vienna-born professor of pharmacology at Stanford University, was co-sponsored by the Israeli Consulate in Los Angeles and the Henrietta Szold chapter of Hadassah in Los Angeles.[32] The show opened at the Beverly-Fairfax Jewish Community Center on May 17, to commemorate Israel's first anniversary. Comprised of one hundred works on paper, the exhibition introduced Los Angeles audiences to the work of six well-established artists who had trained in Germany before emigrating to Palestine in the 1930s.[33] Among the works on display were watercolors of Tel Aviv during the Israeli War of Independence and woodcuts depicting Jerusalem, images that provided viewers at least a glimpse of the faraway nation of Israel. The show was well received not only by the *Los Angeles Times* but, apparently, by a cross-section of the local Jewish community.[34] Kolb's collection appeared in a similar exhibition in San Diego in 1950, arranged by the Jewish Center Lecture Bureau of the National Jewish Welfare Board.[35]

Similar efforts by Jewish impresarios of Israeli art were unfolding elsewhere in the country in the first years after Israel's founding, in venues far removed from the hushed confines of American art museums. At Gimbel Brothers department store in Philadelphia in April 1952, for instance, an exhibition of nineteen Israeli painters—including established artists Marcel Janco, Moshe Castel, Nahum Guttman, and Moshe Mokady—was arranged by a local rabbi, Gerson Brenner, in cooperation with Mokady (the Israeli Minister of Culture). Later that year, the exhibition traveled to the YMHA in New York. (Brenner, the rabbi-cum-impresario, also made reproductions of some of the exhibited works, "so that copies could find their way in to American homes," with the proceeds going directly to the artists.)[36] That same spring, the Jewish community center of Elmira, New York, organized a "Festival of Israeli Arts and Culture" intended to provide the local community, Jewish and non-Jewish, a glimpse of the new Israeli culture. There, individual booths displaying Israeli stamps, tourism posters, jewelry, crafts, and books joined an exhibit of more than one hundred paintings by Israeli artists.[37] Among the visitors to the exhibition were local schoolchildren, brought from Elmira's public schools for a special children's program. The center's executive director noted that the festival was the institution's "first major program on Israel in which the philanthropic theme was entirely absent, and in which the emphasis was on the positive artistic and cultural development of the Israeli people."[38] The goal of the festival was educational, the mood celebratory; the small admission charge went toward production costs.

Exhibitions arranged by American Jewish aficionados of Israeli art often fulfilled educational, philanthropic, and even entrepreneurial aims simultaneously. Both the Gimbel Brothers and Beverly-Fairfax exhibitions, for example, were conceived as fundraising ventures. The career of Murray S. Greenfield, a leading entrepreneur of Israeli art, provides an illuminating example of the multiple impulses motivating boosters of Israeli art in post-war America. His career as an impresario took root and flourished within a specifically Jewish world and began with his efforts to find buyers for the paintings of a fellow aliyah-bet volunteer, probably William "Sonny" Weintraub.[39]

Greenfield's first exhibition of Israeli art in the United States was held at Grossinger's, a kosher resort in the Catskills frequented by Jewish vacationers.[40] Ultimately settling in Israel, Greenfield owned art galleries in Israel and New York, and began distributing Israeli art to a range of exhibitors across the United States beginning in the late 1950s. He lent works from his collection to local synagogues, community centers, department stores, colleges, and museums in an effort to broaden the market for Israeli art.[41] Greenfield characterized his work as fundamentally altruistic, an instrument of economic and cultural development in that the sale of paintings would not only benefit Israel monetarily, but would "help build a cultural bridge" between Israel and the United States.[42] In this light, the aesthetic merits of individual works or artists were less important than the larger project of celebrating and supporting Israel while contributing to American Jewish communal initiatives—and, in Greenfield's case, to building a successful business.

In the parallel world of the professional art establishment, Israeli art was also garnering new admirers. For example, a number of American galleries organized one-person exhibitions of Israeli artists, including Mordecai Ardon, Moshe Castel, Yehoshua Kovarsky, and Zvi Gali, beginning in the late 1940s.[43] In 1953, *Seven Painters of Israel,* the first group exhibition of Israeli art in a major American art institution, opened at the Boston Institute for Contemporary Art and traveled to the Metropolitan Museum of Art, among other museums.[44] The exhibition's curator (and director of the Boston museum), James S. Plaut, billed it as "the first full-scale manifestation of contemporary Israeli painting" to appear in America.[45]

What was noteworthy about the group exhibition, in fact, was not its scope, but its organization by a professional curator and its appearance in several major art venues. Yet, even *Seven Painters* was indebted to Jewish organizational muscle and was designed to do more than excite viewers' aesthetic faculties. The American Fund for Israel Institutions (AFII, precursor to the AICF) served as institutional patron to the exhibition. Plaut described *Seven Painters* as "a salutary undertaking in the realm of cultural exchange," encapsulating perfectly the AFII's mission as a culture-focused philanthropy. True to the organization's exalted aims, the exhibition garnered attention in the highest circles—indeed, *Seven Painters* was informally endorsed by representatives of both the Israeli and American governments.[46] A brief but positive review of the exhibition in *Art News* reflected the notion, so central to the AFII's work, that Israeli art, as the product of a "portentous nation," was more than the sum of its parts.[47] The title of the *Art News* review, "Seven Israeli Ambassadors," succinctly conveyed the potential diplomatic function of culture in the postwar context.[48]

By the early 1960s, the AICF had found its advocate at the Museum of Modern Art in the person of William C. Seitz, associate curator of painting and sculpture exhibitions. A painter and professor of art history at Princeton University, Seitz had joined MoMA's staff in 1960, where he soon organized major exhibitions on Monet and on assemblage art.[49] It is unclear when Seitz first became interested in organizing an exhibition of Israeli art. By early 1962, however, the curator had visited Israel in a professional capacity, surveying the scene and lecturing, and was impressed by what he saw there.[50] Ultimately, Seitz viewed the work of more than seven hundred Israeli artists in New York, Paris, and London, in addition to the "studios, galleries, exhibitions, and kibbutzim throughout Israel."[51]

Seitz selected artworks for the upcoming show with the utmost care, for he knew that the amassed works would be seen "not only by my colleagues but also by other extremely knowledgeable people with whom the reputation of Israeli art is not very high."[52] He felt strongly that the critical reception of Israeli art in America was at stake. In essence, Seitz was preparing a rejoinder to those who would still banish the work of contemporary Israeli artists to the Modern's auditorium gallery (a scenario proposed by a member of MoMA's exhibition committee in 1949).[53] Seitz ultimately included artworks that he felt would best represent the inchoate national school of art that he encountered in Israel.[54] Among the selected artists were Yaacov Agam, a pioneer of op art, and Yigael Tumarkin, an up-and-coming multimedia sculptor, as well as a number of artists that had established their reputations in Israel in the 1940s and 1950s.

According to the critical consensus, *Art Israel* garnered the high reputation for Israeli art that Seitz felt it deserved. The show won plaudits from several prominent critics in the New York press, including Stuart Preston at *The New York Times* and Emily Genauer at the *New York Herald Tribune*, as well as earning largely positive reviews in *Art News* and the *Los Angeles Times*.[55] Critics discussed the participants' formal vocabularies admiringly and located the assembled artists largely within the "cross-currents of internationalism."[56] They praised individual artists whose works they regarded as unique and inventive.

Those with more extensive knowledge of Israeli art noted that, in neglecting many contemporary experimentalists and seminal modernists alike, the collection did not do full justice to Israel's diverse art scene. Meir Ronnen, art critic for the *Jerusalem Post*, noted several oversights and worried in the pages of *Midstream* magazine that "New York's critics may find [*Art Israel*] a little behind the times."[57] Curator and critic Alfred Werner, meanwhile, lamented that "the present show cannot possibly provide more than a hint of what is going on in Israeli studios.[58] Despite its shortcomings, Werner opined, most Americans would undoubtedly find *Art Israel* "a revelation," as the first "significant group show" of Israeli art since *Seven Painters* in 1953.[59]

For Ronnen and Werner, both active in Jewish cultural spheres, *Art Israel* was particularly notable as an alternative to the standard amateur displays of Israeli art and as a challenge to its usual nonprofessional admirers. Werner breathed a sigh of relief that *Art Israel*'s curator was a bona fide scholar of art history who not only transcended Israeli factionalism but also surpassed "the limited knowledge and sensitivity of the parochial association[s]" generally sponsoring local exhibitions of Israeli art.[60] Ronnen, meanwhile, sniffed that "[t]he average visitor" to *Art Israel* "may be a lover of Israel rather than a lover of art" and, as such, "may be horrified to find that there is only one realist in the whole show." For such an audience, the exhibition would seem "quite *avant-garde*," he remarked, heaping disdain on Israeli art's typical American Jewish fans.[61] In this light, the AICF, *despite* its base in the organized Jewish community, had scored a significant aesthetic victory.

Yet nonprofessionals within the American Jewish community continued to engage in exactly the sort of cultural brokering and publicity work that Werner and Ronnen decried and that, in fact, remained essential to the AICF's agenda too. The activities of exhibition organizer Kathryn M. Yochelson provide a case in point. Trained as a public school teacher, Yochelson became an aficionado of Jewish art and began lecturing publicly on the topic in the late 1940s while living in Buffalo, New York, with her husband. At that time, she took up correspondences with two influential experts on Israeli art, Elias Newman and Haim Gamzu, as well as cultivating a friendship with Edgar Schenck, director of the esteemed Albright Art Gallery in Buffalo. In 1953, Schenck enlisted Yochelson's aid in bringing *Seven Painters of Israel* to Buffalo.[62] Yochelson rooted her efforts firmly in the Jewish community: more than seventy Jewish communal leaders agreed to serve on a Jewish Community Sponsoring Committee, co-chaired by Yochelson, and the United Jewish Federations of Buffalo also sponsored the exhibition.[63]

Figure 5.1. Four admirers of Israeli art view the Adas Israel Israeli Art Exhibition in Washington, D. C., in March 1964. Kathryn Yochelson, collector and organizer of the exhibition, is second from left. Photograph by Mel Chamowitz. The Kathryn Yochelson Archive, Collection of Yeshiva University Museum.

At the same time that MoMA's William Seitz was preparing for the *Art Israel* exhibition, Yochelson, now living in Washington, D.C., was invited by the rabbi of a local congregation to organize an exhibition of Israeli art there. Mounted in honor of the sixteenth anniversary of Israel's independence and sponsored in part by the Israeli government, the *Israel Art Festival* at Adas Israel Congregation displayed works lent by two New York art dealers.[64] More diverse stylistically than the upcoming exhibition at MoMA, it was also less committed to the avant-garde of the Israeli art scene. Rather, selected artists hailed from various generations and currents of Israeli art.[65] Different in organization, appearance, and venue from its museum-world counterpart, the *Israel Art Festival* distinguished itself in another regard: it was a fundraiser, intended to benefit the synagogue's Fine Arts Committee, which Yochelson headed.

Local art critics writing in the *Washington Star* and the *Washington Post* pronounced the *Israel Art Festival* at Adas Israel Congregation a failure, dismissing it as a middling, derivative collection and lamenting the "rank dilettantism" of its organization.[66] To Yochelson, however, such critics were missing the point entirely. "The purpose of [the Adas Israel] exhibit," she explained in a rebuttal to the *Washington Post*, "was not to compete with art galleries. Rather, it was an expression of human values. . . . No one pretended to label this 'great' art. The work was shown in this synagogue to commemorate the sixteenth anniversary of a courageous nation."[67]

For the synagogue committee that planned the show, an exhibition of Israeli art was meant to perform a symbolic, celebratory function within the Jewish community and, in addition, to serve as a spur to reinvestment within that community. Indeed, the exhibition was intended not only to commemorate Israel's achievements, but to further the practical goals of Adas Israel's Fine Arts Committee—first among them, to "advise in the embellishment and beautification of the Synagogue."[68] This included the acquisition of a permanent collection of art for the congregation. In this regard, at the very least, the exhibition was a success. Sales of art from the *Israel Art Festival* amounted to $646.09—hardly a tremendous sum, but one that increased the congregation's art fund by 45 percent. With the augmented funds, the congregation promptly ordered "a beautiful bronze and glass cabinet," to house "important historic Adas Israel documents."[69]

This episode exemplifies the general attitude toward Israeli art among many of its American Jewish promoters in the postwar period. American Jewish impresarios—the educators, communal leaders, entrepreneurs, and organizations that sponsored and arranged many exhibitions of Israeli art in the first two decades after Israel's establishment—treasured Israeli art not simply for its aesthetic worth, but for what it signified. This art symbolized many things for its American Jewish admirers: the flowering of Jewish culture in the land of Israel, the triumph of the Zionist political project, and the vibrant religious heritage of the Jewish people, to name a few. So, too, did American Jews greet Israel's musical emissaries with a heightened sense of their value, beyond the realm of aesthetics.

ISRAELI MUSICAL EMISSARIES IN AMERICA

As was the case with Israeli art, there was, in the years after Israel's establishment, a flourish of activity among American Jewish sponsors and lovers of Israeli music. Professional and amateur groups across the country were busy presenting Israel-themed folk, liturgical, and concert music. In Washington, D.C., for example, the cantor and choir of Adas Israel Congregation joined the Hillel Chorale of George Washington University in a concert of works "illustrating the character of ancient liturgical Hebrew music, Jewish folk music and the spirited songs of modern Israel," after Friday evening services in February 1949.[70] In the 1948–49 season, the Columbus Symphony Orchestra performed Israeli composer Menahem Mahler-Kalkstein's *Folk Symphony*; students from Hunter College, Columbia University, and Brooklyn College, meanwhile, presented "Hebrew concert music and folk dances" to local audiences.[71]

Some performances featured works inspired by Israel but composed by Americans, such as Jacob Weinberg's *Hechalutz* (*The Pioneer*) and A. W. Binder's *Israel Reborn*. Both *Hechalutz* and *Israel Reborn* were performed in New York, the former (in excerpts) at Carnegie Hall and the latter at the 92nd Street Y, under the auspices of the National Jewish Music Council during its annual music festival in the spring of 1949. The council also presented a "Salute to Israel Day" and a radio program entitled "The New Road," which told the story of Holocaust survivors en route to Palestine against a soundtrack of Israeli folk songs and an orchestral medley by various artists.[72] The following year, the council's National Jewish Music Festival—with the participation of one thousand local Jewish communities—prominently featured the work of Israeli composers.[73] According to the *American Jewish Year Book*, "Israel's influence was the strongest single factor in Jewish musical life during the 1949–1950 season."[74]

Reporting on the Jewish music scene in *Commentary*, Kurt List, a Vienna-trained composer and editor of *Listen* magazine, perceived a new nationalistic fervor among American Jews. Though he saw that American Jews were displaying a sincerely joyful response to Israel's establishment in their musical tastes, List felt that such nationalist proclivities on the part of musicians and audiences was misguided. Music in the folk style reigned supreme in the popular taste, for "[t]he folk tune," in contrast to more abstract musical styles, could "be counted on to rouse the audience's political emotions."[75] One problem was that the music was stale; according to List, many of the pieces most beloved by American Jews were written in the decades before 1948, "[finding] their way to larger audiences and public approval only in the year in which the Jewish state became a reality."[76] Worse, the overuse of folk themes in the contemporary context served to cut Jewish music off from international currents, according to List. "[P]arochialization," he wrote, "is the enemy of art."[77]

Whether works of art or amateur trifles, Palestinian folk songs had in fact been reaching American listeners for years. Songs were likely to arrive via individual Zionist *shlichim* (emissaries), returning tourists (including professional composers and musicians), and the occasional visiting performer. Songs were generally learned by ear or circulated in "poorly-edited, poorly-printed" collections that made up in enthusiasm what they lacked in professionalism.[78] According to this informal system of musical dispersion, there was "not a Zionist in the United States who in the past fifty years was not exposed at meetings, conventions, congresses, and at all public functions, large or small, to the folk songs of Palestine," wrote one commentator, herself a patron of Israeli music.[79] Palestinian folk songs "were the 'love potion' of the American Zionist for *Eretz* [the Land of Israel]."[80] So common was this informal chain of transmission, in fact, that it provoked a tussle between Israeli and American composers over the rights to arrange such folk songs; Issachar Miron, the composer of "Tzena, Tzena," sued two American composers and a publisher in 1951 in an American court for "alleged illegal arrangement" of his popular melody.[81]

According to another commentator, American Jews were so enamored of folksy Palestinian tunes that the new symphonic music arising in Israel seemed destined to fall on deaf ears. In 1949, Peter Gradenwitz, a music critic living in Tel Aviv, launched a full-scale attack in *Commentary* magazine on what he saw as the commercialization of Israeli folk and symphonic music in the United States and American Jewish ignorance of the "genuine" musical expressions arising from the ranks of Israel's young composers. Recoiling in horror at the memory, Gradenwitz recalled happening upon a music shop in Manhattan in the summer of 1948 displaying an album of Haganah folk songs and another of "inferior café songs" entitled *Tel Aviv Hit Parade*. Both albums were deplorable, according to the author, with over-orchestrated arrangements that rendered even familiar songs unintelligible.[82] Since "both Jews and non-Jews in America seem very interested in the cultural efforts of Israel," Gradenwitz mused, it was "hardly surprising that the worst sentimentalism and cheapest nationalism prevail[ed] in the 'Palestinian' music turned out for American consumption."[83]

Equally disappointing to Gradenwitz was the quality of live Israeli concert music in America. Attending a concert of so-called Palestinian music in New York, Gradenwitz was surprised to encounter a program comprised mostly of American-penned music, with Palestine being represented by an aging composer working in a style redolent of Hasidic Eastern Europe. "I can imagine . . . that the music played must have stifled all desire on the part of the audience to hear any more music from Palestine," Gradenwitz wrote, concluding that, "a similar sort of thing must be going on all over the country."[84]

By these standards, at least, the appearance of the Israel Philharmonic Orchestra (IPO)—established in 1936 by Bronislaw Huberman—offered an unprecedented opportunity both to educate audiences musically and to stoke the enthusiasm of American Jews for Israel. The AICF had included the IPO on its list of beneficiaries since the foundation's earliest years, and through the 1950s and 1960s the IPO was consistently receiving the largest amounts of the AICF's funds annually. Of the top ten beneficiaries in 1955, for example, the IPO received $125,000, while the second-highest-ranking recipient of funds, the Tel-Aviv Museum, received $33,000.[85] In 1960, the combined funds raised for the IPO and its American tour topped $200,000; the Bezalel Museum, second in the funding hierarchy that year, received $150,000 in kind (i.e., in the form of artworks donated by Americans to the museum).[86]

As in all areas of its work, the AICF developed a two-pronged approach to its musical patronage: one goal for Israel, another for America. Its mission in Israel, above all, was to use music as an instrument in the integration of recent immigrants into Israeli society. This was a major theme in the foundation's magazine, *Israel Life and Letters*. If music was an international language capable of bridging nations, it could be employed in a similar capacity within immigrant nations such as Israel which faced the task of blending disparate cultures and traditions into a coherent, cohesive whole. For the masses of new immigrants, most of whom did not know Hebrew and many of whom were illiterate, music was one of the most accessible of cultural forms. With this goal in mind—and with substantial support from the AICF—the Israeli government had overseen the formation of immigrant choirs in 130 settlements throughout the country by the early 1960s, with plans to expand that number to two hundred.

The AICF's complementary mission in America was to develop wide and enthusiastic audiences for Israel's musical artists while garnering support for the training of young Israeli musicians in American conservatories. To this end, the AICF adopted the IPO as its primary ambassador of Israeli musical culture to American audiences. As usual, the AICF framed its philanthropic interventions in the sphere of Israeli music as a fulfillment of American idealism in the postwar world. Music was an art form that, transcending language, served the purpose of bridging, rather than exacerbating, differences. Along with demonstrating the centrality of culture to a nation's survival, the IPO's appearance in the United States would, according to an AICF supporter, "aid in the development of the American concept of brotherhood."[87] The foundation also expected the IPO to convey the idea, by example, "that any nation that can produce such a wonderful cultural product must be a nation of free men like our own."[88]

According to this reasoning, an American alliance with Israel followed naturally from the cultural kinship between the two nations, as demonstrated by the IPO. It was a theme echoed again and again, and not only by the AICF. Upon the arrival of the IPO in New York, for example, the Israeli Consul there offered his hope that the tour would "foster friendship between the people of Israel and those of the North American continent."[89] Likewise, a writer for the *Chicago Daily Tribune*, alerting readers to the IPO's upcoming concert, reflected on the nature of music as a bond between men and nations. "[I]t is to the glory of music that spiritual kinships endure and flourish . . . even when in other areas of human activity there may be discord or tragic bloodshed," he wrote, looking forward to the "new companionship of anthems" that would soon resound in Chicago's Orchestra Hall when the "Star Spangled Banner" and "Hatikvah" were played side by side during the concert program.[90]

The IPO embarked on its first tour of the United States in December 1950, making its way to audiences in forty cities. "People stood in line for hours to buy tickets," one delighted supporter of the Israeli symphony orchestra reported, adding that even "people who are not the usual concert loving public, who seldom buy a ticket to hear a symphony orchestra, came to hear the Israel Orchestra."[91] Why? According to this observer, ticket buyers "felt that this was the first time in the history of the Jews that they could witness a new 'emissary,' a herald, that could be compared to the Levite choirs of the time when the Temple was standing in Israel."[92]

As this sentiment suggests, it was impossible for many audience members and critics to separate the orchestra's formal prowess from its symbolic resonance and its emotional impact. Observers expressed amazement at the orchestra's rapid development as an institution, particularly in light of the hardships that its musicians had endured during World War II, the period of civil war in Palestine and the Arab-Israeli War in 1948. Reviewing the first of two sold-out performances in Chicago, critic Claudia Cassidy noted that "Hatikvah," the Israeli national anthem, sounded "like a hymn after a victorious battle counted its dead." While Cassidy found the IPO "a good orchestra with a warm, resilient tone," she understood that the audience's "thunderclaps of applause, shouts, and whistles, [and] general rejoicing," at the evening's conclusion were a response to more than the music. "It was natural," Cassidy admitted, that in the case of the IPO, "a good performance should stir the attendant uproar of a great one."[93]

The IPO returned to the United States in the fall of 1960 for another multicity North American tour. While some reviews, such in that of the *New York Times*, focused singularly on issues of musical interpretation and performance, there was, nearly ten years later, still a tendency to analyze the impact of the IPO in more than aesthetic terms. Noting that the orchestra had once been dubbed by an American diplomat "Israel's best ambassador abroad," the reviewer in the New York *World-Telegram and Sun*, Louis Biancolli, concurred that the IPO had indeed "conveyed a heartwarming message of good will and culture" in its program at the Metropolitan Opera House. The IPO was not only representative of general good will between nations, however. Composed at its inaugural concert of "men who had fled the Nazi horror," Biancolli was awed by the orchestra's development in a matter of decades into "one of the elect" with the "strength and cohesion . . . of an orchestra twice its age" as well as a "community sense of poetry, and a heart."[94]

Similar treatment was accorded other AICF-sponsored Israeli musical groups appearing in the United States. Israel's Rinat Choir toured in 1962, kicking off its "goodwill tour" of the United States with a performance at the White House.[95] Rinat was apparently the first foreign group to receive a Scroll of Honor from the National Cultural Center (later the John F. Kennedy Center for the Performing Arts) in Washington, D.C.[96] In 1964, Gadna, the Israel National Youth Symphony, also visited America on an AICF-sponsored tour. The symphony orchestra, populated with members of the youth battalions of the Israel Defense Forces, was welcomed to New York by Mayor Robert Wagner, who praised them as "the greatest musical talent of a country to which [*sic*] music and life are inseparable" as well as declaring a "Salute to Gadna Week" in the city.[97] The *New York Times*'s Raymond Ericson, in his review of the symphony's debut performance in New York, proclaimed Gadna a "first-rate ensemble," and a testament to the amazing cultural vitality of "a nation as young and small as Israel."[98] Louis Biancolli of the *New York World-Telegram*, who had written enthusiastically about the IPO, found the group "a living symbol of the stamina of survival" and declared that, if "there are concerts that are noble in what they are and concerts that are noble in what they symbolize," the Gadna debut was both at once.[99] (Biancolli admitted weeping when the orchestra played Oedoen Partos's *In Memoriam*, a tribute to the six million Jews murdered in the Holocaust.) And Henry Beckett, writing in the *New York Post*, named the orchestra's debut "one more achievement of the small State of Israel." Impressed by Gadna's "poise, discipline, [and] devotion" Beckett expressed concern—obviously well founded—that their "appealing story," "youthful freshness," and "mission" might actually distract audiences from the group's substantial musical accomplishments.[100]

Recalling the fervent response to concerts of the Israel Philharmonic Orchestra on its home soil, prominent American rabbi Ira Eisenstein wrote that Israeli audiences, "through their cheers and their vociferous applause," had expressed "the triumph of their cause, the vindication of their sacrifices."[101] On the eve of the IPO's first United States tour in 1950, Eisenstein had worried that American Jewish audiences would not understand the tremendous significance of the event. He feared that American Jews might use the opportunity to display cultural superiority over the Israelis. "If that's going to happen," Eisenstein concluded, "I don't want to be there."[102]

Eisenstein need not have worried. American audiences apparently greeted the IPO and other Israeli musical emissaries with passionate approval, a cathartic response noted (and sometimes shared) by critics attending performances. Writing of the response to the appearance of the Gadna Orchestra, the Milwaukee Jewish Welfare Fund—a significant contributor to the AICF—claimed that the local Jewish community was "delighted . . . and very proud. We looked upon them almost as though they were our children."[103] While the AICF articulated its support for Israeli musical institutions in terms of broad American values and goals, the foundation understood that American Jews in particular took abundant pride in the IPO's achievements. As one AICF-affiliated observer noted, "Wherever the Israel Philharmonic Orchestra appeared, it brought respect and prestige to the American Jewish community." For that alone, he wrote, the AICF had earned the "everlasting gratitude" of American Jews.[104]

"AS HUMAN BEINGS, AS LOVERS OF THE ARTS, AS ZIONISTS": AMERICAN JEWS AS CULTURE BOOSTERS

For the preeminent corporate patron of Israeli culture in America, the America-Israel Cultural Foundation, sponsorship of Israeli art and music in the United States advanced American imperatives. In both internal and public statements, the AICF repeatedly cast Israel's cultural exports as envoys from a struggling but resilient outpost of Western civilization with cultural aspirations similar to America's own. The leaders and allies of the AICF insisted that appreciation of and support for Israeli culture (and hence, Israel) was not only fully consonant with American norms, but also furthered America's expanding democratic mission in the Cold War world. This supposition underlay the AICF's sponsorship of the two most visible group exhibitions of Israeli art in the museum world in this period, *Seven Painters of Israel* and *Art Israel*, as well as its sponsorship of American tours by the Israel Philharmonic Orchestra and other musical groups. This logic was rooted not only in Cold War liberalism, however, but also in the cultural zeitgeist, at a time when appreciation for and consumption of "high" culture—at such venues as art museums and concert halls—was becoming a significant facet of American middle-class behavior. In the cultural climate of postwar America, upwardly mobile audiences sought to educate themselves about the world around them while buttressing their belief in "universal values that united all human beings across time and space," as Christina Klein has written.[105] The AICF premised its domestic agenda upon this belief.

The AICF's public profile reached its apotheosis in the mid-1960s with the opening of the foundation's own cultural center in a five-story, Stanford White–designed mansion on Fifth Avenue in New York City. Fulfilling a function often taken up by foreign consulates, the AICF's Israel Culture House was intended to be the major venue in the United States—indeed, in the entire Western Hemisphere—for Israel's fine and performing arts. (This ambitious gambit was undercut, however, by restricting access to performances to the relatively small pool of AICF members, as well as by the onerous cost of maintaining the historic building.)[106]

At the same time, the AICF embodied a particularly American Jewish agenda that depended for its success upon the efforts its Jewish leadership, membership and fundraising base. The organization's activities in the United States were premised upon the notion that American Jewry had a special responsibility to nurture and promote Israeli culture—albeit to the lasting benefit (as the organization argued) of all humankind. There is evidence that the AICF was well suited to American Jewish communal priorities in the postwar period. We can glean this, in part, from the organization's ability to gracefully weather the downward turn in communal philanthropic giving in the 1950s: while American Jewish contributions to Israel (primarily through the United Jewish Appeal) declined markedly in the years immediately following the War of Independence, reflecting a diminished sense of crisis after Israel's victory, allocations to the AICF from Jewish welfare funds decreased less drastically.[107] This information provides partial but compelling evidence that the American Jewish community believed in the worth of the AICF's cultural mission. "The ability of the [AICF] to maintain itself in the welfare fund communities can be traced, to a large extent, to the growth of the community relations program and an extension of services rendered," reported the authors of the AICF's 1953 loan prospectus. Alongside such innovations as limited membership drives and the publishing of *Israel Life and Letters*, "the presentation of Israel concerts, the circulation of art . . . exhibitions, [and] the national tours of the Israel

Philharmonic Orchestra . . . all combine[d] to educate the American community on the need for cultural assistance to Israel and to identify the [AICF] with this need."[108]

Furthermore, it appears that local Jewish communities had an increasing hand in the organization of the AICF's Israeli cultural events. In Rochester, New York, for example, the Sisterhood of Temple B'rith Kodesh partnered with the Rochester Civic Music Association to bring the IPO to town, while the appearance of the Rinat Choir in Harrison, New York, was co-sponsored by the Harrison Jewish Community Center, Temple Israel of White Plains, and the Westchester Reform Temple of Scarsdale.[109] Indeed, the AICF established outposts in Los Angeles, Chicago, Cincinnati, and Boston in the 1950s in order to foster a closer working relationship with local Jewish communities that had shown significant interest in the foundation's projects.[110] To this end, the AICF also established a women's division in the late 1950s with dues-paying members in New York and Cincinnati; they organized the American premiere of the Israeli dance troupe Inbal and took partial responsibility for the IPO's debut in New York.[111]

It is easy to forget, in retrospect, that the foundation took both a strategic risk and an imaginative leap in shifting its focus strictly to the cultural sphere. Back in 1942, the organization produced an internal report acknowledging possible difficulties in fulfilling its developing cultural mission. The foundation, "because of its nature and essence, cannot meet on anything like equal terms with Hadassah for example, or [the] Jewish National Fund . . . it will never produce slogans or catch-words. Our organization will probably for years to come not penetrate fully to the broad masses of people," the report warned.[112] Nonetheless, the report conveyed that it was precisely through a program of cultural outreach—exemplified by the high-profile tours of Israeli culture that were to become the AICF's bread and butter—it would be possible to attract not only the interest of communal leaders, but also the support of Jewish communities across the country. This, indeed, seems to be exactly what happened.

Whether or not they affiliated with the AICF, American Jewish enthusiasts of Israeli art and music acted as significant promoters of Israeli culture both in local Jewish communities as well as in the wider public sphere in the postwar years. American Jews embraced Israeli art and music for its symbolic resonance—and also for its instrumental worth. In Pittsburgh, for example, an exhibition of Israeli art featuring twenty-nine "leading artists" accompanied the opening of the local 1965 fundraising campaign of the United Jewish Federation. The artwork, available for purchase to those attending the kickoff event, offered buyers the tantalizing double prospect of supporting Jewish communal initiatives (including significant aid to Israel) and garnering cultural capital in the eyes of the public. "Several of [the works]," the Pittsburgh *Jewish Chronicle* noted, had "already been acquired by the Museum of Modern Art, the Brooklyn Museum, the Boston Museum of Fine Arts, and the Fogg Museum at Harvard for their permanent collections."[113] This proclamation suggests the pride with which many American Jews greeted Israeli culture as it met with increasing critical acclaim.

The symbolic and pragmatic functions that Israeli high culture performed for American Jews seem, in many cases, to have outweighed its merit as creative endeavor. Critics of the Jewish culture scene in America such as Alfred Werner and Meir Ronnen (in the field of art) and Kurt List and Peter Gradenwitz (in the field of music) were dismayed by this phenomenon. In a review of the 1952 exhibition arranged by Rabbi Gerson Brenner, Lionel Reiss, writing in *The Reconstructionist*, sounded a similarly critical note; it was clear to him that "most of the pictures are sentimental mementoes to be hung on American walls as a reminder of some place or scene of the Holy Land." He concluded by reminding his readers that, "Works of art have a greater function than just that," that "[a]rt should awaken us to new horizons."[114] Likewise mulling American Jews' role as indiscriminate consumers of Israeli culture, Shlomo Katz, editor of *Midstream* magazine, encouraged his intended audience to cultivate greater expectations. For now, he wrote, "there is still much excitement about Israel, and little criticism of the cultural products that come from there."[115] "As the years pass," he continued, "we want from Israel more than the folk songs of some exotic foreign land. We expect, in all the manifestations of its culture an answer to the universal values and problems that characterized Jewish existence for millennia. The political Israel is one answer to the problems of exile and return, the meaning of history, fulfillment at the end of time. . . . In its cultural manifestations, too, Israel must seek and provide these answers."[116] American Jews, in this light, were not yet asking the right questions.

Despite his own misgivings about the uncritical nature of the American Jewish relationship with Israeli art, critic Alfred Werner was ultimately sympathetic to the yearning that Israeli culture satisfied among its American Jewish champions. He wrote that, despite considerable room for growth and improvement, Israeli art deserved the devoted attention of the public. "[D]o we, as human beings, as lovers of the arts, as Zionists, as American Jews have to wait for the moment when Israel will be sufficiently developed . . . to bestow upon the world gifts so astonishing . . . that the eyes of the entire art world will be directed to it?" The answer, Werner implied, was a decided "no." "It is fascinating and edifying to study Israeli art even while its products may be second or even third rate," he concluded.[117]

Boosters of Israeli art and music in the American Jewish community appeared to agree. For them, organizing, sponsoring, and visiting exhibitions and concerts featuring Israel's cultural emissaries provided an unparalleled opportunity to publicize and celebrate Israel's achievements, to argue for Israel's value to America, and to exercise their own blossoming roles as cultural impresarios. For American Jewish champions of Israel, as, indeed, for many professional critics, Israeli cultural achievements constituted not simply an artistic victory, but a triumph over history itself.

CONCLUSION

It is clear that Israel emerged as a significant cultural touchstone in American Jewish life in the immediate postwar decades. To understand the phenomenon, however, I contend that one must take seriously the cultural project in which American Jews of the postwar era, particularly in the organized community, were engaged, and why they immersed themselves in that cultural project in the first place. Cultural institutions (i.e., magazines, arts foundations, museums) and cultural events (such as book festivals, folk dance programs, concerts, and art exhibitions) were becoming key vehicles through which American Jews constructed their lives as Jews—or a significant portion of their lives, at least. In these years, American Jews were abandoning urban ethnic neighborhoods en masse for the suburban frontier, a corollary to their increasing professionalization and affluence after World War II. Searching for communal coherence, a majority of American Jews joined suburban synagogues, as has been well documented. They also created and partook of cultural activities that felt genuinely "Jewish" in some sense but which were not necessarily premised upon deep Jewish literacy or religious commitment. Reading a book with a Jewish theme, displaying (and shopping for) Judaica at a synagogue gift shop, learning a Jewish dance, attending a concert of Jewish music: for a posturban, postimmigrant minority population, participating in these practices created Jewish time and Jewish space and solidified specifically Jewish networks.

It was in this context, I contend, that many American Jews grappled with the existence of Israel in the first postwar decades. It is true that international travel was more frequent, reliable, and affordable than ever before, making it easier to visit Israel firsthand. So, too, was the Israeli government busy devising currency schemes and building new hotels, all designed to "take the austerity out of a visit to Israel."[1] Indeed, the annual number of tourists to Israel rose considerably in this period: in 1950, Israel greeted more than thirty thousand visitors, twice as many as the year before;[2] in 1958, the ten-year anniversary of Israel's establishment, a "record total" of 75,158 visited;[3] by 1966, the numbers had leapt to an estimated three hundred thousand visitors annually.[4]

There were those in the organized Jewish community who felt that a personal encounter with Israel would be enormously beneficial, to both

American Jews and Israelis. The Reform and Conservative movements, for example, had instituted pilgrimages to Israel among the rabbinate and laity by the early 1950s.[5] "The American Jew has no intention of abandoning his own land," wrote one proponent of travel to Israel, "but he will return home [from Israel] . . . with a more enlightened and enthusiastic report of life" in the Jewish state. In this light, the American Jewish visitor to Israel would not simply satisfy his own personal curiosity, but would be better equipped to "speak with conviction based on fullness of knowledge and understanding, not out of some romanticized version of Zionist idealism," and to be "the best ambassador Israel could possibly have to plead its cause."[6] Yet no more than one-third of the American Jewish population chose to travel to Israel in these years.[7] Rather, for many American Jews, engaging with Israel in the cultural realm was a crucial channel through which they came to know, or to feel that they knew, Israel.

Proponents of Israel in the organized American Jewish community in particular hoped that, in helping American Jews integrate Israel into their cultural milieu as middle-class Americans, this population would come to see Israel as relevant to their own lives. This feeling, in turn, could be harnessed to any number of projects: educating Jewish youth and buttressing their Jewish identities, strengthening the health of Zionism as a movement, raising money for Jewish communal initiatives (including, but not limited to, aid to Israel), and advocating on Israel's behalf in the public sphere. As with any population, only a relatively small number of American Jews could claim to be cultural producers—as writers or as choreographers, for example. Many more, however, were active consumers of cultural goods and participants in the cultural arena. The foot soldiers in the field of culture were those who discussed *My Promised Land* in their book clubs, danced the hora at Hanukkah parties, paraded in an Israeli dress for a Hadassah fundraiser, or admired a painting by Israeli artist Moshe Mokady at the local Jewish community center.

Why did masses of American Jews engage in such practices? As I have argued, creating and participating in Israel-centered cultural practices was a means, for many, of expressing pride in the Jewish state and, by extension, in the Jewish people as a whole. Such practices helped postwar American Jews explore and shape their own Jewish identities; they functioned as vehicles for articulating and celebrating Jewish difference, within limits, in postwar American society. At the same time, there were other motives at work. Promoting Israel in the American cultural realm served American Jews as a means of announcing full participation in postwar American life. Often, when American Jews took part in Israel-themed cultural activities, they were doing so in the public realm, with an eye to how such engagements appeared to non-Jews. For many involved in such activities, the promotion and consumption of Israel in the cultural realm signified the sophistication and largesse of the American Jewish community. Proponents also claimed publicly that Israel's cultural achievements, nurtured by American Jews, were an absolute boon to human civilization.

In this context, American Jews cultivated a brand of transnational cultural patronage and consumption in this period that they felt suited America's cultural responsibilities in the postwar world. Many of Israel's American Jewish impresarios acted on the belief, prominent among arts, media, and government elites, that cultural exchange between nations and among ethnic and religious groups was key to garnering allies and winning the Cold War. Thus, groups such as the America-Israel Cultural Foundation argued that their cultural stewardship of Israel was not simply a matter of Jewish self-interest, but a means of buttressing democracy in the Middle East and thus securing American interests in that volatile region. In positioning Israel as an inspiring and enriching factor in American Jewish life at mid-century, writers, arts philanthropists, and Hadassah members, among others, propagated the idea that Israel, a new, impoverished Middle Eastern nation of uncertain geopolitical worth to the United States, was in fact a cultural analogue to America. Proclaiming Israel as a struggling democracy with a shared religious, ethical, and cultural tradition with the West, American Jews crafted support for Israel as a complement to America's Cold War aims.

To what extent was the cultural work of an AICF politically imbricated with the work of the U.S. government at the time? To be sure, some Jewish intellectuals served as key operatives in what Frances Stonor Saunders has called the "cultural Cold War," the U.S. government's co-option and mobilization of intellectuals and artists as covert propagandizers for anticommunism.[8] However, there are no explicit indications (at least none that I have found) that Israel's American Jewish impresarios—i.e., the actors examined in this book—were working closely or systematically with the State Department, the United States Information Agency, or the CIA.[9] It is worth noting that (according to Saunders) the CIA's network of contacts in the field of culture—especially among the philanthropic foundations—was still, in many ways, a bastion of white Anglo-Saxon Protestant privilege. So while anticommunist American Jewish intellectuals played an important role in deploying Cold War cultural propaganda, the world in which their propaganda projects unfolded was hardly a seedbed of Jewish communal activity. In addition, when compared to the rest of the Middle East, Israel appears to have received very little attention in the field of public diplomacy during the Cold War. Indeed, as historian Nicholas J. Cull has pointed out, one of the USIA's goals in the Middle East in this period was "to combat America's image as the sponsor of Israel by playing up support for Arab regimes and stressing points at which the U.S. had gone against Israeli wishes, as in the extension of aid to Arab countries."[10]

This suggests that, as far as the American government was concerned, American patronage of Israeli culture, and the encouragement of cultural exchange between America and Israel, was not urgently important in winning the Cold War. At the very least, then, we can say that American Jewish boosters of Israeli culture, implementing communal resources to encourage cultural exchange with and appreciation of Israel, found themselves in a climate congenial to their overall cultural project. In the public mind, "culture" and "internationalism" often went hand in hand, one reinforcing the other—and both, it seemed, to the benefit of America.

Israel was indeed influencing American Jewish culture in the first postwar decades, evident not only in the pro-Israel rhetoric of much of the leadership of the organized community but also in the practices of everyday American Jews. Taking stock of American Zionism just seven years after Israel's establishment, one commentator found that expressions of pride in Israel had already become commonplace in many settings. As of 1955, examples of the new mindset

> range[d] from the introduction of regular prayers for Israel in the Orthodox synagogue to the normalcy of the appearance of the . . . Israeli flag at Jewish gatherings. . . . They [were] seen in the little synagogue art shops, in the Israeli Seder plates and pictures in homes committed to Judaism, in the substitution of the *hora* . . . for the *sher* (East European dance) at weddings and other *simhot* (celebrations) where notions of middle-class dignity [did] not inhibit Jews from expressing joy in Jewish dance forms.[11]

Likewise, in *Israel Today*, the first textbook on the contemporary Jewish state written for young Reform Jews (published in 1964), authors Harry Essrig and Abraham Segal portrayed the penetration of Israel into the everyday lives of their readers. According to the authors, cultural practices were central to this phenomenon. They wrote:

> American Jews have always united for charity work and welfare work, and for defense against anti-Semitism. But unity for Zionism does something that welfare and defense activities could not do. For example, Israel interests more Jews in Hebrew and Jewish history, in Jewish music, literature, art, dance, crafts. Because of

Israel, a growing number of American Jews give their children Hebrew names, study Hebrew in public high schools and colleges, dance the hora at weddings, try Israeli recipes in new Jewish cookbooks. The Hebrew language, Zionist ideas, Israeli songs and dances are studied in all types of Jewish schools. . . . Many synagogues use Israeli music in worship, raise funds for Israel, exhibit Israeli art, buy Torah covers and ornaments from Israel, offer courses on Israeli life and problems. Books, articles, movie, radio and TV programs, news reports about Israel appear almost daily around us.[12]

Essrig and Segal explained that participating in such activities, and living in the Jewish environment shaped by them, provided American Jews "a tremendous boost in morale . . . Israel's story has made us more willing, more proud, to be Jews."[13]

It is striking that, in a textbook designed for Reform religious schools, the authors were careful to stress that this development characterized Jewish life in all its variety, including "Orthodox, Reform, Conservative, 'non-religious' socialist and labor groups, and 'unattached' Jews who belong to no special group."[14] Essrig and Segal also intimated that support for Israel was not an end in itself. Support for Israel was significant, as the authors' comments imply, because it made the American Jewish population into a cohesive community and because it inspired participation in Jewish life in America. The "unity" the authors cite appears, at the very least, as a unity of experience—most American Jews, they suggested, had encountered Israel in their lives in similar ways, through a particular set of cultural practices.

There were many indications, too, that this new mentality was permeating mainstream American culture. Just as nonfiction and fiction books conveyed overwhelmingly positive images of the Jewish state, American mass media served as an important means of transmitting such representations to a broad swath of the American public. *Time* magazine, for example, featured David Ben-Gurion admiringly in cover articles no less than three times in the first decade of Israel's existence.[15] Israel had its enthusiasts on television as well: with the participation of the Zionist Organization of America, national television personality Ed Sullivan marked the third anniversary of Israel's establishment in a special broadcast of *The Toast of the Town* (the precursor to *The Ed Sullivan Show*), filmed at Madison Square Garden with twenty thousand in attendance.[16]

In a more sober vein, the prominent radio and television journalist Edward R. Murrow spent two weeks in Israel in 1956, transmitting daily radio broadcasts and preparing material for an episode of his acclaimed television program *See it Now* on tensions between Israel and Egypt, which aired in March. (He returned for brief reports from Israel in the wake of the Suez War in October.) Murrow, by his own and others' accounts, was a staunch admirer of Israel. His sympathy for the country stemmed primarily from his biblical literacy—he was raised as a Quaker in North Carolina—and from his exposure to the plight of European Jewish refugees as a young assistant secretary at the Emergency Committee in Aid of Displaced German Scholars and then as a journalist in Europe during World War II. His radio report of witnessing the liberation of Buchenwald was a powerful, early contemplation of the Holocaust for a mass audience. (A colleague later recalled that his encounter with Buchenwald "deeply colored his attitude toward Israel.")[17]

While some American Jews apparently balked at *See It Now*'s even-handed approach to the impending Suez crisis (with journalist Howard K. Smith providing the Egyptian perspective), those who tuned in to Murrow's dispatches from the Jewish state encountered an intriguing and admirable Israel of biblical landscapes and idealistic but battle-ready young kibbutzniks.[18] Even if the size of the regular viewing audience for *See It Now* was relatively small for all but a few landmark broadcasts, Murrow's gravitas, authority, and comparatively wide reach as a public figure ensured Israel a sympathetic hearing—and viewing—in living rooms across the country.[19]

American viewers encountered contemporary Israel, too, in the nationally televised broadcasts of the Israeli trial of Nazi war criminal Adolf Eichmann in 1961. Daily transmissions of the four-month trial, along with supplementary news coverage, offered many Americans their first taste of contemporary Hebrew, while providing sympathetic images of Holocaust survivors and other Israeli citizens.[20] Hannah Arendt's rumination on the trial in her book *Eichmann in Jerusalem* (1963) and the heated response to it, especially among Jewish intellectuals and communal leaders, constitutes its own chapter in the annals of postwar American Jewish culture.[21] For Arendt the political philosopher, the trial provided an opportunity to dissect, in the person of Adolf Eichmann, the means by which an advanced, bureaucratized civilization perpetrated genocide against its fellow citizens, as well as a chance to probe the collective political failures of the genocide's chief victims. In analyzing the trial as a public spectacle, Arendt also accused the Israeli government of using the trial to its own political ends, as a case for Israel's very existence (because the Jewish state had enabled the Jews, at last, "to hit back," as Arendt summed it up).[22] She did not address the trial's reception among the global public, including, of course, American Jews.

But a slightly earlier book, by a decidedly lesser-known figure, provides at least a glimpse of how American Jews greeted and understood the Eichmann trial at the time, in personal terms. Shula Hirsch's *An American Housewife in Israel*, published in 1962, found the Los Angeles–born, Long Island (New York) based homemaker at the gates of the Beit Ha'am (House of the People) in Jerusalem during the trial. (Hirsch spent the summer of 1961, with her American husband and children, living in Tel Aviv.) In the book, Hirsch described finagling her way into the courtroom, where she found that, "[t]he setting was the same as I had seen on television in New York, with Eichmann sitting guarded in his glass cage." She recalled contemplating the figure of Eichmann there:

> I could visualize the blood of guilt oozing from his fingertips. I could see that he had all the physical features of a human. . . . But, I could not possibly imagine what he consisted of internally to have acted in such a barbaric, inhuman, cold-blooded manner. As I peered through his glass cage, I could visualize millions of my people being herded into the showers with the gas turned on and I could hear the murmuring from their lips of the "Shmah prayer" as they met their untimely deaths.[23]

Hirsch concluded her trip to Jerusalem with a visit to Theodor Herzl's grave and the national military cemetery on Mount Herzl, a look at King David's tomb on Mount Zion, and a tour of synagogues; the Eichmann trial was but one installment in the author's grand tour of the young state of Israel.

Yet this passage on the trial, nestled within a clumsily written example of the women's interest subset of the "Israel book" genre, is prime evidence that American Jews "got it"—that is, that Ben-Gurion's central lessons about the Holocaust were finding a ready audience. Chief among these lessons was the idea that the Holocaust, though unprecedented in scale, was the culmination of centuries of antisemitism in the Diaspora; also, that only the Jewish state could speak for the martyred millions, and only Israel could ensure that nothing like it would ever happen to the Jews again. By the early 1960s, many Jews appeared less eager to draw universal implications from the Holocaust, seeing within it, instead, an "entire concept of victimhood" that served increasingly as a "springboard for political action and . . . political legitimation" of Jewish group survival.[24] In this light, American Jews no longer viewed Israel mainly as an exemplar of enlightened Jewish culture—and, indeed, as a paragon of Western civilization not only in the Middle East but in the entire postwar world—but, rather, as the sole watchdog for and protector of Jews everywhere, by any means necessary.

Hirsch's book, with its chirpy "housewife's-eye view" of the Jewish state (as the dust jacket proclaimed), serves as a reminder, too, of how much has changed in the intervening years. Considering Israel's rosy image and growing popularity in American culture in these years, it has become easy to trivialize the artifacts of postwar American Zionism simply as 1950s kitsch. American Jewish attitudes toward Israel have changed since the "honeymoon" of the postwar period, as Israel itself has undergone seismic political shifts and American Jews have grown more comfortable expressing disapproval of some Israeli policies.[25] (In fact, by the early 1960s, some American Jewish intellectuals and leaders were already challenging an idealized relationship with Israel, as Michael Staub has shown.)[26] Aesthetics have changed, too. The culture of postwar American Jews can appear as quaint rather than cool; for some, it is something to be enshrined in museum collections (at best) or forgotten in flea market bins (at worst). (For a particularly thorough evocation of the material culture of this era—including the preponderance of Israeli-made goods in American Jewish households—I refer readers to Ethan and Joel Coen's film *A Serious Man*.)

Even at the time, the Zionist culture of the "Hadassah set" came in for its fair share of ribbing. In a short story published in *Commentary* in 1951, for example, Meyer Levin gently lampooned a group of American Jewish suburbanites who, brainstorming at their regular, joint poker game–Hadassah meeting, decide to raffle a Cadillac to raise money for Israel. Written in the voice of one of the neighborhood husbands, "After All I Did for Israel," is, in part, a send-up of the middle-of-the-road American Zionism of the postwar period, exemplified by Hadassah. "[A]ll these gatherings and rummages and teas . . . help give the girls an activity," the narrator writes of his wife and her fellow Hadassah members, comparing them to "kids selling lemonade."[27] While admitting that the local wives did end up raising "quite a few pennies" on Israel's behalf, the narrator implies that such activities properly functioned much like their neighbors' admired "big modernistic house": that is, as the requisite, superficial accessories of suburban life.[28] (In the story, this tidy scenario is upended when the narrators' teenage son and daughter vigorously espouse the Zionist idealism they find latent in their parents' leisure-time activities—a foreshadowing, perhaps, of the countercultural battles to come within the Jewish community of the late 1960s.)

The condemnation of postwar American Zionism as feminized—and therefore, according to some, intrinsically problematic—is a warped reflection of historical reality: in the postwar period, women played crucial roles as institution builders, cultural producers, and cultural arbiters in the American Jewish community. This book presents further evidence that this was, in fact, the case. Alongside this dismissal of 1950s American Zionism is a different critique, also premised on gender tropes, that has taken firm root in the scholarly and popular imagination alike. According to this line of reasoning, a mythic vision of Israel as unremittingly muscular and heroic, exemplified by the wildly popular novel *Exodus* (1958) and its blockbuster movie adaptation (1960), had a hegemonic grip on the American Jewish imagination in the postwar period. Without a doubt, the golden-boy swagger of Paul Newman's Ari Ben Canaan encapsulated a vision of Israel that was immensely appealing to American audiences. The likeness of Israel shaped by postwar American Jews was richer and more complex than these common indictments allow, however.

In their roles as cultural impresarios, postwar American Jews crafted an elastic Israel that could seemingly be all things to all people—teenagers and housewives, art lovers and business entrepreneurs, Zionists and non-Zionists, Jews and non-Jews. To be sure, American Jewish "boosters" of the Jewish state were eager to portray Israel as a heroic land of tough, fighting "new Jews." Within the cultural sphere, American Jews also forged images of Israel, however, as a laboratory for womanly fulfillment; a spur to interethnic and international brotherhood in the age of the atom bomb; a player in the international arts scene; and even as an ally in the spread of free-market capitalism (to name a few). This elastic Israel accorded perfectly with the simultaneously communalist and integrationist sensibilities of the postwar moment, as many American Jews sought to revitalize and strengthen Jewish life after the Holocaust while winning unprecedented levels of acceptance and admiration among non-Jewish Americans.

While postwar American Jews were certainly preoccupied with the ongoing process of acceptance in American society, and Israel's possible role in that regard, they were, at the same time, fully absorbed in the communal tasks at hand: to fulfill their new responsibilities as the religious, intellectual, and organizational heart of Diaspora Jewry in the wake of the Holocaust. In this light, Israel's birth, far from signaling the eclipse of the organized Jewish community in America (as staunch Zionists had held), augured a new era of cultural and communal growth for American Jewry. While culture and community are not one and the same, there is no doubt that shifts in American Jewish culture effected changes in communal priorities, and vice versa. Thus, to name an example from the fourth chapter of this book, members of Hadassah and the America-Israel Chamber of Commerce and Industry, in attempting to match American Jewish influence to Israeli needs, both altered the nature of American Jewish material culture and reoriented the community's organizational priorities. In flexing financial and political muscle on behalf of Israel's economic health, these American Jewish women and men emerged not only as tastemakers but also as pro-Israel consumer-advocates.

The literature on Jews as consumers—cultural, religious, and ethnic—has been influential in American Jewish historiography, and with good reason. Historians such as Andrew Heinze and Jenna Weissman Joselit have argued, compellingly, that consumption has served as a primary means by which Jewish immigrants became American. Scholars who grapple with the role of consumption in molding American Jewish life have also examined how consumerist behavior and mentalities have shaped Judaism as an

American religion, suited to the capitalist democracy in which American Jews live. Consumption, in this light, is a crucial mechanism through which American Jews and others have shaped their everyday habits, idioms, and identities—communal and individual. In a broad sense, as Marilyn Halter has written, "[w]hereas at one time the relationship between human beings and material objects resulted in identities that were acquired with the possessions one inherited, in modern times, people most often construct their own identities and define others through the commodities they purchase."[29]

Existing scholarship is less clear about how the Jewish-directed consumption of American Jews may have cohered, consciously or not, with the contemporaneous national discourse about America's place in the world and about the role of consumption in securing America's domestic and foreign policy goals. To what extent is Jewish consumption a cultural act, shaping the identities, aesthetics, and lived experience of everyday American Jews? To what extent is Jewish consumption a political tool, to be wielded in pursuit of policies that benefit specific sectors of local, national, and global populations? The answer is that consumption—of goods and of culture—is, and has been, both.[30] But there is much more to learn about the interplay of consumption, culture, and politics. In looking closely at American Jews' passion to promote and consume Israel in postwar culture, we may begin to see afresh the cords drawing American Jews as consumer-activists, in a new mode, to the arena of political power. The cultural sphere, too, can provide channels through which American Jews and others in American society may accrue and deploy political capital.

Israel's birth set in motion a complex process of cultural adjustment and innovation among American Jews that, in turn, fostered a re-formation of American Jewish identity. Israel began to play an increasingly crucial symbolic role for American Jews after the 1967 Arab-Israeli War, as they sought not simply to maintain but to actively emphasize cultural difference within American society.[31] The emergence of an overwhelmingly pro-Israel worldview among the organized American Jewish community—a development characteristic of the post-1967 era—was, in part, a response to the explosive political and cultural realignments within American life in the late 1960s. This book presents evidence, however, that American Jewry's increasingly muscular political attachments to Israel beginning in the late 1960s were premised on the cultural work of the preceding two decades. Considering Israel's increasing relevance within postwar American Jewish culture, we may begin to see the assertive Zionism of the latter decades of the twentieth century as an organic and cumulative development rather than a revolutionary break with what came before.

There is a paradox at the heart of this phenomenon: on the one hand, the cultural work of the first postwar decades provided American

Jews a sense of intimacy with Israel which, I believe, laid the foundations for the cathartic, "survivalist" political rhetoric and behavior characteristic of the post-'67 period. On the other hand, the integrationist, liberal spirit with which so much of that cultural work was undertaken was increasingly ill-suited to the militantly pro-Israel stance of the later postwar era. The zeitgeist changed, but the foundations remained.[32]

It is important to remember that, for many of the postwar actors investigated here, Israel—as a means of outreach as well as a communal cause—served a conciliatory rather than incendiary role. In the process of reinventing Israel as an intrinsic component of American Jewish culture in the years between 1948 and 1967, many American Jews of the postwar era came to insist, and to believe, that Israel belonged to all Americans. In this way, American Jews succeeded in domesticating Israel, transforming the Jewish state from terra incognita to a recognizable entity. Israel's American Jewish impresarios—serving as cultural ambassadors to their community and to their fellow Americans—insisted on Israel's relevance to America and shaped an image of Israel as a valued and trusted American friend. This development changed American Jewish life indelibly and influences the American relationship with Israel to this day.

NOTES

CHAPTER ONE. INTRODUCTION

1. Ida M. Barkan, "Memories of the Future," *Women's League Outlook* 33, no. 1 (Fall 1962): 10.

2. Ibid.

3. For analyses of American Jews' cultural engagements with the Yishuv (Jewish settlement in Palestine) in the prestate period, see Jeffrey Shandler, "Producing the Future: The Impresario Culture of American Zionism before 1948," in *Divergent Jewish Cultures: Israel and America*, ed. Deborah Dash Moore and S. Ilan Troen (New Haven: Yale University Press, 2001), 53–71, and Jeffrey Shandler and Beth S. Wenger, eds., *Encounters with the "Holy Land": Place, Past and Future in American Jewish Culture* (Hanover and London: The University Press of New England, 1997).

4. Rafael Medoff, "Recent Trends in the Historiography of American Zionism," *American Jewish History* 86, no. 1 (1998): 134.

5. For a succinct presentation of this perspective, as well as recent objections to it, see Jonathan D. Sarna, *American Judaism: A History* (New Haven: Yale University Press, 2004), 315–17.

6. "Major Program Recommendations: Some Suggested Highlights for Local Celebrations," 14–19, in "Planning the Local Community Celebration," File 6, Box 806, I-337, American Jewish Historical Society (hereafter AJHS).

7. Ibid., 19.

8. Herbert H. Lehman, "Why Israel's Tenth Anniversary Should Be Observed," 3, in "Planning the Local Community Celebration," File 6, Box 806, I-337, AJHS.

9. Ibid., 2–3.

10. Irving Miller, "For an All American Celebration," 6, in "Planning the Local Community Celebration," File 6, Box 806, I-337, AJHS.

11. Edward S. Shapiro, *A Time for Healing: American Jewry since World War II* (Baltimore: Johns Hopkins University Press, 1992), 204–208; Gerald Sorin, *Tradition Transformed: The Jewish Experience in America* (Baltimore: Johns Hopkins University Press, 1997), 195–96, 214; and Sarna, *American Judaism*, 334–37.

12. Shapiro, *A Time for Healing*, 207.

13. Sarna, *American Judaism*, 333, 335.

14. Stephen J. Whitfield, "Value Added: Jews in Postwar American Culture," in *A New Jewry? America Since the Second World War, Studies in Contemporary Jewry:*

An Annual VIII, ed. Peter Y. Medding (New York and Oxford: Oxford University Press, 1992), 77.

15. See, for example, Yosef Gorny, *The State of Israel in Jewish Public Thought: The Quest for Collective Identity* (New York: New York University Press, 1994); Ben Halpern, *The Idea of the Jewish State*, 2nd edition (Cambridge: Harvard University Press, 1969); Daniel Elazar, *Community and Polity: The Organizational Dynamics of American Jewry*, revised ed. (Philadelphia: Jewish Publication Society, 1995); Melvin I. Urofsky, *We Are One! American Jewry and Israel* (Garden City, NY: Anchor Press/ Doubleday, 1978).

16. Deborah Dash Moore, *To the Golden Cities: Pursuing the American Jewish Dream in Miami and L.A.* (Cambridge: Harvard University Press, 1994), 260.

17. Michelle Mart, *Eye on Israel: How America Came to View Israel as an Ally* (Albany: State University of New York Press, 2006).

18. M. M. Silver, *Our Exodus: Leon Uris and the Americanization of Israel's Founding Story* (Detroit: Wayne State University Press, 2010), 111.

19. Ibid., 19. Pointing to American Jewry's failure "to organize a substantive instrument for publicity work and lobbying" (23) on behalf of Israel as evidence of "the public silence of American Jews regarding Israel during the 1950s" (22), Silver largely overlooks the cultural sphere (aside from *Exodus*) as a site of public engagement with Israel. I argue, in contrast, that the spectrum of cultural practices described in this book provided exactly the "mechanisms and self-confidence needed" (24) to express solidarity with Israel publicly, even before *Exodus* was published.

20. Arthur A. Goren, *The Politics and Public Culture of American Jews* (Bloomington: Indiana University Press, 1999), 188.

21. Peter L. Hahn, *Caught in the Middle East: U.S. Policy Toward the Arab-Israeli Conflict, 1945–1961* (Chapel Hill: University of North Carolina Press, 2004), 28.

22. See Hahn, *Caught in the Middle East*, 32–143; Zvi Ganin, *An Uneasy Relationship: American Jewish Leadership and Israel, 1948–1957* (Syracuse: Syracuse University Press, 2005), 153–55; and Mart, *Eye on Israel*, 33–36.

23. Mart, *Eye on Israel*, 53–64; Bat-Ami Zucker, *U.S. Aid to Israel and Its Reflection in* The New York Times *and* The Washington Post, *1948–1973: The Pen, the Sword, and the Middle East* (Lewiston, NY: The Edwin Mellon Press, 1992), 45–51; 153.

24. See, for example, Naomi W. Cohen, *American Jews and the Zionist Idea* (Jerusalem: KTAV Publishing House, 1975), 14–23; Goren, *The Politics and Public Culture of American Jews*, 146–64; and Mark A. Raider, *The Emergence of American Zionism* (New York: New York University Press, 1998), 69–124.

25. Jacob Blaustein, "Israel Through American Eyes," speech printed in pamphlet published by the American Jewish Committee, 11. File VV-4-28, Series 4, Subject File III, Collected Business and Personal Papers of Louis and Jacob Blaustein (Ms. 400), Milton S. Eisenhower Library Special Collections, Johns Hopkins University.

26. Goren, *The Politics and Public Culture of American Jews*, 192. For further examples of this attitude, see Mart, *Eye on Israel*, 72–75, 81–82, 136–37, and 151–54.

27. Cohen, *American Jews and the Zionist Idea*, 101–102; Ganin, *An Uneasy Relationship*, 182–217.

28. Kennedy used the phrase in conversation with Golda Meir, then foreign minister of Israel. The quotation, recorded in a secret memorandum, is as follows: "The United States . . . has a special relationship with Israel in the Middle East really comparable only to what it has with Britain over a wide range of world affairs." Kennedy went on to say, however, that neither the United States nor Israel could "afford the luxury of identifying Israel [among other countries] as our exclusive friends" in the Middle East; such an approach would alienate potential Arab allies in the region whose friendship was important to American security (and thus, he argued, to Israel's security as well). "Document 121: Memorandum of Conversation, Palm Beach, Florida, December 27, 1962, 10 a.m.," in *Foreign Relations of the United States, 1961–1963, Volume XVIII: Near East 1962–1963*, ed. Nina J. Noring (Washington: Government Printing Office, 1995), 276–83.

29. Cohen, *American Jews and the Zionist Idea*, 110–12 and 130–34; Arlene Lazarowitz, "Different Approaches to a Regional Search for Balance: The Johnson Administration, the State Department, and the Middle East, 1964–1967," *Diplomatic History* 32, no. 1 (January 2008): 25–54.

30. Nathan Reich, "The Year in Retrospect," *American Jewish Year Book* 49 (1947–48): 107.

31. For a comprehensive survey of American Jewry's engagements with and attitudes toward Israel since 1948, see Jack Wertheimer, "American Jews and Israel: A 60-Year Retrospective," *American Jewish Year Book* 108 (2008): 3–79.

32. The Zionist Organization of America (ZOA) was particularly hard hit in this regard. Before 1948, the ZOA was the chief centrist-Zionist group in the United States and the largest American Zionist organization. Its membership declined from a peak of 250,000 in 1948 to less than one hundred thousand in following years. Saul S. Friedman, "Zionist Organization of America," in *Jewish American Voluntary Organizations*, ed. Michael N. Dobkowski (New York: Greenwood Press, 1986), 510; Melvin I. Urofsky, *We Are One! American Jewry and Israel*, 278–97. And see the *American Jewish Year Book* throughout the late 1940s and early 1950s for yearly summaries of the state of organized American Zionism.

33. If, in the period before 1948, "Zionism's actual base of support . . . extended into virtually every organized group in the American Jewish population . . . many of which were not formally Zionist," organized American Zionism played a crucial role in this development. The Israeli government swiftly displaced American Zionism's leadership in the realms of politics and fundraising after May 1948, however. Samuel Halperin, *The Political World of American Zionism* (Detroit: Wayne State University Press, 1961), 301. See also Ganin, *An Uneasy Relationship*, for a detailed study of the interrelationship among the American Zionist movement, the non-Zionist leadership of the organized community, the White House, and the Israeli government in the first decade of Israeli statehood.

34. See Gorny, *The State of Israel in Jewish Public Thought*, 54–78.

35. Thomas A. Kolsky, *Jews Against Zionism: The American Council for Judaism, 1942–1948* (Philadelphia: Temple University Press, 1990), 201.

36. In September 1949, *Reader's Digest*, the popular general interest magazine, published opposing articles on Israel, American Jewry, and the "dual loyalty" question by Alfred M. Lilienthal ("Israel's Flag Is Not Mine") and Abba Hillel Silver ("The

Case for Zionism"). See Ganin, *An Uneasy Relationship*, 12–13. Likewise, in the spring of 1950, historian Oscar Handlin and journalist Dorothy Thompson argued either side of the issue in an exchange on "Israeli Ties and U.S. Citizenship" in *Commentary*. Dorothy Thompson, "America Demands a Single Loyalty: The Perils of a 'Favorite' Foreign Nation," *Commentary* 9 (March 1950): 210–19, and Oscar Handlin, "America Recognizes Diverse Loyalties: 'External' Ties Are Not Necessarily Dangerous," *Commentary* 9 (March 1950): 220–26. For a contemporaneous analysis of American Jewish responses to the dual loyalty question, see Marshall Sklare and Benjamin B. Ringer, "A Study of Jewish Attitudes toward the State of Israel," in *The Jews: Social Patterns of an American Group*, ed. Marshall Sklare (Glencoe, IL: The Free Press, 1960), 443–45.

37. Ganin, *An Uneasy Relationship*, 81–104, 117–21, 137–41.

38. Wendy L. Wall, *Inventing the "American Way": The Politics of Consensus, From the New Deal to the Civil Rights Movement* (New York: Oxford University Press, 2008). According to Wall, this mid-century consensus was a political project rather than a historical actuality; the rhetoric stressing national harmony masked significant differences among sectors of the population, who did disagree on national priorities and the best methods for achieving particular economic, social, and political goals.

39. Michael E. Staub, *Torn at the Roots: The Crisis of Jewish Liberalism in Postwar America* (New York: Columbia University Press, 2002).

40. For more on the intellectual development of the idea of cultural pluralism in American public discourse, particularly as an American Jewish preoccupation and desideratum, see Daniel Greene, *The Jewish Origins of Cultural Pluralism: The Menorah Association and American Diversity* (Bloomington: Indiana University Press, 2011).

41. For a concise overview of these developments, see Hasia R. Diner, *The Jews of the United States, 1654 to 2000* (Berkeley: University of California Press, 2004), 283–88.

42. Ibid., 287.

43. Ibid., 261.

44. Riv-Ellen Prell, "Community and the Discourse of Elegy: The Postwar Suburban Debate," in *Imagining the American Jewish Community*, ed. Jack Wertheimer (Hanover, NH, and London: Brandeis University Press and the University Press of New England, 2007), 70.

45. Ibid., 76–78; and see Edward S. Shapiro, *A Time for Healing: American Jewry since World War II*, 151–53. Two classic contemporaneous works on postwar American society and culture that undoubtedly influenced this discourse were David Riesman, *The Lonely Crowd: A Study of the Changing American Character* (New Haven: Yale University Press, 1950) and William H. Whyte, *The Organization Man* (New York: Simon and Schuster, 1956).

46. Hasia R. Diner, "Before 'The Holocaust': American Jews Confront Catastrophe, 1945–62," in *American Jewish Identity Politics*, ed. Deborah Dash Moore (Ann Arbor: The University of Michigan Press, 2008), 83–116.

47. Ibid., 103.

48. Eli Lederhendler, *New York Jews and the Decline of Urban Ethnicity, 1950–1970* (Syracuse: Syracuse University Press, 2001), 63–92; Samuel C. Heilman,

Portrait of American Jews: The Last Half of the Twentieth Century (Seattle: University of Washington Press, 1995), 8–46.

49. Riv-Ellen Prell introduces this term in her essay, "Community and the Discourse of Elegy," 67–69.

50. Jeffrey Shandler, "What Is American Jewish Culture?" In *The Columbia History of Jews and Judaism in America*, ed. Marc Lee Raphael (New York: Columbia University Press, 2008), 348–49.

51. Shapiro, *A Time for Healing*, 200. Shapiro is correct to point out that the American-born, postwar generation of American Jews "did not speak Yiddish, avoided European-style Orthodox synagogues, were not attracted to the working-class world of Yiddish socialism, and had only a passing acquaintance with Hebrew and Yiddish writers and thinkers" (195). To suggest that this list constitutes the litmus test for Jewish cultural viability or for a "cultural" Jewish identity, however, is to exalt American Jewish immigrant culture as the sole paradigm of authenticity. It is helpful to remember, too, that the *Yiddishkayt*/Jewishness of the immigrant generation was itself a novel product, a creative adaptation to American life, like the postwar Jewish culture that followed. See, for example, Jeffrey Shandler, *Adventures in Yiddishland: Postvernacular Language and Culture* (Berkeley: University of California Press, 2006), 73–82.

52. Several volumes on *Commentary* and its significance have appeared in recent years, including Nathan Abrams, *Norman Podhoretz and Commentary Magazine: The Rise and Fall of the Neocons* (New York: Continuum, 2010), Benjamin Balint, *Running Commentary: The Contentious Magazine that Transformed the Jewish Left into the Neoconservative Right* (New York: PublicAffairs, 2010), and Murray Friedman, ed., *Commentary in American Life* (Philadelphia: Temple University Press, 2005). See also Steven J. Zipperstein, "*Commentary* and American Jewish Culture in the 1940s and 1950s," *Jewish Social Studies*, New Series 3, no. 2 (Winter 1997): 18–28.

53. Shapiro, *A Time for Healing*, 70–71.

54. Arnold Band has written of *Marjorie Morningstar* and *Exodus* as two of the three "most significant samples" of the popular fiction genre in American Jewish culture (216). The third is the musical *Fiddler on the Roof* (1964). Arnold J. Band, "Popular Fiction and the Shaping of Jewish Identity," in *Jewish Identity in America*, ed. David M. Gordis and Yoav Ben-Horin (Los Angeles: The Wilstein Institute of the University of Judaism, 1991): 215–25. See also Stephen J. Whitfield, "Value Added: Jews in Postwar American Culture," 72. According to Whitfield, Israel's outsized imprint on American Jewish culture began with the publication of *Exodus*; I argue in this book that Israel surfaced as a key reference in American Jewish culture in the decade before *Exodus*'s publication in 1958.

55. Jeffrey Shandler and Elihu Katz, "Broadcasting American Judaism: The Radio and Television Department of the Jewish Theological Seminary," in *Tradition Renewed: A History of the Jewish Theological Seminary*, ed. Jack Wertheimer (New York: The Jewish Theological Seminary, 1997), 363–401; Julie Miller and Richard I. Cohen, "A Collision of Cultures: The Jewish Museum and the Jewish Theological Seminary, 1904–1971," also in *Tradition Renewed*, 310–61. Several other museums opened in the first postwar decades as well, serving as harbingers of the explosion in

such venues in the later decades of the twentieth century. These museums included Temple Emanu-El in New York (which received the core of its collection in
1945), the reconceived Jewish Museum in New York (1947), the Temple Museum
of Congregation Emanu-El in San Francisco (1947), Hebrew Union College's public
collection at the Blenheim Memorial Library in Cincinnati (1950), B'nai B'rith's
museum of Jewish history (now the B'nai B'rith Klutznick National Jewish Museum)
in Washington, D.C. (1957), and the Magnes Museum in Berkeley, California (1962).

While some museums benefited from the bequests of individual collectors,
others—including many local synagogue collections—expanded their holdings in the
postwar period through the dissemination of Nazi-looted Judaica recovered by the
U.S. Army. The Synagogue Council of America was involved in this restoration
and distribution project and encouraged synagogues across the country to "set aside
museum-like nooks to house these doubly sacred objects and to tell the story of the
destruction of Jewish life in Europe." Hasia R. Diner, *We Remember With Reverence
and Love: American Jews and the Myth of Silence After the Holocaust, 1945–1962* (New
York and London: New York University Press, 2009), 37.

56. "National Foundation for Jewish Culture (NFJC)," in *Jewish American
Voluntary Organizations*, ed. Michael N. Dobkowski (New York: Greenwood Press,
1986), 345.

57. Stuart Svonkin, *Jews Against Prejudice: American Jews and the Fight for
Civil Liberties* (New York: Columbia University Press, 1997), 188. These and related
cultural activities were organized by the American Jewish Congress's Commission
on Jewish Affairs and its Women's Division.

58. See "An American Synagogue for Today and Tomorrow: Statements Made
at Conference of the Union of American Hebrew Congregations," *Architectural
Record* 102 (September 1947): 99; and Synagogue Architects Consultant Panel of
the Union of American Hebrew Congregations, *The American Synagogue: A Progress
Report; Proceedings, Second National Conference and Exhibit on Synagogue Architecture*,
ed. Rabbi Eugene J. Lipman and Myron E. Schoen (New York: UAHC, 1958); Janay
Jadine Wong, "Synagogue Art of the 1950s: A New Context for Abstraction," *Art
Journal* 53, no. 4 (Winter 1994): 37–43; Abram Kanof, "The Tobe Pascher Workshop
1956–1986," in *Moshe Zabari: A Twenty-Five Year Retrospective*, ed. Nancy M. Berman
(New York: The Jewish Museum and Los Angeles: The Hebrew Union College
Skirball Museum, 1986), 6–17.

Commentary magazine, among other American Jewish publications, published
articles on synagogue art and architecture in its pages in the early postwar years, invit-
ing preeminent architects, art historians, and critics to discuss the new aesthetic possibilities and their moral resonances. See, for example, Rachel Wischnitzer-Bernstein,
"The Problem of Synagogue Architecture: Creating a Style Expressive of America,"
Commentary 3 (March 1947): 51–55; Percival and Paul Goodman, "Modern Artist
as Synagogue Builder: Satisfying the Needs of Today's Congregations," *Commentary* 7
(January 1949): 233–41; and William Schack, "Synagogue Art Today: I: Something
of a Renaissance," *Commentary* 20 (December 1955): 548–53. The art press—particularly *Architectural Record* and *Progressive Architecture*—also devoted attention to
the subject throughout the first postwar decades.

59. A. W. Zelomek, *A Changing America: At Work and Play* (New York: Wiley,
1959), 120–31.

60. Alvin Toffler, *The Culture Consumers: A Controversial Study of Culture and Affluence in America* (New York: St. Martin's Press, 1964), 8.

61. Ibid., 10.

62. August Heckscher, *The Public Happiness* (New York: Atheneum, 1962), 292.

63. James T. Patterson, *Grand Expectations: The United States, 1945–1974* (New York and Oxford: Oxford University Press, 1996), 61, 70–71; 313–17.

64. Ibid., 321; Zelomek, *A Changing America*, 79–104.

65. Patterson, *Grand Expectations*, 67–70.

66. For example, in the post–World War II years American Jews entered the white collar professions at higher rates than non-Jews; by the late 1950s, the median income among American Jews was more than 30 percent higher than that of non-Jews. See Barry Chiswick, "The Labor Market Status of American Jews: Patterns and Determinants," *American Jewish Year Book* 85 (1985): 135–38.

67. Shandler, "What Is American Jewish Culture?" 348–49.

68. Toffler, *The Culture Consumers*, 34–35.

69. Albert Isaac Gordon, *Jews in Suburbia* (Boston: Beacon Press, 1959), 79.

70. Ibid., 78.

71. David Boroff, "Jewish Readers and Jewish Writers," *Congress Bi-Weekly* 27, no. 19 (December 19, 1960): 3.

72. Aleisa R. Fishman, "Keeping Up with the Goldbergs: Gender, Consumer Culture, and Jewish Identity in Suburban Nassau County, New York, 1946–1960" (PhD Diss.: American University, 2004), 134–36.

73. Christina Klein, *Cold War Orientalism: Asia in the Middlebrow Imagination, 1945–1961* (Berkeley: University of California Press, 2003), 23.

74. Nicholas J. Cull, *The Cold War and the United States Information Agency: American Propaganda and Public Diplomacy, 1945–1989* (Cambridge: Cambridge University Press, 2008), 114–17.

75. In addition to Klein's, other important studies of Cold War–era cultural production and discourse in the United States include Walter L. Hixson, *Parting the Curtain: Propaganda, Culture, and the Cold War* (New York: St. Martin's Griffin, 1998); Melani McAlister, *Epic Encounters: Culture, Media, and U.S. Interests in the Middle East, 1945–2000* (Berkeley: University of California Press, 2001), Frances Stonor Saunders, *The Cultural Cold War: the CIA and the World of Arts and Letters* (New York: The New Press, 2001), and Cull, *The Cold War and the United States Information Agency*.

76. Jonathan D. Sarna, *American Judaism*, 334; Elazar, *Community and Polity*, 107.

CHAPTER TWO. BEFORE *EXODUS*

1. Herbert Sonnenfeld and Pierre van Paassen, *Palestine: Land of Israel* (Chicago: Ziff-Davis, 1948), 8.

2. Ibid., 22, 23, 27.

3. Horace Kallen's book about the Jewish settlement in Palestine, *Frontiers of Hope*, was published in 1929; *Palestine To-day and To-morrow: A Gentile's Survey*

of Zionism, by John Haynes Holmes, a Unitarian minister of national renown, was published in the same year. See Arthur A. Goren, *The Politics and Public Culture of American Jews*, 174.

4. Samuel Halperin, *The Political World of American Zionism*, 258–59.

5. Sonnenfeld and van Paassen, *Palestine: Land of Israel*, 19.

6. The authors and titles that follow appear under the subject heading "Israel" in the subject and title index 1947–1951 of the *Book Review Digest* 1951 (H. W. Wilson Co., 1951): J. Garcia-Granados, *Birth of Israel* (1948); I. F. Stone, *This Is Israel* (1949); B. M. Bloomfield, *Israel Diary* (1950); J. Dunner, *Republic of Israel* (1950); R. E. McGill, *Israel Revisited* (1950). An even longer list of titles appears under the subject heading of "Palestine," in the 1947–1951 Subject and Title Index.

7. Herbert Poster, "Literature," *American Jewish Year Book* 51 (1950), 207; Milton Himmelfarb, "Israel Omnibus," *Commentary* 10 (1950): 608.

8. Himmelfarb, "Israel Omnibus," 608.

9. Carl Alpert, "American Books on Zionism and Israel, 1949–1950," *Jewish Book Annual* 9 (1950–51), 23.

10. Americans generally appeared to be buying increasing numbers of books in this period. According to John Tebbel, the American book publishing industry experienced an unprecedented boom beginning in 1944–45 and continuing through the 1950s. John Tebbel, *A History of Book Publishing in the United States*, vol. IV, *The Great Change, 1940–1980* (New York and London: R. R. Bowker, 1981), 50–61; 722. For contemporaneous discussions of the health of the publishing industry, see, for example, David Dempsey, "In and Out of Books," *New York Times*, September 9, 1951, BR5; David Dempsey, "Quality (Culture) Plus Quantity (Readers) Pays Off," *New York Times*, January 3, 1956, 261; Ray Shaw, "Book Boom," *Wall Street Journal*, September 26, 1961, 1; and Philip Shabecoff, "Publishers Busy With Mergers, New Marketing Ideas and Sales," *New York Times*, January 8, 1962, 127.

11. The summaries of yearly activities of the Jewish Book Council between 1946–1952, published in the *Jewish Book Annual* (volumes 6–11) and drawing upon surveys conducted by the council, show a steady growth in programming and participation among a wide spectrum of the organized American Jewish community, particularly in regard to Jewish Book Month. In his report on the year 1948–49, for example, Philip Goodman cited "constant requests for guidance in the selection of books and the building of Jewish libraries and collections." Philip Goodman, "The Jewish Book Council of America in 5709 (1948–49)," *Jewish Book Annual* 8 (1949–1950), 109.

12. Ibid.

13. See Philip Goodman, "The Jewish Book Council of America in 5711 (1950–1951)," *Jewish Book Annual* 10 (1951–52), 52.

14. Philip Goodman, "The Jewish Book Council of America in 5710 (1949–1950)," *Jewish Book Annual* 9 (1950–51), 72.

15. Goodman, "The Jewish Book Council of America in 5711 (1950–1951)," 53.

16. Ibid., 54.

17. "News of the Week [Jewish Publishers to Emphasize Sales]," *Publishers' Weekly* 164, no. 15 (October 10, 1953), 1567.

18. "Shop Talk," *Publishers' Weekly* 155, no. 15 (April 9, 1949), 1619.

19. Critic Harold U. Ribalow, for example, cited comparatively low sales figures in a skeptical assessment of the health of Israel books, while Trude Weiss-Rosmarin, editor of the *Jewish Spectator*, described a decline in the market for Jewish books more generally in the early 1950s. See Ribalow, "Zion in the Book Stores," *Jewish Frontier* 19, no. 1 (March 1952): 16–19, and Weiss-Rosmarin, "The Plight of the Jewish Book," *Jewish Spectator* 17, no. 9 (October 1952): 5–6; and see also Carl Alpert, "American Books on Zionism and Israel, 1950–1951," *Jewish Book Annual* 10 (1951–52): 15. According to Alpert, the situation had stabilized by 1951. Carl Alpert, "American Books on Zionism and Israel, 1951–1952," *Jewish Book Annual* 11 (1952–53), 19.

20. The rapidly diminishing Yiddish press in the United States did not appear to be particularly interested in the Israel books flooding the American book market. For example, no reviews of prominent examples of books about Palestine/Israel by Ruth Gruber, George Fielding Eliot, Jorge Garcia-Granados, or I. F. Stone appeared in the Yiddish periodical press in the late 1940s, at least according to Sophie Udin's comprehensive index of publications on Palestine and Zionism. Sophie A. Udin, *Palestine and Zionism: A Three Year Cumulation, January 1946–December 1948: An Author and Subject Index to Books, Pamphlets, and Periodicals* (New York: Zionist Archives and Library of Palestine Foundation Fund, 1949). Two of the remaining Yiddish daily newspapers, the *Forverts* (*Jewish Daily Forward*) and the *Tog* (*Day*) also apparently paid little attention to this genre, even as each provided extensive and ubiquitous coverage of events in Israel and regularly offered news and reviews of other new books in Yiddish, Hebrew, and English. One exception to this is Chaim Weizmann's autobiography, *Trial and Error*, which the *Forverts* serialized beginning in January 1949, translated into Yiddish (from English) by M. Osherovitsh.

21. Paul Breines, *Tough Jews: Political Fantasies and the Moral Dilemma of American Jewry* (New York: Basic Books, 1990).

22. Mart, *Eye on Israel*, 53–84; Michelle Mart, "Tough Guys and American Cold War Policy: Images of Israel, 1948–1960," *Diplomatic History* 20, no. 3 (Summer 1996): 357–80.

23. McDonald insisted in his book that his wife and his daughter lived little better than most Israelis, despite his lofty position as U.S. ambassador to Israel. In one passage, the author describes his daughter Bobby's attempt to provide a "typically American" turkey dinner one Saturday night during their residency in Israel. Finding that "turkeys . . . were more rare than the proverbial hen's teeth in Israel," his daughter procures from a kibbutz the only two turkeys within twenty miles of Tel Aviv; when the turkeys arrive after the local butcher has closed for Shabbat, the family recruits a staff member to shoot the turkey with a pistol. "Bobby served an excellent dinner," McDonald reported, "while the surviving turkey cackled defiance outside the window." James G. McDonald, *My Mission in Israel* (New York: Simon and Schuster, 1951), 161.

24. See chapter 1, footnotes 69, 70, and 71. It is worth noting that in his talk before the Women's National Book Association (cited above), Mortimer Cohen specifically mentioned three national Jewish women's organizations (Hadassah, the National Council of Jewish Women, and the National Federation of Temple Sisterhoods) as major promoters of Jewish books. The *Jewish Book Annual*, too,

provides sporadic but compelling evidence of this phenomenon. In his report on the Jewish Book Council of America in 1948–49, for example, Philip Goodman devoted special attention to the participation of Jewish women's organizations in promoting and celebrating Jewish Book Month; he singled out eight national organizations here, including Zionist stalwarts Hadassah and Mizrachi Women. The Jewish Book Council also included among its specialized titles a publication called *Reading Circles for Women*. (There was no counterpart publication for Jewish men.) Goodman, "The Jewish Book Council of America in 5709 (1948–49)," *Jewish Book Annual* 8 (1949–1950): 111; Goodman, "Jewish Book Council of America in 5712 (1951–52)," *Jewish Book Annual* 11 (1952–53): 193.

25. Americans journeying abroad in increasing numbers in the nineteenth century published travel literature about the Holy Land, and this literature, in turn, introduced American audiences to a body of common tropes about the land and its denizens. Books such as William C. Prime's *Tent Life in the Holy Land* (1857) and William McClure Thomson's *The Land and the Book* (1859) wed Protestant pilgrimage with wilderness adventure and found an avid audience in the United States. Prime, Thomson, and others described the Palestinian landscape as an authentic record of biblical times while simultaneously conveying the notion that the land suffered under its Jewish and Muslim inhabitants, bereft of God's blessing. For more on American travelers to the Holy Land in the nineteenth century and the books they wrote about those travels, see John Davis, *The Landscape of Belief: Encountering the Holy Land in Nineteenth-Century American Art and Culture* (Princeton: Princeton University Press, 1996), 27–52; Lester I. Vogel, *To See A Promised Land: Americans and the Holy Land in the Nineteenth Century* (University Park: The Pennsylvania State University Press, 1993), 39–93, 105; and McAlister, *Epic Encounters*, 13–20.

26. For more on this history, see Gershon Greenberg, *The Holy Land in American Religious Thought, 1620–1948: The Symbiosis of American Religious Approaches to Scripture's Sacred Territory* (Lanham, MD, New York, and London: University Press of America, 1994).

27. These books include Millar Burrows's *Palestine Is Our Business* (1949), Willie Snow Ethridge's *Going to Jerusalem* (1950), Bertha Spafford Vester's *Our Jerusalem, An American Family in the Holy City—1881–1949* (1950), T. Cuyler Young, *Near Eastern Culture and Society* (1951), Alfred Lilienthal, *What Price Israel* (1953), Virginia Gildersleeve, *Many a Good Crusade: Memoirs* (1954), and Elmer Berger, *Judaism or Jewish Nationalism: the Alternative to Zionism* (1957).

28. Morrell Heald, *Transatlantic Vistas: American Journalists in Europe, 1900–1940* (Kent, OH, and London: The Kent State University Press, 1988), xi; Edwin Emery, *The Press and America: An Interpretive History of the Mass Media* (Englewood Cliffs, NJ: Prentice-Hall, 1972), 483–88.

29. Michael Emery, *On the Front Lines: Following America's Foreign Correspondents Across the Twentieth Century* (Washington, DC: The American University Press, 1995), 215; Mart, *Eye on Israel*, 23–52 and 53–84.

30. Eliot's book about Israel, *Hate, Hope, and High Explosives: A Report on the Middle East*, was published in 1948. Vincent Freimarck, "George Fielding Eliot," *American National Biography Online*; and "George Fielding Eliot, 76, Dies; Military Writer of World War II," *New York Times*, April 22, 1971, 44.

31. Poster, "Literature," 207.

32. Douglas Martin, "Robert St. John, 100, Globe-Trotting Reporter and Author," *New York Times*, February 8, 2003. St. John's career as a foreign correspondent for NBC was cut short after his name appeared in *Red Channels*, the publication purporting to expose communist sympathizers in broadcast journalism.

33. Robert St. John, *Shalom Means Peace* (Garden City, NY: Doubleday, 1949), 3.

34. Diner, *We Remember With Reverence and Love*, 180–87.

35. Jorge Garcia-Granados, *The Birth of Israel: The Drama as I Saw It* (New York: Knopf, 1948), 100.

36. I. F. Stone, *This Is Israel* (New York: Boni and Gaer, 1948).

37. Several American GIs penned books in the 1950s about their service on behalf of Israel. Titles that deal exclusively with the role of American volunteers who participated in illegal immigration operations and who fought in the Jewish underground and in the Arab-Israeli War of 1948 include Murray Gitlin's *The Embarkation* (1950), Daniel Spicehandler's *Let My Right Hand Wither* (1950), Erwin Arnovitz's *Of Blood and Oil* (1951), and Isaac Zaar's *Rescue and Liberation* (1954). According to Aviva Halamish, the story of American volunteers is absent from early Israeli accounts of the period, which exclusively stressed the heroic roles of members of the Palmach or the Mossad. Aviva Halamish, "American Volunteers in Illegal Immigration to Palestine, 1946–1948," *Jewish History* 9, no. 1 (Spring 1995): 101–102.

38. The sole note of true dismay sounded by St. John was in response to his meeting with Menachem Begin, former leader of the paramilitary organization known as the Irgun. In response to Begin's argument that the ends (terrorism) justified the means—and whose methods "were repugnant to a majority of Israelis as well as to most people, anywhere, who believe in law and order," according to the author—St. John cited an abuse of his beloved greeting, "shalom" (188). "Shalom means peace," he wrote, "but the word had a hollow ring when Beigin [*sic*] said it" (188).

39. Clifton Daniel, "Israeli Vignettes," *New York Times*, January 30, 1949, BR10.

40. M. M., "Newsmen Tell of Palestine's Peace Quest," *Los Angeles Times*, April 3, 1949, D4.

41. Gerold Frank, "The Israelis at Home," review of *Shalom Means Peace*, by Robert St. John, *New York Herald Tribune Weekly Book Review*, February 20, 1949, 4.

42. Poster, "Literature," 207. In this case, Poster was noting criticisms of not only *Shalom Means Peace* but also Garcia-Granados's *Birth of Israel* and Stone's *This Is Israel*.

43. Alice Hackett, "PW Forecast for Buyers," *Publishers' Weekly*, 155, no. 2 (January 8, 1949), 143.

44. "Candidates for the Best Seller List" [annotated listing], *Publishers' Weekly* 155, no. 15 (April 9, 1949), 1625, and *Publishers' Weekly* 155, no. 18 (April 30, 1949), 1825. Interestingly, Israelis were among St. John's most avid readers. Reporting on the reading public in Israel, critic Alfred Werner noted that *Shalom Means Peace* was a popular current events title among the general public, along with biographies of Roosevelt and Stalin and the memoirs of King Abdullah of Jordan. According

to another commentator on the Israeli literary scene, St. John, despite a soft-boiled take on contemporary Israeli affairs, had apparently ruffled feathers "in high places over what is regarded as 'the abuse of confidence.'" Alfred Werner, "A Literary Letter About Israel," *New York Times*, October 15, 1950, BR17; Gertrude Samuels, "Reading and Writing About Israel," *New York Times*, October 9, 1949, BR37.

45. The *New York Herald Tribune* sent the author to visit the Middle East with the United Nations Special Committee on Palestine in the summer of 1947, where she began writing about the saga of the *Exodus* as well as taking photographs for *Life* magazine. See Ruth Gruber, *Exodus 1947: The Ship that Launched a Nation*, formerly titled *Destination Palestine* (New York: A. A. Wyn, 1948; New York: Random House, 1999), xvii. See also "Destination Palestine," *The New Republic* 118 (February 9, 1948): 14–18; "Sidetrack to Palestine," *Colliers* 120 (November 22, 1947): 8, 22–23; "Shabbat in Tel Aviv," *Commentary* 9 (February 1950): 159–62, and "Hebrew as She is Spoke," *Commentary* 10 (November 1950): 466–69.

46. For an autobiographical overview of Gruber's career, see *Witness: One of the Great Foreign Correspondents of the Twentieth Century Tells Her Story* (New York: Schocken Books, 2007). In his foreword to the book, Richard Holbrooke credits Gruber as the source of the plot of Uris's *Exodus* (xi).

47. Gruber, "A Bread-and-Butter Note," *Israel Without Tears* (New York: A. A. Wyn, 1950), unpaginated.

48. Ibid., 173.

49. "Tips for the Bookseller," *Publishers' Weekly* 158, no. 13 (September 23, 1950), 1401; "A Calendar of Important Spring Books and Spring Promotions," *Publishers' Weekly* 157, no. 4 (January 28, 1950), 541.

50. Alice Hackett, "PW Buyers' Forecast," *Publishers' Weekly* 158, no. 18 (October 28, 1950), 1967.

51. Gerold Frank, review of *Israel Without Tears*, by Ruth Gruber, *New York Herald Tribune Book Review*, December 17, 1950, 4; Hal Lehrman, Review of *Israel Without Tears*, *New York Times*, December 31, 1950, 11.

52. C. H. Voss, review of *Israel Without Tears*, *Churchman* 16 (December 1, 1950), 164.

53. For more on the role of the rise of travel literature—the writing and reading of it—as a middle-class pursuit, see William W. Stowe, *Going Abroad: European Travel in Nineteenth-Century American Culture* (Princeton: Princeton University Press, 1994).

54. Golda Meir (as told to Judith Krantz), "At Home in Jerusalem," *Good Housekeeping* 145 (July 1957): 68–69.

55. Readers of postwar women's magazines would not have been surprised by the tenor of the article; according to historian Joanne Meyerowitz, popular magazines in the postwar period frequently published articles championing women as successful public figures, their authors expressing "overt admiration for women whose individual striving moved them beyond the home" (231). The *Good Housekeeping* piece on Meir encapsulates perfectly a postwar popular literature that "advocated both the domestic and the nondomestic, sometimes in the same sentence" and in which "domestic ideals coexisted in ongoing tension with an ethos of individual achievement" (231). Joanne Meyerowitz, "Beyond the Feminine Mystique: A Reassessment

of Postwar Mass Culture, 1946–1958," in *Not June Cleaver: Women and Gender in Postwar America, 1945–1960*, ed. Joanne Meyerowitz (Philadelphia: Temple University Press, 1994), 229–62. See also the introduction to *A Jewish Feminine Mystique?: Jewish Women in Postwar America*, ed. Hasia R. Diner, Shira Kohn, and Rachel Kranson (New Brunswick and London: Rutgers University Press, 2010), 1–12, and Anita Shapira, "Golda: Femininity and Feminism," in *American Jewish Women and the Zionist Enterprise*, ed. Shulamit Reinharz and Mark A. Raider (Waltham: Brandeis University Press, 2005), 303–12.

56. Nell Ziff Pekarsky, "Shopping, Swapping, *Shepping Nahas* in Israel," *Hadassah Newsletter* 32, no. 6 (March 1952): 6.

57. *Hadassah Newsletter* 28, no. 7 (April 1948): 3.

58. Shira Klein, "An Army of Housewives: Women's Wartime Columns in Two Mainstream Israeli Newspapers," *Nashim* 15 (2008):101.

59. Biographical statement ("Mrs. Molly Lyons Bar-David"), 2. File A-B, RG15/ Operations and Functions/Series: Speakers' Bureau/Biographical profiles/1950–1975 A-L, Hadassah Archives.

60. By the late 1960s, Bar-David was also Israel correspondent for the *Winnipeg Free Press*. Biographical statement, 2.

61. Molly Lyons Bar-David, *My Promised Land* (New York: G. P. Putnam's Sons, 1953), 294.

62. Ethel Dexter, review of *My Promised Land*, by Molly Lyons Bar-David, *Springfield Republic*, December 20, 1953, 10C.

63. A. D., review of *My Promised Land*, *San Francisco Chronicle*, November 29, 1953, 8.

64. C. J. Roth, review of *My Promised Land*, *Library Journal* 78 (November 15, 1953): 2028. With its domestic perspective and light touch with both familial and historical crises, *My Promised Land* appears, in retrospect, as an entry (albeit an unusual one) into the nascent "literature of domestic chaos," in Laura Shapiro's formulation (145). First published in popular women's magazines at mid-century, innovated and perfected by such writers as Shirley Jackson, Ernestine Gilbreth Carey, and Erma Bombeck, this genre of best-selling books translated the everyday travails of its harried housewife narrators into droll tales of postwar domesticity. While Bar-David's memoir is rarely laugh-out-loud funny, as are the best examples of the genre, it shares more than a few genes with the domestic chaos literature of the day. Laura Shapiro, *Something From the Oven: Reinventing Dinner in 1950s America* (New York: Viking Penguin, 2004).

65. For McDonald, the Bible provided the philosophical bedrock for his own work in Israel, underscoring what he felt to be the special mission of the Jewish state. McDonald never divulged to which Christian denomination he belonged, but, aside from his admiration for the pope, culminating in two visits to the Vatican (described in the book), his sensibilities were those of a mainline American Protestant at mid-century: The Bible was the blueprint for moral order in the world, and America was the architect of that order.

66. Mary Clawson's *Letters from Jerusalem* more nearly matches the distinguishing marks of the domestic chaos genus. Maintaining an amused tone throughout, *Letters* features "rambunctious but witty children," a "laconic but witty" husband,

and a "beset but witty" housewife, hallmarks of the genre, as Laura Shapiro has written (*Something from the Oven*, 150).

67. Mary Clawson, *Letters from Jerusalem* (London and New York: Abelard-Schuman, 1958), unpaginated.

68. To some reviewers at least, Clawson's unmitigated admiration for Israel was problematic. "Mrs. Clawson's naive and completely uncritical enthusiasm is somewhat disturbing," wrote a critic in the *Saturday Review*, noting that "it is doubtful that the thoughtful Israeli himself would . . . welcome such an unconstructive and starry-eyed approach to his country" (J. W., review of *Letters from Jerusalem*, by Mary Clawson, *Saturday Review* 41 [April 26, 1958]: 28). The *Times Literary Supplement*, meanwhile, agreed that "the chorus of praise and admiration becomes almost monotonous," in an otherwise positive review (*Times* [London] *Literary Supplement*, September 12, 1958, 516).

69. Clawson, *Letters From Jerusalem*, 224.

70. Norma Mayron, "Israeli Kitchen," *Women's League Outlook* 33, no. 3 (March 1963): 26.

71. Willetta Bar-Illan, "From Tzimmes to Homus: The Dawn of Israeli Cuisine," *Hadassah Magazine* 42, no. 4 (1961): 6.

72. Dorothy Rossyn, "Culture in Cookery," *Hadassah Magazine* 46, no. 9 (May 1965): 12–13.

73. Quentin Reynolds, "Land of a Determined People," review of *Watch for the Morning*, by Thomas Sugrue, *New York Times*, October 1, 1950, 215.

74. Titles appear in the cumulative indices of the *Book Review Digest* published in 1956, 1961, and 1966.

75. Solomon Kerstein, "American Books on Israel and Zionism 1955–1956," *Jewish Book Annual* 14 (1956–57): 94.

76. Mordkhe Rudavsky, "James Grover McDonald," (in Yiddish) *der amerikaner (Jewish American)* 46, no. 38 (July 9, 1948): 2.

77. Norma H. Goodhue, "Despite Hardship, Israel Seeks More Immigrants, Writer Tells Hadassah," *Los Angeles Times*, January 29, 1952, B1.

78. Ribalow, "Zion in the Book Stores," 17.

79. Ibid.; "Film Head Voices Israel Aid Appeal," *Los Angeles Times*, December 19, 1949, A3; "Hadassah Benefit Set," *New York Times*, November 15, 1957, 23. Several writeups in *Publishers' Weekly* noted Gruber's significant presence on the lecture circuit; see footnote 49, above.

80. "Today's Events," *The Washington Post and Times Herald*, February 26, 1959, C17; "Author to Speak," *The Washington Post and Times Herald*, May 15, 1958, D5; "Today's Events," *The Washington Post and Times Herald*, September 14, 1959, B4.

81. Frederic G. Melcher, "The Need for Better Statistics," *Publishers' Weekly* 155 (January 8, 1949): 132.

82. Roland Gelatt, "Bogus Best Sellers," *Saturday Review of Literature* 32, no. 13 (March 26, 1949): 20–22.

83. Putnam, for example, would not provide hard numbers to the industry about two of its titles that were among the top three best-sellers of 1949, Mika

Waltari's *The Egyptian* and Sholem Asch's *Mary*. "Best Sellers of 1949," *Publishers' Weekly*, 157, no. 3 (January 21, 1950): 235.

84. "What Shall We Do About Best Seller Lists?" *Publishers' Weekly* 155, no. 11 (March 26, 1949): 1399.

85. Ribalow, "Zion in the Book Stores," 17.

86. On Doubleday & Co., see John William Tebbel, *A History of Book Publishing in the United States*, vol. 4: *The Great Change*, 105–17.

87. On A. A. Wyn, see "Books and Authors," *New York Times*, May 22, 1945, 17; "Aaron Wyn, 69, Publisher, Dead," *New York Times*, November 5, 1967, 86.

88. Ribalow, "Zion in the Book Stores," 17; "A Calendar of Important Spring Books and Spring Promotions," 541.

89. "135 Leading Campaigns of the Fall Season," *Publishers' Weekly* 164, no. 12 (September 19, 1953): 1144–45. *My Promised Land* was not listed among the titles in this survey.

90. I have not found sales numbers for Bar-David's *My Promised Land*.

91. Mrs. Samuel Fox, "From Hadassah's Bookshelves," 6, *The Bulletin of the Los Angeles Chapter of Hadassah*, May 1949. File: Chapter Newsletters, 1949–1995, Box 2B, RG 15, Hadassah Archives.

92. "Order This Book Now," *The Bulletin of the Los Angeles Chapter of Hadassah*, November 1948, 11. File: Chapter Newsletters, 1949–1995, Box 2B, RG 15, Hadassah Archives.

93. David Boroff, "Jewish Readers and Jewish Writers," *Congress Bi-Weekly* 27, no. 19 (December 19, 1960): 3.

94. Alice Payne Hackett and James Henry Burke, *80 Years of Best Sellers, 1895–1975* (New York: R. R. Bowker, 1977), 178, 196.

95. See, for example, Andrew Furman, *Israel Through the Jewish-American Imagination* (Albany: State University of New York Press, 1997), 39–58; Moore, *To The Golden Cities*, 227–61; Mart, *Eye on Israel*, 169–76; Douglas Little, *American Orientalism: The United States and the Middle East Since 1945*, 3rd ed. (Chapel Hill: The University of North Carolina Press, 2008), 25–32; and Arnold J. Band, "Popular Fiction and the Shaping of Jewish Identity," 215–25.

96. Moore, *To the Golden Cities*, 243.

97. Beverly Kaplan Feiges, "In Praise of 'Exodus,' " letter to the editor, *Hadassah Newsletter* 39, no. 5 (January 1959): 11.

CHAPTER THREE. HORA HOOTENANNIES
AND YEMENITE HOEDOWNS

1. Carl Alpert, "An Experience in Cultural Relationships," *The Reconstructionist* 8, no. 10 (June 26, 1942): 12.

2. Ibid., 14.

3. Ibid.

4. Ibid.

5. Dvora Lapson, "Dance in the Jewish School," *The Reconstructionist* 17, no. 17 (December 28, 1951): 23.

6. John Martin, "Folk-Dance Boom," *New York Times*, February 23, 1941, SM10.

7. Anthony Shay, *Choreographing Identities: Folk Dance, Ethnicity, and Festival in the United States and Canada* (Jefferson, NC, and London: McFarland, 2006), 31–32.

8. Martin, "Folk-Dance Boom," SM10.

9. Nina Spiegel, "Jewish Cultural Celebrations and Competitions in Mandatory Palestine, 1920–1947" (PhD diss., Stanford University, 2001), 185–86.

10. Ibid., 179.

11. Dina Roginsky, "Sixty Years to the First Dalia Conference, 1944–2004: Changes in Israeli Folk Dance," *Dance Now* 11 (November 2004): 97. See also Spiegel, "Jewish Cultural Celebrations and Competitions in Mandatory Palestine," 176–79.

12. Mordecai M. Kaplan, *Judaism as a Civilization: Toward a Reconstruction of American-Jewish Life* (New York: Macmillan, 1934; Philadelphia: Jewish Publication Society, 1994), 203.

13. For more on Kaplan, see Mel Scult, *Judaism Faces the Twentieth Century: A Biography of Mordecai M. Kaplan* (Detroit: Wayne State University Press, 1993); and Emanuel S. Goldsmith et al., *The American Judaism of Mordecai M. Kaplan* (New York: New York University Press, 1990).

14. "A Hebrew Arts Project," 2, File 7, Box 2, Moshe Davis Papers, Ratner Center for the Study of Conservative Judaism, Jewish Theological Seminary. For more on the Hebrew youth movement and Hebrew culture, see, for example, Davis's series of essays, "Letters on Hebrew Culture," published in *Niv* in the late 1930s. Moshe Davis, "Letters on Hebrew Culture," (in Hebrew) *Niv* 3, no. 1 (Tishrei 5699 [September 1938]): 9–11; 3, no. 2 (Cheshvan 5699 [October 1938]): 4–5; 3, no. 3 (Kislev 5699 [November 1938]): 2–4; and 3, no. 4 (Tevet 5699 [December 1938]): 7–8. See also Alan Mintz, "The Divided Fate of Hebrew and Hebrew Culture at the Seminary," in *Tradition Renewed: A History of the Jewish Theological Seminary*, vol. II, ed. Wertheimer, 81–112.

15. Corinne Chochem, "Artists in Search of Their People," *The Reconstructionist* 12, no. 20 (February 7, 1947): 21; and see Pauline Koner, "Chochem, Corinne," in *Jewish Women in America*, ed. Paula E. Hyman and Deborah Dash Moore (New York: Routledge, 1998), 226.

16. Ruth R. Goodman with Ruth P. Schoenberg, "Dance: Israeli Folk Dance Pioneers," in *Jewish Women in America*, 295. And see Naomi M. Jackson, *Converging Movements: Modern Dance and Jewish Culture at the 92nd Street Y* (Hanover: University Press of New England/Wesleyan University Press, 2000), 177, 183.

17. For more on the "Benderly boys," see Jonathan Krasner, *The Benderly Boys and American Jewish Education* (Waltham: Brandeis University Press, 2011).

18. Goodman and Schoenberg, "Dance," 295.

19. Lapson, "Dance in the Jewish School," 23. See also Dvora Lapson, "The Jewish Dance," *The Reconstructionist* 10, no. 8 (May 26, 1944): 13–17.

20. Ibid., 24.

21. Judith Brin Ingber, *Victory Dances: The Story of Fred Berk, A Modern Day Jewish Dancing Master* (Tel Aviv: Israel Dance Library; Minneapolis: Emmett Publishing, 1985), 14–24.

22. Fred Berk, interview by Judith Brin Ingber, transcript of tape recording, April 21–26, 1979, Dance Collection of the New York Public Library for the Performing Arts, 108. In the 1950s, Berk went on to establish a teacher training workshop in Israeli folk dance at the 92nd St. Y and one at Camp Blue Star in Hendersonville, North Carolina, as well as forming Hebraica, an Israeli folk dance troupe made up of twelve teenagers that Berk had chosen from his classes at the Y. See also Ingber, *Victory Dances*, and Jackson, *Converging Movements*, 202–203.

23. Fred Berk, *Guide for the Israeli Folk Dance Teacher* (American Zionist Youth Foundation, 1979), 6. Reprinted from *Hora* newsletter, Fall 1972.

24. Ibid.

25. Ingber, *Victory Dances*, 86. At one point, Berk had suggested forming a committee (much like the Folk Dance Committee in Israel) that would judge which dances should be taught and unify the teaching of them. Nothing came of the plan, which Berk later came to see as misguided and unrealistic in a country as big and diverse as the United States. Fred Berk, interview with Judith Brin Ingber, transcript of tape recording, April 21–26, 1979, Dance Collection of the New York Public Library for the Performing Arts, 9.

26. See, for example, Fred Berk and Lucy Venable, *Dances from Israel in Labanotation* (1963, rev. 1967); Dvora Lapson and Gert Kaufman, *New Israeli Dances* (New York: Jewish Education Committee of New York, 1948); Florence E. Freehof, *Tips on Teaching Folk Dancing* (New York: Bloch, 1948) and *New Dances From Israel* (New York: Bloch, 1960); Miriam Lidster, "Israeli Folk Dances" (Festival Workshop, San Francisco); Jewish National Fund publications "Shavuot Sheaves" (1953) and "Summer Camp Guide" (1953); and Alisa Wirtz, *Dances of Israel* (New England Zionist Youth Commission, n.d.).

27. Sturman, for example, an organizer and participant in the first Dalia Festival, was a returning staff member at the influential Folk Dance Camp in Stockton, California, in the 1950s and 1960s, at Camp Hess Kramer in Malibu, California, and in the folk dance institute at Roosevelt University in Chicago (to name a few venues). According to one source, her folk dance cycle inspired by the biblical Song of Songs emerged as one of the most popular and enduring contributions to the international folk dance repertoire in America. See *Viltis* 16 (October/November 1957): 14; *Viltis* 17 (March/April 1958): 25; *Viltis* 21, no. 1 (May 1962): 7; and Goodman and Schoenberg, 295. For an overview of some of the major Israeli folk dance figures, many of whom taught in the United States in this period, see Judith Brin Ingber, "Shorashim: The Roots of Israeli Folk Dance," in *Seeing Israeli and Jewish Dance*, ed. Judith Brin Ingber (Detroit: Wayne State University Press, 2011), 99–169.

28. Ben Zion Schreiber, "The Brandeis Camp Institute, An American Jewish Educational Institution," *The Reconstructionist* 15, no. 7 (May 13, 1949), quoted in Ingber, *Victory Dances*, 58–59.

29. Quoted in Ronald Kronish, "John Dewey's Influence on Jewish Education in America: The Gap Between Theory and Practice," *Studies in Jewish Education* 1 (1983): 188.

30. See, for example, "Is IZFA Zionist?" [Letter to the Editor], *The Student Zionist* (March 1949); "Discussion on IZFA's Future," *The Student Zionist* (May 1950); and Bernie Brown, "Uganda, 1952," *The Student Zionist* (Spring 1952): 30–33. Jewish Student Organizations Collection, AJHS.

31. For more on the diminishing fortunes of *halutziut* in America, see Arthur A. Goren, *The Politics and Public Culture of American Jews*, 165–85.

32. "The Future of the Zionist Youth Movement: A Symposium," *Furrows* 20, no. 3 (March/April 1964): 11.

33. Summary of presidential address, Report, Student Zionist Organization 13th Annual Convention, 1966, File 7, Box 49, RG I-61, AJHS.

34. Don Schiller, "Future of Young Judaea," *Furrows* 20, no. 3 (March/April 1964): 18.

35. "Wanted—A Broadening of Boger Chinuch," *Ohalenu* (n.d.), 20. According to the table of contents, the article was written in 1950 and reprinted in this issue. B'nei Akiva of North America, Nearprint Special Topics, American Jewish Archives (hereafter, AJA).

36. Chaim Gunner, "An Evaluation of the American Movement," in "Twenty-Five Years of Hashomer Hatzair: An Evaluation," 3, File 5, Box 1, Hashomer Hatzair Records (Mss 281), AJA. On the differences in ideology and approach of Habonim and Hashomer Hatzair, see Arthur Aryeh Goren, "Epilogue: On Living In Two Cultures," in *Divergent Cultures*, ed. Moore and Troen, 339. The essay is a personal reflection on his coming of age in Habonim in the immediate postwar years.

37. "Tochnit Kovshim" (training manual), 14, File 4, Box 2, Hashomer Hatzair Records, AJA.

38. Leonard Fein, "We Did Not Know That We Were Our Parents' Children," in *Builders and Dreamers: Habonim Labor Zionist Youth in North America*, ed. J. J. Goldberg and Elliot King (New York: Herzl Press, 1993), 144.

39. David Hajdu, *Positively 4ᵗʰ Street: The Lives and Times of Joan Baez, Bob Dylan, Mimi Baez Fariña and Richard Fariña* (New York: North Point Press, 2001), 117.

40. Daniel Elazar, "*Detroit, the Early 1950s*: 'Habonim Was Looked at as a Bit Wild,'" in *Builders and Dreamers*, ed. Goldberg and King, 173.

41. Mordecai Richler, "*Montreal, 1947*: 'We Danced the Hora in the Middle of the Street,'" in ibid., 127, 128.

42. Marion Magid, "*New York, the Early 1950s*: 'It Was Inefficient, Gentle, and Decent,'" in ibid., 167, 169.

43. Ibid., 168, 169.

44. Ibid., 169.

45. Elazar, "'Habonim Was Looked at as a Bit Wild,'" 173.

46. Barry Friedman, interview with author, July 20, 2005.

47. A short Purim play, "The Saga of Shushine Creek," composed by a Habonim member in 1953, included songs written to the tunes of an eclectic medley of American popular and folk songs, from "Red River Valley" to "Joe Hill," but also included the Israeli folk songs "Finjan" and "Artzah Alinu." Likewise, in the Purim issue of *Haboneh* in 1954, regular contributor Osher Epstein published a poem, "Purim on the Purple Sage," which retold the Purim story as a Western-style ballad.

Haboneh 17, no. 2 (November 1952): 20; *Haboneh* 18, no. 5 (March 1954); *Haboneh* 17, no. 5 (February/March 1953); *Haboneh* 18, no. 5 (March 1954). Box 9, Jewish Student Organizations Collection, AJHS.

48. In these years, it became standard practice for local chapters of the various Zionist youth movements to develop a *chug rikkud*, which would meet regularly to learn and practice, as did the other special interest groups in areas like dramatics and arts and crafts. The *chug rikkud* would receive instruction periodically from folk dance instructors within the movement, such as Young Judaea's Aryeh Cooper, or from Israeli emissaries such as Ayalah Goren, who was first sent to the United States in 1949 by the Jewish Agency for the express purpose of teaching Israeli folk dance to Zionist organizations and other Jewish and non-Jewish groups. Ayalah Goren, e-mail correspondence with author, January 17, 2008.

49. Ronnie Cohen, "The Neshef Is What We Remember Most," in *Builders and Dreamers*, ed. Goldberg and King, 199.

50. *Young Judaean* 47, no. 4 (January 1959): 20, Box 49, Jewish Student Organizations Collection, AJHS. In this issue, Club Golda Meir of Chattanooga and Club Ner Tamid of Waco both reported learning Israeli songs and dances.

51. One proponent of mixed Israeli folk dancing at the time cited a recent reaction in B'nei Akiva against mixed dancing, which suggests that the issue was far from resolved. "Wanted—A Broadening of Boger Chinuch," 21.

52. Clara Frieder, telephone conversation with author, August 18, 2005; and Barry Friedman, interview with author, July 20, 1995.

53. Camp Moshava brochure, no date. B'nei Akiva of North America, Nearprint Special Topics, AJA.

54. Barry Friedman, interview with author, July 20, 1995.

55. *Young Judaean* 42, no. 7 (April 1954); *Young Judaean* 39, no. 7 (April 1952); *Young Judaean* 41, no. 4 (January 1953); and *Young Judaean* 42, no. 7 (April 1954), Box 49, Jewish Student Organization Collection, AJHS.

56. There are many examples of these sorts of activities in the pages of *Haboneh*, the movement's periodical, including participation in a Jewish Tercentenary Program in Cleveland; in an Israel Independence Day celebration in Providence in 1954; in a community-wide Hanukkah festival in Vancouver in 1962; and in Baltimore's annual "All Nations Day" in 1963. See *Haboneh* 19, no. 1 (November 1954): 20, *Haboneh* 18. no. 7 (May/June 1954): 17, both in Box 9, Jewish Student Organizations Collection, AJHS; and *Haboneh* 26, no. 3 (Spring 1962): 16, *Haboneh* 28, no. 2 (December 1963), both in Box 10, Jewish Student Organizations Collection, AJHS.

57. "We 'Could Have Danced All Night,' " *Young Judaean* 52, no. 1 (November 1963): 20, Box 50, Jewish Student Organizations Collection, AJHS.

58. Program, Sixth Annual Israel Dance Festival, Archives of the Israeli Dance Institute (hereafter, IDI).

59. Irwin M. Schor, "Twelfth Annual Israel Folk Dance Festival," *Hora* 1, no. 3 (Spring 1963), unpaginated, IDI.

60. Yearly program festivals in the collection of the Israeli Dance Institute include information about the participating groups as well as providing an overview of the content of each program.

61. Frances Zynstein, "Reflections of the V'ida," *Furrows* 15, no. 4 (January 1960): 9–10, Box 10, Jewish Student Organizations Collection, AJHS.

62. Isabelle K. Goldstein, "Israel Folk Dance in Philadelphia," *Hora* 1, no. 1 (October 1962), unpaginated; and "Israel Folk Dance in Boston," *Hora* 1, no. 3 (Spring 1963), unpaginated, IDI.

63. See Emily Alice Katz, "Pen Pals, Pilgrims, and Pioneers: Reform Youth and Israel, 1948–1967," *American Jewish History*, 95, no. 3 (September 2009): 249–76.

64. Richard Kraus, *Folk Dancing: A Guide for Schools, Colleges, and Recreation Groups* (New York: Macmillan, 1962), 5–6.

65. V. F. Beliajus, "Folk Dance Toward Brotherhood," *Religious Education* 53, no. 1 (January/February 1958): 60.

66. "Pacific Folk Dance Camp (Stockton)," *Viltis* 21, no. 1 (May 1962): 19–20. And see Lisa Lekis, "Folk Dance Flourishes in California!" *Dance Magazine* 29 (January 1955), 41.

67. See, for example, "Pacific Lutheran University Folk Dancers," *Viltis* 19, no. 3 (September/October 1960): 19; "Norwalk, Darien to Note U.N. Week," *New York Times*, October 21, 1962, 26; and "Club Activity" section, *Viltis* 23, no. 6 (March/April 1965): 20.

68. Myers, "Israel Dances in America," *Recreation* XLVI-A, no. 3 (June 1953): 152.

69. Lisa Lekis, "Folk Dance Flourishes in California!" 41.

70. Patricia Mooney Melvin, "Building Muscles and Civics: Folk Dancing, Ethnic Diversity and the Playground Association of America," *American Studies* 24, no. 1 (Spring 1983): 93.

71. Quoted in ibid., 94.

72. Esther Brown, "New Vitality From Ancient Roots," *Dance Magazine* 28 (February 1954), 39, 40.

73. V. F. Beliajus, "The Ethnic Situation," *Viltis* 19 (January/February 1960): 4.

74. Lekis, "Folk Dance Flourishes in California!" 39.

75. For a contemporaneous account of this phenomenon, see Howard Taubman, "Cold War on the Cultural Front," *New York Times*, April 13, 1958, SM12. See also Hixson, *Parting the Curtain*; Cull, *The Cold War and the United States Information Agency*; Richard T. Arndt, *The First Resort of Kings: American Cultural Diplomacy in the Twentieth Century* (Dulles, VA: Potomac Books, 2005); and Saunders, *The Cultural Cold War*.

76. Ernest Sisto, "US Folk Dancers to Tour in Japan," *New York Times*, March 7, 1956, 35.

77. Editorial, *Journal of the International Folk Music Council* 8 (January 1956): 2.

78. Anthony Shay, *Choreographic Politics: State Folk Dance Companies, Representation, and Power* (Middletown, CT: Wesleyan University Press, 2002), 59. Shay explicitly uses the term *Golden Era* to describe the status of state-sponsored dance companies in the Cold War years (3).

79. Gila Melandoff Zalon, an important young dancer in the Israeli folk dance scene at the time, received lessons directly from Inbal: "They would teach us the

Yemenite movements, so we would really learn how to do it," she recalled. Gila Zalon, interview with author, July 20, 2005.

80. Winthrop Sargeant, "Musical Events [Yemenite Hoedown]," *New Yorker*, January 18, 1958, 92–93. For contemporaneous reviews of Inbal, see John Martin, "Dance: Vital Art," *New York Times*, January 12, 1958, X19; "Dancers of Israel," *Time*, January 20, 1958, 64; Walter Arlen, "Inbal Dance Troupe Fascinates at Ritz," *Los Angeles Times*, October 29, 1959, C8–9.

81. Rudolf Orthwine, "A Message for the New Year," *Dance Magazine* 32 (January 1958), 26.

82. Ibid.

83. Program, First Israeli Folk Dance Festival and Context, IDI. A suite of dances "from many lands," presented by various Zionist youth groups, does appear on the program of the twelfth annual festival, from 1963. These dances were listed as Russian, Arabic, Chassidic, Yemenite, and Israeli. An explanatory note appearing in the program ("Israeli folk dance is nurtured by many roots"), however, suggests that participants chose to include these dances to explicate the diverse sources of Israeli folk dance rather than to celebrate the folk traditions of other groups.

84. Viola Hegyi Swisher, "'In the Light of a Kindred Humanity,'" *Dance Magazine* 41 (March 1967), 49; and see Cathy Curtis, "Folk Dance Festival Taking Its Last Kicks," *Los Angeles Times*, January 4, 1989. Curtis gives 1947 as the date of the festival's founding.

85. Freehof, *Guide for Israeli-Jewish Folk Dancers*, 27.

86. Fred Berk, "A Dissenting View: About Folk Dance," *Dance Magazine* 31 (December 1957), 90.

87. Sherm Hantor, "The Old and New Meet in Dance," *The Minnesota Daily*, *Ivory Tower Edition*, Monday, April 15, 1957, 11. Clipping in Hillel Records, File: Israel-America Club programming, 1953–1961, Box D02 S15 CH, Upper Midwest Jewish Archives.

88. Myers, "Israel Dances in America," 152, 154.

89. "Pacific Lutheran University Folk Dancers," 19.

90. See, for example, Beata Mueller, "The Churches and the Creative Arts," *National Council Outlook* 4 (January 1954): 15, 22; John W. Simons, "The Church and the Arts," *Commonweal* 61 (November 5, 1954): 135–37; "The Heavies and the Heroes," *Christian Century* 75 (January 8, 1958): 38–39; "Great Arts Speak Language of Soul," *Christian Century* 75 (December 24, 1958): 1476; and Marvin P. Halverson, "If the Arts Are to Return," *Christian Century* 78 (December 20, 1961): 1525–28.

91. For more on the role of dance in American Christianity, see Margaret Fisk Taylor, "Creative Rhythmic Movement As a Religious Education Art," 47–51, and Elizabeth Crone Brown, "Developing the Creative Power Through Dance," 56–57, both in *Religious Education* 53, no. 1 (January/February 1958); and Ann Dirksen, "Introduction to Religious Dance," *Dance Magazine* 36 (March 1962), 14–17, 68.

92. Taylor, "Creative Rhythmic Movement As a Religious Education Art," 48.

93. Moshe Davis, "The Dance: What It Means to Me—A Religious Interpretation," *Dance Magazine* 31, no. 6 (June 1957), 22. Davis continued, "Under the impact of Western civilization, the individual personality is often imprisoned

by external forces. . . . This has occurred in religious life, too, in the area where personal expression should be supreme. Individualized chanting in prayer has been sublimated into uniform congregational singing and personalized movement has been inhibited by the demand of group decorum and 'solidity.' "

94. Miriam Teplitz, " 'To See Ourselves As Others See Us': The Experience of our National Program Chairman at a Church Family Encampment," *Women's League Outlook* 28, no. 2 (December 1957): 12, 14.

95. Ibid., 12.

96. Donald Duncan, "The Views of a Church," *Dance Magazine* 32 (September 1958), 67–68; and Kristi Dawn Brubaker, "Dance Festivals in the Church of Jesus Christ of Latter-day Saints" (MA thesis, UCLA, 2000).

97. Evelyn Cox, "USA Mormon Youth Tour Israel As Israeli Folk Dancers," *Young Judaean* 53, no. 1 (November 1964): 9–11, Box 50, Jewish Student Organization Collection, AJHS.

98. For more on Israel in Mormon theology and eschatology, see Greenberg, *The Holy Land in American Religious Thought, 1620–1948,* 227–58.

99. "Israel Folk Music and Dance In Clog-Time Tune Setting," *Viltis* 21, no. 1 (May 1962): 16–17.

100. Ibid., 16.

101. The Folk Dancer, based in Flushing, Queens, appointed Fred Berk, Katya Delakova, and Zafra Tatcher as musical supervisors; Manhattan-based Tikva Records was also supervised by Berk. Folkcraft, in Newark, New Jersey, produced records with the guidance of Dvora Lapson and Rivka Sturman, while the Israel Music Foundation, with offices in New York and Tel Aviv, was also supervised by Lapson. Folkways Records, a better-known specialty label, produced *Dances of the World's People,* with Ronnie and Stu Lipner, and *Israel Dances* (music by Oranim Zabar), with Edna Ashuah. See Freehof, *Guide for Israeli-Jewish Folk Dancers,* 24.

102. As Barbara Kirshenblatt-Gimblett has pointed out, Jews were central to the folk music scene in America in the postwar years, as "composers, performers, agents, and managers." The Elektra and Folkways labels were helmed by American Jews: Jac Holzman and Leonard Ripley ran the former company, while Moses Asch founded the latter. Barbara Kirshenblatt-Gimblett, "Sounds of Sensibility," *Judaism* 47, no. 1 (Winter 1998): 66.

103. Oranim Zabar's albums for Elektra include *Shalom* (1958), *On the Road to Elath* (1958), *Hora! Songs and Dances of Israel* (1960), and *A Town Hall Concert* (1961); other Israeli music records include *A Concert with Hillel and Aviva* (1959), *Sabra, The Young Heart of Israel* (Ron and Nama, 1960); *The Dudaim* (1961), and *Sing Along In Hebrew* (Maccabee Singers, 1962). Elektra's catalogue from these years is available online: http://www.bsnpubs.com/elektra/. Accessed January 17, 2014.

104. Theodore Bikel, *Theo: The Autobiography of Theodore Bikel* (New York: HarperCollins, 1994), 154. Kirshenblatt-Gimblett writes that Bikel (along with concert performer Martha Schlamme) helped delineate "a place for Jewish music within an international folk music scene." His work with Geula Gill and his own performances and recordings of Israeli folk music no doubt played an important role in securing a broad audience for Israeli folk music in America in the 1950s and 1960s. Kirshenblatt-Gimblett, "Sounds of Sensibility," 68.

105. Promotional letter from Eris Productions, October 1, 1958, File: Folk Song—General, 1959–1960, Box 7, Events, Education Department, Archive of 92nd St. Y. The Bureau represented more than sixty Israeli performing artists in America, including "folk and interpretive dancers, opera and folk singers, concert pianists, violinists, guitarists, accordionists, pantomime-comedians, actors, [and] narrators."

106. Yarkoni, "one of the most prominent Israeli popular artists in the Jewish Diaspora," had first won fame in Israel during the War of Independence. She moved to the United States in the 1950s to establish a career as a pop artist, recording several albums for CBS/Columbia and also performing regularly in nightclubs and cafes. See Motti Regev and Edwin Seroussi, *Popular Music and National Culture in Israel* (Berkeley: University of California Press, 2004), 83–85.

107. "Some of the Performances and Achievements of Geula Gill Trio," undated publicity material, Events, Education Department, Archives of the 92nd St. Y.

108. "Music and Dance of Israel," *Rhapsody*, Canadian Broadcasting Corporation, July 5, 1959, *MGZIA 4-3613, Dance Collection of New York Public Library for the Performing Arts.

109. According to Gila (Melandoff) Zalon, Carrigan had been a member of Berk's Merry-Go-Round dancers as well, a dance troupe for children that drew heavily upon the Israeli folk dance repertoire. Gila Zalon, interview with author, July 20, 2005.

110. Jerry Herman with Marilyn Stasio, *Showtune* (New York: Donald I. Fine Books, 1996), 37.

111. Leo Lurman, "At the Theatre," *Dance Magazine* 35, no. 11 (November 1961), 28.

112. *Saturday Review of Literature* 44 (November 4, 1961), 32; *Time*, October 20, 1961, 64; Howard Taubman, "Theatre: All 'Milk and Honey' at the Martin Beck," *New York Times*, October 11, 1961, 52.

113. Quoted in Lurman, "At the Theatre," 29.

114. Herman, *Showtune*, 45, 55.

115. John S. Wilson, "In Search of a Musical," *New York Times*, January 28, 1962, 85; Herman, *Showtune*, 40.

116. Wilson, "In Search of a Musical," 85.

117. Minutes of Mercaz Habonim, October 30, 1956, File 750, Box 67, Records of the Labor Zionist Organization of America, Archives of the YIVO Institute for Jewish Research.

118. Some heroes of the folk scene included Israeli folk songs in their repertoires in these years. The Weavers, for example, recorded an English-language version of Issachar Miron's "Tzena, Tzena," which rose to second place on the Billboard charts in 1950. See Ari Y. Kelman, "Hear Israel," *Tablet Magazine*, January 7, 2011, http://www.tabletmag.com/jewish-arts-and-culture/music/55172/hear-israel. Accessed January 17, 2014.

CHAPTER FOUR. A CONSUMING PASSION

1. The Book-of-the-Month Club, founded in 1926 by Harry Scherman, an advertising executive and former journalist for the *American Hebrew*, became "an

enduring feature of the cultural landscape and the progenitor of dozens more book clubs and other 'of-the-month' marketing devices," as Joan Shelley Rubin has written. Rubin, *The Making of Middlebrow Culture* (Chapel Hill: The University of North Carolina Press, 1992), 96. And see Janice A. Radway, *A Feeling for Books: The Book-of-the-Month Club, Literary Taste, and Middle-Class Desire* (Chapel Hill: The University of North Carolina Press, 1997).

2. Advertisement for Israel Gift of the Month Club, *Hadassah Magazine* 47, no. 3 (November 1965): 11.

3. Ibid.

4. As Jack Wertheimer has noted, "At no time since Israel's establishment has a majority of Jews ever been to the Jewish state." Jack Wertheimer, "American Jews and Israel: A Sixty-Year Retrospective," 37.

5. Andrew R. Heinze, *Adapting to Abundance: Jewish Immigrants, Mass Consumption, and the Search for American Identity* (New York: Columbia University Press, 1990); Jenna Weissman Joselit, *The Wonders of America: Reinventing Jewish Culture, 1880–1950* (New York: Hill and Wang, 1994); Barbara Kirshenblatt-Gimblett, "Kitchen Judaism," in *Getting Comfortable in New York: The American-Jewish Home, 1880–1950*, ed. Susan L. Braunstein and Jenna Weissman Joselit (New York: The Jewish Museum, 1990), 76–105. For a contemporaneous critique of the increasing centrality of consumption in Jewish religious life, see Jonathan D. Sarna, *People Walk on their Heads: Moses Weinberger's Jews and Judaism in New York* (New York: Holmes and Meir, 1991).

6. See, for example, Jeffrey Shandler and Beth S. Wenger, " 'The Site of Paradise': The Holy Land in American Jewish Imagination," in *Encounters With the "Holy Land": Place, Past and Future in American Jewish Culture*, ed. Jeffrey Shandler and Beth S. Wenger (Hanover and London: The University Press of New England, 1997), 11–40.

7. Lizabeth Cohen, *A Consumers' Republic: The Politics of Mass Consumption in Postwar America* (New York: Vintage Books, 2003), 119.

8. Ibid., 126–27.

9. See Matthew Frye Jacobson, *Barbarian Virtues: The United States Encounters Foreign Peoples at Home and Abroad, 1876–1917* (New York: Hill and Wang, 2000).

10. According to the *Jerusalem Post*, "both the popular appeal of Israel exhibitions . . . and their commercial achievements [had] greatly increased," by the late 1950s, while dropping costs for vendors at the fairs had made it possible "to expand activity abroad despite relatively modest budget allocations." "Israel Fairs Are Carefully Planned," *Jerusalem Post*, May 6, 1958, 5. See also "Israel Participating in Eight International Fairs," *Israel Economic Bulletin* 6, no. 9–10 (August 1954): 13; "Israel Exhibits at World Trade Fair," *American-Israel Economic Horizons* 12. no. 7 (July 1960): 11.

11. On the structure of the Israeli economy at this time, see Michael Wolffsohn, *Israel: Polity, Society, and Economy, 1882–1986: An Introductory Handbook*, trans. Douglas Bokovoy (Atlantic Highlands, NJ: Humanities, 1987), 205–71, and Nachum T. Gross, "The Economic Regime during Israel's First Decade," in *Israel: The First Decade of Independence*, ed. S. Ilan Troen and Noah Lucas (Albany: State University of New York Press, 1995), 231–41.

12. For an overview of the Israeli government's early strategies in securing aid from the United States, and American government's response, see Hahn, *Caught in the Middle East*, 79–82. In regard to American Jewish philanthropic contributions to Israel at the time, see Menahem Kaufman, "Envisaging Israel: the Case of the United Jewish Appeal," in *Envisioning Israel: The Changing Ideals and Images of North American Jews*, ed. Allon Gal (Detroit: Wayne State University Press, 1996), 219–27, and Ernest Stock, "Philanthropy and Politics: Modes of Interaction between Israel and the Diaspora," in *Israel: The First Decade of Independence*, ed. Troen and Lucas, 699–711. Welfare funds contributed to the United Jewish Appeal (the majority of which were disbursed to the United Israel Appeal) reached a peak of $150 million during the War of Independence. In the next several years, lacking a similarly dramatic rallying point, American Jews contributed diminishing funds to the UJA (and thus to Israel). The Appeal hit its low point—$60 million—in 1955. Kaufman, "Envisaging Israel," 224.

13. See Deborah Dash Moore, "Bonding Images: Miami Jews and the Campaign for Israel Bonds," in *Envisioning Israel*, ed. Allon Gal, 254–67.

14. For an overview of the organization's membership numbers and activities in the postwar period, see Deborah Dash Moore, "Hadassah," *Jewish Women in America: An Historical Encyclopedia*, eds. Paula E. Hyman and Deborah Dash Moore (New York: Routledge, 1997), 576–77 and 579–81. For a more detailed analysis of Hadassah's success in replacing lost members in this period, see Rebecca Boim Wolf, " 'It's Good Americanism to Join Hadassah': Selling Hadassah in the Postwar Era," in *A Jewish Feminine Mystique?*, ed. Diner, Kohn, and Kranson, 65–67. See also *American Jewish Women and the Zionist Enterprise*, ed. Shulamit Reinharz and Mark A. Raider (Waltham: Brandeis University Press, 2005).

15. Shandler and Wenger, " 'The Site of Paradise': The Holy Land in American Jewish Imagination," 34.

16. See, for example, Wolffsohn, *Israel: Polity, Society, and Economy*, 259–61, and Nadav Halevi, "Perspectives on the Balance of Payments," in *The Israeli Economy: Maturing Through Crises*, ed. Yoram Ben-Porath (Cambridge: Harvard University Press, 1986), 249–51.

17. See Jenna Weissman Joselit, "Bezalel Comes to Town: American Jews and Art," *Jewish Studies Quarterly* 11, no. 4 (2004): 354–65.

18. Ads for these and other distributors appear frequently in American Jewish publications in this period.

19. "What the Buyers Say . . ." *Israel Economic Horizons* 5, no. 6–7 (June/July 1953): 5.

20. Ibid.

21. "Linen Products to Be Sold Here," *Israel Economic Horizons* 6, no. 3 (March 1954): 5.

22. "Handwoven Rugs by New Israelis To Be Sold In Fifth Avenue Store," *Israel Economic Horizons* 6, no. 12 (December 1954): 8.

23. The photograph accompanies the article, "Raincoat Sales Reach Large Volume in First Year," *Israel Economic Horizons* 4, no. 5 (May 1952): 6.

24. "Boston Store Features Israel," *Israel Economic Horizons* 3, no. 4 (April 1951): back page.

25. Ibid.

26. "Demand for Israel Handicrafts Increases Steadily Throughout U.S.," *Israel Economic Horizons* 6 (October 1954): 6; "1400 Stores Throughout U.S. Sell Novel Made-in-Israel Gift Items," *Israel Economic Horizons* 6 (March 1954): 5; Israel Wolsky, "Giftware, Food Imports Rise," *American-Israel Economic Horizons* 14, no. 1 (January 1962): 11.

27. "Israel Store Opens in Detroit," *Israel Economic Horizons* 4, no. 3 (March 1952): 6; "First All-Israel Store in New York," *American-Israel Economic Horizons* 12, no. 10 (October 1960): 8.

28. For overviews of this phenomenon, see Sarna, *American Judaism*, 282–93; Leon Jick, "The Reform Synagogue," 102–104, and Jack Wertheimer, "The Conservative Synagogue," 123–32, both in *The American Synagogue: A Sanctuary Transformed*, ed. Jack Wertheimer (Hanover and London: Brandeis University Press and the University Press of New England, 1987); Michael A. Meyer, *Response to Modernity: A History of the Reform Movement in Judaism* (Detroit: Wayne State University Press, 1988), 353–84.

29. Eugene J. Lipman and Myron E. Schoen, eds., *The American Synagogue: A Progress Report; Proceedings, Second National Conference and Exhibit on Synagogue Architecture*, (New York: UAHC, 1958). See also Joellyn Wallen Zollman, "Shopping for a Future: A History of the American Synagogue Gift Shop" (PhD diss., Brandeis University, 2002), 66–68.

30. "Modern Drama, Art, Music, Dance Expressing Faith at San Francisco Biennial," *American Judaism* 15, no. 2 (Winter 1965–66): 12–14.

31. For more on the Book and Art Service, see Zollman, "Shopping for a Future," 40–41; on Zamir, see "Seminary Minstrels Bring Israel to Synagogues," *United Synagogue Review* 11, no. 2 (Spring 1958): 16–17, and Sid Konikoff, "Alienated? Disoriented?" *Women's League Outlook* 37, no. 4 (Summer 1967): 8, 14; on the repertory theater, see "Spotlight on Jewish Drama," *United Synagogue Review* 15, no. 4 (Winter 1963): 32.

32. Reports of such programs appear in issues of *United Synagogue Review* and *American Judaism*, the lay magazines for the Conservative and Reform movements, respectively.

33. "Modern Drama, Art Music, Dance Expressing Faith at San Francisco Biennial," 13.

34. Myron E. Schoen, "We Are Fast Catching Up," *American Judaism* 15, no. 1 (Fall 1965): 31.

35. "Spotlight on Jewish Drama," 32; Israel M. Goldman, "Art and the Synagogue," *United Synagogue Review* 11, no. 3 (Autumn 1958): 14.

36. To this end, for example, the Reform movement instituted a Joint Committee on Ceremonies in 1936. During the interwar period, both the Reform movement's National Federation of Temple Sisterhoods and the Women's League for Conservative Judaism developed special programs and exhibitions intended to encourage the purchase and use of modern, aesthetically pleasing Jewish ceremonial objects in the home. See Zollman, "Shopping for a Future," 33–38, and Joselit, *The Wonders of America*, 154–69.

37. Shonie B. Levi and Sylvia R. Kaplan, *Across the Threshold: A Guide for the Jewish Homemaker* (New York: Farrar, Straus and Cudahy and the National Women's League of the United Synagogue of America, 1959), 8.

38. "Sisterhood Topics," *American Judaism* 11, no. 2 (Winter 1961): 44.

39. Jenna Weissman Joselit, "The Jewish Home Beautiful," in *The American Jewish Experience*, ed. Jonathan D. Sarna, 2nd ed. (New York and London: Holmes and Meier, 1997), 236–44; see also Barbara Kirshenblatt-Gimblett, "Kitchen Judaism."

40. Betty D. Greenberg and Althea O. Silverman, *The Jewish Home Beautiful* (New York: The Women's League of the United Synagogue of America, 1950 [1941]), 13.

41. Ibid., 8.

42. National Women's League of the United Synagogue of America, *Proceedings of the Biennial Convention, 1950–1952*, 179.

43. Nurith Kenaan-Kedar, "The Metal Arts and Crafts Industry in the First Two Decades of Israel's Independence," in *Modern Creations from an Ancient Land: Metal Craft and Design in the First Two Decades of Israel's Independence* (in Hebrew and English) (Tel Aviv: Eretz Israel Museum and Jerusalem: Yad Itzhak Ben-Zvi, 2006), vii–xv.

44. See, for example, Stephanie Rains, "Celtic Kitsch: Irish-America and Irish Material Culture," *Circa Art Magazine* 107 (Spring 2004): 52–57; Marilyn Halter, *Shopping for Identity: The Marketing of Ethnicity* (New York: Schocken Books, 2000); Paul R. Mullins, *Race and Affluence: An Archaeology of African America and Consumer Culture* (New York: Kluwer Academic/Plenum Publishers: 1999); and Robert Orsi, *The Madonna of 115th Street: Faith and Community in Italian Harlem* (New Haven: Yale University Press, 1985).

45. David Morgan, *Visual Piety: A History and Theory of Popular Religious Images* (Berkeley: University of California Press, 1998), 152–80.

46. Colleen McDannell, *Material Christianity: Religion and Popular Culture in America* (New Haven and London: Yale University Press, 1995), 4.

47. Vanessa L. Ochs, *Inventing Jewish Ritual* (Philadelphia: The Jewish Publication Society, 2007), 103.

48. The National Women's League established a separate Ceremonial and Gift Shop division in 1951; by 1953, the department counted 425 synagogue gift shops among its affiliates. National Women's League, *Proceedings of the Biennial Convention*, 175.

49. Ibid., 65.

50. Zollman, "Shopping for a Future," 183, 174, 187.

51. Ibid., 189–90.

52. Quoted in ibid., 111.

53. Forty-three percent of Sklare and Greenblum's respondents claimed to have Israeli objects at home, while only 39 percent claimed to have Shabbat candlesticks—essential ritual objects for observant Jews. Asked to remember their childhood homes, only 18 percent of respondents recalled having objects from the Holy Land. The authors also noted that Israeli objects were usually not acquired in Israel itself, but were likely to have been purchased at synagogue gifts shops, Jewish bookstores, and department stores. Marshall Sklare and Joseph Greenblum, *Jewish Identity on the Suburban Frontier: A Study of Group Survival in the Open Society* (New York: Basic Books, 1967), 229.

54. Quoted in Zollman, "Shopping for a Future," 190.

55. Esther L. Fink, "Suggestions for a Gift Shop," *Women's League Outlook* 22, no. 1 (September 1951): 24.

56. Transcript of the Seventeenth Biennial Assembly (1948), p. 213, File: 2.213, Box 4, Women of Reform Judaism Records (MSS 73), AJA.

57. Ibid., 219.

58. This view of the promotion and consumption of Israeli goods as an altruistic economic intervention—not simply as an act of charity, but as a bid to help grow another nation's economy—presents an intriguing counterpoint to the Christian domestic practices described by Morgan and McDannell, which do not explicitly connect the domestic sphere with the global economic marketplace or the professionalized philanthropic sector.

59. Miriam Fierst and Lili Eller, "Who Is She?: An Appraisal of the Composite Hadassah Member," *Hadassah Newsletter* 39 no. 2 (October 1958): 9.

60. Etta Rosensohn, president of Hadassah in 1952–53, used the term *human rehabilitation* in reference to the organization's Youth Aliyah project; the concept applies equally well to Hadassah's efforts in the crafts industry and vocational education, described below. See Moore, "Hadassah," 577. See also Erica B. Simmons, *Hadassah and the Zionist Project* (Lanham, MD: Rowman and Littlefield, 2006).

61. "Gifts from Israel for Americans," *Hadassah Newsletter* 29 no. 1 (September 1948): 8.

62. Eliezer Whartman, "Made In Israel: Israel Exports to U.S. Increasing,". *Hadassah Newsletter* 35, no. 3 (November 1954): 5.

63. Molly Lyons Bar-David, "Israel Crafts: A Rich Inheritance," *Hadassah Newsletter* 33, no. 1 (September 1952): 6, 14.

64. Mordecai Ardon-Bronstein, "Art: It's Function in Israel," *Hadassah Newsletter* 33, no. 5 (January 1953): 13.

65. Sylvia Satten Banin, "Israel Makes It America Buys It," *Hadassah Newsletter* 38, no. 2 (October 1957): 4.

66. Jennie C. Lowenthal, letter to the editor, *Hadassah Newsletter* 39, no. 7 (March 1959): 13.

67. Mrs. Alexander [Julia] Dushkin, "Vocational Guidance," seminar speech, February 13, 1947, File: Mrs. Dushkin Correspondence re: Brandeis Vocational Center, 1947–1948, Box 6, Hadassah Vocational Education Records (RG 6A), Hadassah Archives.

68. Minutes of the Youth Aliyah and Palestine Youth Services Committee Meeting, March 1, 1949, File: Minutes—Palestine Youth Services Committee, Box 4, Hadassah Vocational Education Records, Hadassah Archives. Apparently, the first fashion show to appear at a Hadassah national convention was actually comprised of clothing designed by professional Israeli fashion designers; after that, the annual convention's fashion show showcased the work of students at the Seligsberg School. See Shirli Brautbar, *From Fashion to Politics: Hadassah and Jewish American Women in the Post World War II Era* (Boston: Academic Studies Press, 2012), 94.

69. "So—You're Going to Have a Hadassah Fashion Show!" December 23, 1949, p. 1, File: Correspondence re: Hadassah Institute of Fashion and Design, Box 6, Hadassah Vocational Education Records, Hadassah Archives.

70. Ibid., 2.

71. Report by Helen Kittner, File: Reports—Financial, Histories—Five and Ten Year Chronologies 1946–1958, Box 2, Hadassah Vocational Education Records, Hadassah Archives.

72. "For the Fashion Show Commentary," 3, included in packet "So—You're Going to Have a Hadassah Fashion Show!" File: Correspondence re: Hadassah Institute of Fashion and Design, Box 6, Hadassah Vocational Education Records, Hadassah Archives.

73. Ibid., 2.

74. Ibid., 3.

75. Ibid.

76. *Vanity Fair* Program/Hadassah Fashion Show, September 10, 1951, File: Fashion and Design Institute Fashion Show 1951, Events, Box 1, Hadassah Israel Education Services, RG 18, Hadassah Archives.

77. Ibid., 4.

78. Brautbar, *From Fashion to Politics*, 97.

79. Letter from Selma Kalman to Mrs. Neumann, July 7, 1950; letter from Miriam Freund to Helen Kittner, July 13, 1950; and letter from Miriam Freund to Julia Dushkin, August 31, 1950, all in File: Correspondence re: Hadassah Institute of Fashion and Design, 1949–1950, Box 6, Hadassah Vocational Education Records (RG 6A), Hadassah Archives.

80. File: Fashion and Design Institute Fashion Shows, 1952–1955, Box 1, Hadassah Israel Education Services, RG18, Hadassah Archives.

81. Brautbar also makes note of this photograph in her chapter on Hadassah, fashion shows, and beauty culture. Brautbar, *From Fashion to Politics*, 98.

82. Zollman, "Shopping for a Future," 199.

83. For a discussion of tropes about Jewish women in American popular and literary culture, see Harley Erdman, *Staging the Jew: The Performance of an American Ethnicity, 1860–1920* (New Brunswick: Rutgers University Press, 1997), 40–60, and Louis Harap, *The Image of the Jew in American Literature: From Early Republic to Mass Immigration* (Philadelphia: The Jewish Publication Society of America, 1974), 147–88; 194–99; 334–41. Ann Pelligrini has touched upon the fascination with Jewish women's sexuality in fin-de-siècle Europe in "Whiteface Performances: Race, Gender, and Jewish Bodies," in *Jews and other Differences: The New Jewish Cultural Studies*, ed. Jonathan Boyarin and Daniel Boyarin (Minneapolis: University of Minnesota Press, 1997), 108–49.

84. See especially Riv-Ellen Prell, *Fighting to Become Americans: Jews, Gender, and the Anxiety of Assimilation* (Boston: Beacon Press, 1999), 21–57, for a discussion of communal anxiety in the early twentieth century regarding the immigrant Jewish "ghetto girl" as an object of display.

85. See Burke O. Long, *Imagining the Holy Land: Maps, Models, and Fantasy Travels* (Bloomington: Indiana University Press, 2002), 16–28; and Mark C. Carnes, *Secret Ritual and Manhood in Victorian America* (New Haven and London: Yale University Press, 1989), 17–36.

86. Letter from Miriam Freund to Julia Dushkin, August 31, 1950, File: Correspondence re: Hadassah Institute of Fashion and Design, Box 6, Hadassah Vocational Education Records, Hadassah Archives.

87. "Vocational Education Trains in New Skills," Annual Report (1951), 35, File: 1A: Seligsberg School, Box 9, Hadassah Israel Education Services Reports 1950–1974 (RG 6B), Hadassah Archives.

88. Vocational Education Report, Mid-Winter Conference of the National Board of Hadassah, January 20–23, 1952, File: Reports: Financial, Histories 1946–

1958, Box 2, Hadassah Vocational Education Records, Hadassah Archives. As Miriam Freund wrote in 1950, "We want the Fashion Show to go on being what is has been . . . a potent instrument not only for the promotion of vocational education, but also for public relations." Letter from Miriam Freund to regional presidents, July 17, 1950, File: Correspondence re: Hadassah Institute of Fashion and Design 1949–1950, Box 1, Hadassah Vocational Education Records, Hadassah Archives.

89. Ida Boneparth, "Israel Fashions: Dollar Earners," *Hadassah Newsletter* 33, no. 1 (September 1952): 7. While the Women's Division of the Israel Bond Drive began hosting its own annual fashion show in 1955, it was not until 1967 that the show limited itself to the displaying of Israeli fashion alone. Rather, the Israel Bond fashion shows, hosted by local department stores around the country, displayed clothing from countries with friendly ties to Israel. Miriam Fineman, founder of the event and national director of the women's division, convinced some of the most important names in the fashion industry to contribute samples to the show, free of charge, using Israeli textiles as their basis. Helen Rossi, "Whither the Waistline? Unique Israeli Fashions Penetrate World Markets," *Hadassah Newsletter* 39, no. 10 (June 1959): 6; Marylin Bender, "Touring Fashion Show Aids Israel Bond Drive," *New York Times*, May 2, 1963, 58; Ruth Gruber Michaels, "Israel Fashions in U.S.A.," *Hadassah Magazine* 48, no. 2 (October 1966): 28.

90. Brautbar, *From Fashion to Politics*, 96.

91. Dorothy Rossyn, "Convention Report," *Hadassah Newsletter* 39, no. 3 (November 1958): 9, 14.

92. Michaels, "Israeli Fashions in U.S.A.," 8.

93. Untitled report on the Institute of Fashion and Design, File: Fashion and Design Institute Fashion Show, 1951, Box 1, Hadassah Israel Education Services, RG 18, Hadassah Archives.

94. Wolf, "'It's Good Americanism to Join Hadassah,'" 73.

95. Miriam Fierst and Lili Eller, "Who Is She?: An Appraisal of the Composite Hadassah Member," *Hadassah Newsletter* 39, no. 2 (October 1958), 9.

96. Wolf, "'It's Good Americanism to Join Hadassah,'" 72.

97. "Form American Israel Chamber of Commerce to Promote Trade," *Israel Economic Horizons* 5 no. 6–7 (June/July 1953): 6.

98. "Israel: Challenge and Opportunities," opening address to the Third Conference of Bi-National Chambers of Commerce with Israel, published in *American-Israel Economic Horizons* 14, no. 6–7 (June/July 1962): 6–7.

99. "Israel Strengthens Ties with New Nations," *American-Israel Economic Horizons* 11, no. 8–9 (August/September 1959): back page.

100. Rebecca L. Stein, "'First Contact' and Other Israeli Fictions: Tourism, Globalization, and the Middle East Peace Process," in *Palestine, Israel, and the Politics of Popular Culture*, ed. Rebecca L. Stein and Ted Swedenburg (Durham and London: Duke University Press, 2005), 283, footnote 15. The boycott was intended to "weaken Israel's economy and armed forces by limiting her access to foreign markets, sources of arms and supplies, and foreign capital and technical know-how," according to an article on the boycott in the *New York Times*. According to the commissioner-general of the boycott, by 1966, the Arab Boycott Committee had taken action against roughly nine thousand companies, of which nearly 90 percent

ultimately complied with the terms of the boycott. Hedrick Smith, "Arab Boycott Challenging Major U.S. Corporations," *New York Times,* October 17, 1966, 1, 16.

101. "A Chamber Achievement: Start Legislation to Outlaw Arab Boycott," *American-Israel Economic Horizons* 16, no. 10 (October 1964): 3.

102. "Commerce Department Publishes Anti-Boycott Regulations," *American-Israel Economic Horizons* 17, no. 10 (October 1965): 3–4.

103. Harold S. Caplin, "American-Israel Pavilion—Cooperation for an Unusual Project," speech at American-Israeli Chamber of Commerce and Industry luncheon, April 17, 1964, File PO.3: Israel-Brochures, Box 275, New York World's Fair 1965–1965 Corporation Records, 1959–1971, New York Public Library (hereafter NYPL).

104. From comments by Nathan Straus III, "American-Israel World's Fair Corporation," 6, File PO.3: Israel-Brochures, Box 275, New York World's Fair 1965–1965 Corporation Records, 1959–1971, NYPL.

105. "Dedication Ceremony at the New York World's Fair 1964–1965 American-Israel Pavilion, October 14, 1963," 6, File PO.3: Israel-Brochures, Box 275, New York World's Fair 1965–1965 Corporation Records, 1959–1971, NYPL.

106. See Frank J. Murphy, ed., *World's Fair Merchandise Sale Catalog* (New York: George E. Porcell Enterprises, 1965), unpaginated, 1964/1965 World's Fair Collection, Long Island Division, Queens Borough Public Library.

107. "Pavilion at World's Fair Boosts Israeli Exports," *American-Israel Economic Horizons* 16, no. 10 (October 1964): 7.

108. "1959—Record Year for Israeli Exports," *American-Israel Economic Horizons* 12, no. 3 (March 1960), 21.

109. Straus, " 'Aid *and* Trade' Concept Spreading," published excerpt of address by Nathan Straus III, *American-Israel Economic Horizons* 14, no. 5 (May 1962): 5.

110. It is worth noting that the American-Israel Pavilion at the New York World's Fair 1964–65 became embroiled in a controversy about free speech and Middle East politics during the course of the exhibition's run. Officials of the America-Israel World's Fair Corporation demanded that the Jordan Pavilion, sponsored by the Jordanian government, remove a mural depicting the plight of Palestinian refugees and indicting Israel for sowing discord in the region. (They argued that the mural slandered another nation and violated the spirit of the Fair.) This began a prolonged and unresolved public battle about the issue over the next two years among World's Fair bureaucrats, local and national politicians, the American-Israel World's Fair Corporation and other American Jewish organizations, Jordanian officials, and Arab Americans and American Jews who visited the fair or followed the controversy in the press. For a full account of the drama, see Emily Alice Katz, "It's the Real World After All: The American-Israel Pavilion–Jordan Pavilion Controversy at the New York World's Fair, 1964–1965," *American Jewish History* 91, no. 1 (March 2003): 129–55.

111. Ruth Glazer, "The Jewish Object: A Shopper's Report," *Commentary* 12, no. 1 (July 1951): 65.

112. Ibid., 66.

113. Sarah C. Schack, "Every Day in Every Way . . ." *Midstream* 3, no. 2 (Spring 1957): 106.

114. Ibid.

115. Ibid., 108.

116. Ibid., 110.

117. Ibid.

118. "Art Goes to the Synagogue," *American Judaism* 14, no. 3 (Spring 1965): 21.

119. Samuel Heilman, "Jews and Judaica: Who Owns and Buys What?" in *Persistence and Flexibility: Anthropological Perspectives on the American Jewish Experience*, ed. Walter P. Zenner (Albany: State University of New York Press, 1988), 273.

120. Colleen McDannell, "Interpreting Things: Material Culture Studies and American Religion," *Religion* 21, no. 4 (1991), 382.

CHAPTER FIVE. CULTURAL EMISSARIES AND THE CULTURE EXPLOSION

1. "A Cultural Explosion," editorial, *Life*, October 18, 1954, 38.

2. See, for example, C. J. McNaspy, "Culture Explosion," *America*, December 3, 1960, 340–42; "Cultural Centers Are Springing Up in Cities Big and Small," *New York Times*, July 29, 1962, 177; "Bigger than Baseball," *Musical America* 83 (March 1963): 7; "Midwest Culture Boom," *New York Times*, May 7, 1963, 39; Harold C. Schonberg, "Speaking Out [The National 'Culture Explosion' is Phony]," *The Saturday Evening Post*, July 13, 1963, 10, 14; and for a satirical take on the collecting of "culture boom" data, see Roger Angell, "The NCMSB Report," *The New Yorker*, February 20, 1965, 47–48, 50, 53.

3. "This Culture Boom: How Real Is It?" *Changing Times* 19, no. 10 (October 1965): 37.

4. Toffler, *The Culture Consumers*, 19.

5. Ibid., 23.

6. For more on these particular cultural practices, see Richard Brilliant, ed., *Facing the New World: Jewish Portraits in Colonial and Federal America* (New York: Prestel, 1997); and Heinze, *Adapting to Abundance*, 133–44.

7. Radway, *A Feeling for Books*, 161.

8. Toffler, *The Culture Consumers*, 34–35.

9. See chapter 1 for a discussion of this phenomenon.

10. Brochure about the America-Israel Cultural Foundation and the America-Israel Culture House, February 1966. File: Culture House Sale of Building Documents, institutional archives of the America-Israel Cultural Foundation, New York (hereafter AICF).

11. For contemporaneous accounts of Habimah's encounter with America, see Murray Shumach, "Habimah—Without Guns," *New York Times*, April 25, 1948, X1; Alexander Ramati, "Theatre in Israel: Foreign Help Sought in Efforts to Aid Development of Modern Approach," *New York Times*, October 5, 1952, X3; "Habimah Company Arrives for 7-Week Season Here," *New York Times*, January 28, 1964, 25. Contemporaneous coverage of Inbal's American appearances include John Martin, "Dance: Vital Art," *New York Times*, January 12, 1958, X19; Winthrop Sargeant, "Musical Events [Yemenite Hoedown]," *New Yorker*, January 18, 1958,

92–93; "Dancers of Israel," *Time*, January 20, 1958, 64; Walter Arlen, "Inbal Dance Troupe Fascinates at Ritz," *Los Angeles Times*, October 29, 1959, C8–9.

12. Wall, *Inventing the "American Way,"* 244.

13. Ibid., 242, 244. It is important to note that American Jews, as a group, are entirely absent from Wendy Wall's account of the United States' public diplomacy efforts abroad. Wall describes how the American government undertook an immense public diplomacy operation (exemplified by the Letters from America campaign) in the early postwar period to win grassroots allies in contemporary Europe, recruiting the masses—especially those with ancestral ties to the Old World—to serve as everyday ambassadors of American democracy. The absence of Jews from the story is, I believe, not an oversight on Wall's part, but an indication of how little American Jews, with few living relatives in postwar Europe, could theoretically or practically contribute to this campaign as a postimmigrant group.

14. Hixson, *Parting the Curtain*, xiv; and see also Cull, *The Cold War and the United States Information Agency*.

15. Hixson, *Parting the Curtain*, xii.

16. Memorandum from Leon L. Gildesgame to members of the Executive Committee of the AICF, November 2, 1964, 4, File: Leon Gildesgame Correspondence, 1964–1968, AICF.

17. Letter from Itzhak Norman to Alfred Barr, March 22, 1949, William Seitz correspondence, 1964, Israeli art scrapbook (vol. 2), Library of the Musuem of Modern Art [hereafter, Seitz correspondence 1964, MoMA Library]; letter from Monroe Wheeler to Itzhak Norman, May 5, 1949, Seitz correspondence 1964, MoMA Library.

18. "American Support for Constructive Activities in Palestine: The Existing Situation," (April 8, 1939), File: Incorporation Documents, 1939–1974, AICF.

19. "Prospectus for Procurement of $1,000,000 Loan for Four Years Submitted by the American Fund for Israel Institutions," 6, 14, File: Miscellaneous 1950s, AICF.

20. Ibid., 7.

21. Ibid., 15–17.

22. Ibid., 15.

23. Ibid.

24. Benny Morris, *Righteous Victims: A History of the Zionist-Arab Conflict, 1881–2001* (New York: Vintage, 2001), 178.

25. Frank W. Buxton, "Cultural Lend-Lease," *Israel Life and Letters* 7, no. 5 (May 1951): 15.

26. Ibid.

27. Address by Samuel Rubin (January 7, 1957), 1–2, File: Samuel Rubin Correspondence, AICF. See also Samuel Rubin, "A New Orientation," speech reprinted from Annual Meeting of Board of Directors, File: Samuel Rubin Correspondence, AICF.

28. Ibid., 4.

29. Horace M. Kallen, "The American Function of the American Fund," *Israel Life and Letters* (January/February/March/April 1952): 15.

30. Noting a mounting interest in arts patronage in the business world, Toffler wrote that, "Foundations, one of the more curious fruits of the tree of affluence, give away money for an astonishing variety of purposes. . . . By 1963 foundations were

issuing grants at an estimated rate of $820 million a year, up $10 million from the 1960 level. . . . [H]ere, as in the field of business patronage, the amount allocated for cultural purposes was distinctly on the rise both absolutely and relatively." Toffler, *The Culture Consumers*, 172.

31. See, for example, James S. Plaut, "Seven Painters of Israel," *Carnegie Magazine* 27 (March 1953): 86–89; Clement Greenberg, "Art," *The Nation* 166 (March 1948): 84–85; William Schack, "Israeli Painting: After Twenty-Five Years," *Commentary* 15 (June 1953): 593–601; "Seven Israeli Ambassadors," *Art News* 51 (February 1953): 7. Likewise, Israeli artists and critics had been grappling for decades with the question of what constituted "Israeli art" as a national school. The creation of a new national art center in the Land of Israel, in turn, was inextricable from the larger Zionist project of reinventing Jewish culture and society in the Jewish homeland. See Dalia Manor, *Art in Zion: The Genesis of Modern National Art in Jewish Palestine* (London: Routledge/Curzon, 2005); and Yigal Zalmona, "History and Identity," in *Artists of Israel: 1920–1980*, ed. Susan Tumarkin Goodman (New York: The Jewish Museum, 1981), 27–46.

32. In 1957, Kolb donated a substantial collection of graphic art by Jewish artists to Temple Emanu-El in San Francisco, forming the foundation of the synagogue's art museum. Biographical information about Kolb was kindly supplied by Paula Freedman, archivist, Congregation Emanu-El, San Francisco.

33. The artists included were: Jacob Steinhardt, Isidor Ascheim, Ludwig Shwerin, Francisca Baruch, Jacob Pins, and Joseph Budko.

34. According to Deborah Dash Moore, the Beverly-Fairfax exhibition "garnered praise from all segments of the Jewish community"; see "Open Israeli Art Exhibit in L.A. May 17," *California Jewish Voice*, May 13, 1949; "First Israel Art Here; Showing Impressive," *Los Angeles Times*, May 22, 1949; and Moore, *To The Golden Cities*, 208.

35. *Southwestern Jewish Press*, June 9, 1950.

36. *Art Digest* 26 (April 15, 1952), 12; Lionel Reiss, "Oils and Watercolors by Israeli Artists at Y.M.H.A., New York," *The Reconstructionist* 18, no. 17 (December 26, 1952), 28.

37. "Gleanings," *Jewish Community Center Program Aids* 12 (1951–52), unpaginated.

38. Ibid.

39. Meyer Levin, "Israel Picks Up the Art Boom," *New York Times*, July 8, 1962.

40. "Israeli Art Show," *American-Israel Economic Horizons* 18, no. 4 (April 1966): 10.

41. "Israeli Art Sales in U.S. Increase," *American-Israel Economic Horizons* 17, no. 12 (December 1965): 10.

42. "Israeli Art Show," 10.

43. Individual exhibitions are too numerous to list here. *Art News*, the *New York Times*, and the *Los Angeles Times*, among other publications, announced and reviewed such exhibitions throughout this period. For listings of exhibitions in these years for a number of prominent Israeli artists, see Goodman, *Artists of Israel*.

44. "Israeli Art on U.S. Circuit," *Art Digest* 27 (January 15, 1953), 9.

45. Plaut, "Seven Painters of Israel," 86.

46. Ibid.

47. "Seven Israeli Ambassadors," 7.

48. Ibid.

49. See Hilton Kramer, "Art View: A Distinguished Curator Who Linked Scholarship and Art," *New York Times*, March 13, 1977, and "William C. Seitz, Art Scholar, Dies," *New York Times*, October 28, 1974. Seitz established his reputation by advocating for contemporary art at a time when the Modern and the art-historical establishment generally took a more conservative approach to the modern canon.

50. Letter from William C. Seitz to Samuel Dubiner, February 19, 1962, Seitz correspondence 1964, MoMA Library.

51. William C. Seitz, "Introduction," *Art Israel: 26 Painters and Sculptors* (New York: The Museum of Modern Art, 1964; exhibition catalogue), 6.

52. Letter from William C. Seitz to Barry Kernerman, April 26, 1962, Seitz correspondence 1964, MoMA Library.

53. Letter from Philip Goodwin to James Thrall Soby, April 8, 1949, Seitz correspondence 1964, MoMA Library. That *Art Israel*, though organized under MoMA's auspices, was mounted at The Jewish Museum rather than in MoMA's own galleries, suggests that perhaps some ambivalence toward Israeli art did remain, sixteen years later.

54. Seitz, "Introduction," 6, 13.

55. Stuart Preston, "Art: Israeli Show Depicts New National School," *New York Times*, December 8, 1964; Emily Genauer, "Art of Israel—Jewish Museum Exhibit Opening," *New York Herald Tribune*, December 8, 1964, File: Press Releases/News Clippings, AICF; "Art Israel," *Art News* 64 (February 1965): 58–59; William Wilson, "Israel Show a Study in Passion," *Los Angeles Times*, October 2, 1966.

56. Charlotte Willard, "In the Art Galleries," *New York Post*, December 13, 1964, File: Press Releases/News Clippings, AICF.

57. Meir Ronnen, "Art in Israel," *Midstream* 10, no. 3 (November 1964): 51.

58. Alfred Werner, "Melting Pot: Third Phase," *Arts Magazine* 39, no. 4 (January 1965): 45.

59. Ibid., 40.

60. Ibid.

61. Ronnen, "Art in Israel," 51.

62. See Kathryn M. Yochelson, "Golden Threads: Discovering Israeli Art," in *Fruits of a Lifetime: The Kathryn Yochelson Collection of Israeli Art*, ed. Gabriel M. Goldstein and Kathryn M. Yochelson (New York: Yeshiva University Museum, 2002), 9–61.

63. "Israeli Art Exhibit—September 16 to October 18 at Albright Art Gallery," *Buffalo Jewish Review*, September 4, 1953, 8, clipping, File: General: Buffalo: Public Events: 7 Painters of Israel scrapbook 1948–1960, Papers of Kathryn M. Yochelson (hereafter, Yochelson Papers), Yeshiva University Museum (hereafter, YUM).

64. The art dealers were Edith Talbert and Eleanor Richman; see *Israel Chronicle*, March 16, 1964, clipping, File: General: Adas Israel Synagogue Exhibit: Scrapbook 1950s, Box OS2, Yochelson Papers, YUM.

65. Ibid.; and Yochelson, "Golden Threads," 31–32.

66. *Washington Star,* April 26, 1964, clipping, File: General: Adas Israel Synagogue Exhibit: Scrapbook 1950s, Box OS2, Yochelson Papers, YUM; *Washington Post,* April 26, 1964, clipping, File: General: Adas Israel Synagogue Exhibit: Scrapbook 1950s, Box OS2, Yochelson Papers, YUM.

67. *Washington Post,* undated clipping, File: General: Adas Israel Synagogue Exhibit: Scrapbook 1950s, Box OS2, Yochelson Papers, YUM.

68. "General Purposes of the [Adas Israel] Art Committee," File: General: Adas Israel Synagogue Exhibit: Scrapbook 1950s, Box OS2, Yochelson Papers, YUM.

69. Annual Report 1963–1964, Fine Arts Committee, File: General: Adas Israel Synagogue Exhibit: Scrapbook 1950s, Box OS2, Yochelson Papers, YUM.

70. "Arts Program Will Feature Jewish Music," *The Washington Post,* February 26, 1949, 8.

71. Kurt List, "The Folk Revival in Jewish Music: A Report on the 1948–1949 Season," *Commentary* 8, no. 5 (November 1949): 482.

72. Ibid., 481. And see Kurt List, "Music," *American Jewish Year Book* 51 (1950): 228–33.

73. Kurt List, "Music," *American Jewish Year Book* 52 (1951): 186.

74. Ibid., 188.

75. List, "The Folk Revival in Jewish Music," 482.

76. Ibid.

77. Ibid., 484.

78. Ethel S. Cohen, "The Disharmony Between Israeli and American Jewish Composers," *The Reconstructionist* 17, no. 5 (April 20, 1951): 23.

79. Ethel Cohen and her husband, Frank Cohen, founded the Esco Fund, a private foundation dedicated to bettering life in Israel. The development of Israeli musical culture was one of the fund's primary projects; to that end, the Cohens established a program in 1947 for training young Israeli composers in the United States as well as building a concert hall in Kibbutz Ein Gev (completed in 1952). Ethel Cohen, who held a master's degree in musicology from New York University, was also a member of the board of directors of the America-Israel Cultural Foundation. For more on Ethel Cohen and the Esco Fund, see Marianne Sanua, "The Esco Fund Committee: The Story of an American Jewish Foundation," in *America and Zion: Essays and Papers in Memory of Moshe Davis,* ed. Eli Lederhendler and Jonathan D. Sarna (Detroit: Wayne State University Press, 2002), 117–60.

80. Cohen, "The Disharmony Between Israeli and American Jewish Composers," 23.

81. Ibid.

82. Peter Gradenwitz, "Israeli Music in America," *Commentary* 8 (July 1949): 76.

83. Ibid.

84. Ibid., 79.

85. Financial statement, 1955, File: Financial Statements, 1943–1956, AICF.

86. Financial statement, 1960, File: Financial Statements, 1960–1963, AICF.

87. William Heller, "Viewpoint . . . ," editorial, *Israel Life and Letters* 7, no. 3 (March 1951): back page.

88. Ibid.

89. "Israel Orchestra Arrives for Tour," *New York Times*, December 30, 1950, 9.

90. Seymour Raven, "Philharmonic Orchestra from Israel Will Play Twice Here," *Chicago Daily Tribune*, February 4, 1951, F1.

91. Aaron Baron, "In Retrospect: Observations on the Israel Philharmonic Orchestra Tour of America," *Israel Life and Letters* 7, no. 4 (April 1951): 22.

92. Ibid.

93. Claudia Cassidy, "Philharmonic of Israel Given Noisy Acclaim," *Chicago Daily Tribune*, February 11, 1951, 22.

94. Louis Biancolli, "Israel Orchestra at Met," *World-Telegram and Sun*, October 17, 1960, File: Press Releases/News Clippings, AICF.

95. "International Rinat Choir Will Sing in Harrison, N.Y.," *New York Times*, December 1, 1962, 16; Paul Hume, "Skilled Israeli Choir Finally Heard," *The Washington Post-Times Herald*, December 7, 1962, C12.

96. Memorandum from Leon L. Gildesgame to members of the Executive Committee of the AICF, November 2, 1964, 3, File: Leon Gildesgame Correspondence, 1964–1968, AICF.

97. Henry Beckett, "Israel Youth Symphony Wins Carnegie Acclaim," *New York Post*, October 12, 1964, File: Press Releases/News Clippings, AICF.

98. Raymond Ericson, "Youth Symphony of Israel Bows," *New York Times*, October 12, 1964, 36.

99. Louis Biancolli, "Israel Youth Symphony Has Carnegie Hall Debut," *New York World-Telegram*, October 12, 1964, File: Press Releases/News Clippings, AICF.

100. Beckett, "Israel Youth Symphony Wins Carnegie Acclaim."

101. Ira Eisenstein, "What Concerts Do to Israelis," *The Reconstructionist* 16, no. 15 (December 1, 1950): 16.

102. Ibid.

103. Quoted in memorandum from Leon L. Gildesgame to members of the Executive Committee of the AICF, November 2, 1964, 3, File: Leon Gildesgame Correspondence, 1964–1968, AICF.

104. Baron, "Retrospect: Observations on the Israel Philharmonic Tour of America," 22.

105. Klein, *Cold War Orientalism*, 65.

106. Gideon Paz, interview with author, March 2005, New York City. The Israel Culture House closed in the 1970s. And see press release, "Five-Story Town House Will Be Purchased by America-Israel Cultural Foundation; To Become Israel Culture House," March 26, 1965, and undated clipping, "Window on Israel Opened in New York," both in File: Culture House Sale of Building Documents, AICF.

107. Financial information gathered by the organization through 1953 reveals the following trend: after an initial decrease between 1948 (the peak fundraising year for the Jewish federations) and 1951, allotments to the AICF rose incrementally, even as overall contributions to communal welfare funds continued to fall; in practical terms, this meant that while the total communal welfare pool declined by almost half, the AICF declined by only 15 percent. See "Prospectus for Procurement of $1,000,000 Loan for Four Years Submitted by the American Fund for Israel Institutions," 14, 17, File: Miscellaneous 1950s, AICF. The *American Jewish Year*

Book contains information about the annual sums collected by American Jewish fundraising bodies.

108. "Prospectus for Procurement of $1,000,000 Loan for Four Years," 19.

109. A. J. Warner, "Israel Orchestra Concert Stirring," File: Press Releases/News Clippings, AICF; "International Rinat Choir Will Sing in Harrison, N.Y.," 16.

110. Memorandum, Ralph Goldman to Leon Gildesgame, August 29, 1961, B-1, File: Leon Gildesgame Correspondence, 1956–1963, AICF.

111. Ibid., B-3.

112. Undated report, File: Miscellaneous Correspondence, 1942, AICF.

113. "Israeli Art to Highlight UJF Kick-off," *Pittsburgh Jewish Chronicle*, March 5, 1965.

114. Reiss, "Oils and Watercolors by Israeli Artists at Y.M.H.A., New York," 29.

115. Shlomo Katz, "Shepherd Songs [Notes in Midstream]," *Midstream* 6, no. 2 (Spring 1960): 28.

116. Ibid.

117. Alfred Werner, "Art—Israel's New Frontier," *Judaism* (Spring 1958), reprinted in *Art in Judaism: Studies in the Jewish Artistic Experience*, ed. Robert Gordis and Moshe Davidowitz (New York: National Council on Art in Jewish Life, 1975), 104.

CONCLUSION

1. Richard Joseph Covello, "Israel Eases Austerity for Tourists," *New York Times*, December 17, 1950, X25.

2. Ibid.

3. Seth S. King, "Pioneer Land Still," *New York Times*, March 1, 1959, XX27.

4. "Who Travels to Israel?" *Our Age* 8, no. 9 (February 5, 1967): 5. Numbers in the article come from Israel's Ministry of Tourism. The article does not delineate the percentage of Jewish visitors coming from the United States.

5. See Meyer, *Response to Modernity*, 348–49; Maurice N. Eisendrath, "The State of Our Union," April 19, 1953, 13, file 1, box 69, Union of Reform Judaism Records, AJA, and "Semi-Annual Report from President Eisendrath to the Executive Board of the UAHC, June 1952," in *Proceedings of the Union of American Hebrew Congregations* (Cincinnati: Union of American Hebrew Congregations, 1956), 146–65; and Eli Lederhendler, "The Ongoing Dialogue: The Seminary and the Challenge of Israel," in *Tradition Renewed: A History of the Jewish Theological Seminary, vol. II*, ed. Wertheimer, 177–270.

6. Charles I. Glicksberg, " 'Israelization of the American Tourist," *Congress Bi-Weekly* 26, no. 10 (May 25, 1959): 21.

7. See Wertheimer, "American Jews and Israel": 37.

8. These intellectuals include Melvin Lasky, Sidney Hook, and Irving Kristol, among others. Saunders, *The Cultural Cold War*.

9. I am grateful to Emily S. Rosenberg for first directing my attention to this issue.

10. It is also important to note that the Middle East in general received much less attention than did Europe in the postwar years. Cull, *The Cold War and the United States Information Agency*, 145–46.

11. Abraham G. Duker, "The Impact of Zionism on American Jewry," in *Jewish Life in America*, ed. Theodore Friedman and Robert Gordis (New York: Horizon Press, 1955), 316.

12. Harry Essrig and Abraham Segal, *Israel Today* (New York: Union of American Hebrew Congregations, 1964), 270.

13. Ibid., 271. It is well worth noting that, despite the examples mentioned by Essrig and Segal above, few American Jews acquired a deep knowledge of the Hebrew language in this period. See Jonathan Krasner, "The Limits of Cultural Zionism in America: The Case of Hebrew in the New York City Public Schools, 1930–1960," *American Jewish History* 95, no. 4 (December 2009): 349–72.

14. Essrig and Segal, *Israel Today*, 270.

15. Ganin, *An Uneasy Relationship*, 114–115; *Eye on Israel*, 186, footnote 17.

16. "Israel Anniversary Show," *Toast of the Town*, the Museum of Television and Radio, New York.

17. Quoted in A. M. Sperber, *Murrow: His Life and Times* (New York: Freundlich Books, 1986), 253. For more on Murrow, see Sperber and also Joseph E. Persico, *Edward R. Murrow: An American Original* (New York: McGraw-Hill, 1988).

18. Bob Edwards, *Edward R. Murrow and the Birth of Broadcast Journalism* (New Jersey: John Wiley and Sons, 2004), 128; Edward Bliss Jr., ed., *In Search of Light: The Broadcasts of Edward R. Murrow, 1938–1961* (New York: Alfred A. Knopf, 1967), 287–89.

19. For *See It Now*'s ratings, see Anthony R. Fellow, *American Media History*, 2nd ed. (Boston: Wadsworth/Cengage Learning, 2010), 287.

20. Jeffrey Shandler, *While America Watches: Televising the Holocaust* (New York: Oxford University Press, 1999), 114–15 and Deborah E. Lipstadt, *The Eichmann Trial* (New York: Nextbook/Schocken, 2011), 56–106.

21. See, for example, Lipstadt, *The Eichmann Trial*; 148–180; Eli Lederhendler, *New York Jews and the Decline of Urban Ethnicity, 1950–1970* (Syracuse: Syracuse University Press, 2001), 53–62; Shandler, *While America Watches*, 118–21; Peter Novick, *The Holocaust in American Life* (Boston: Houghton Mifflin Company, 1999), 134–42; and Tom Segev, *The Seventh Million: The Israelis and the Holocaust*, trans. Haim Watzman (New York: Hill and Wang, 1993), 357–60, 465. Scholars continue to assess Arendt's articles and book as well as reactions to them at the time. In the last three years alone, scholarship on the subject (in English) includes Adam Sacks, "Hannah Arendt's Eichmann Controversy as Destabilizing Transatlantic Text," *AJS Review* 37, no. 1 (2013): 115–34; Christian Wiese, "'No Love of the Jewish People'?: Robert Weltsch's and Hans Jonas's Correspondence with Hannah Arendt on 'Eichmann in Jerusalem,'" in *German-Jewish Thought Between Religion and Politics: Festschrift in Honor of Paul Mendes-Flohr on the Occasion of His Seventieth Birthday*, ed. Christian Wiese and Martina Urban (Berlin: De Gruyter, 2012), 387–432; *Eichmann in Jerusalem: Fifty Years After*, ed. Kai Ambos (Berlin: Duncker u. Humblot, 2012); and Roger Berkowitz, Jeffrey Katz, and Thomas Keenan, eds., *Thinking in Dark Times: Hannah Arendt on Ethics and Politics* (New York: Fordham University Press, 2010).

22. Hannah Arendt, *Eichmann in Jerusalem: A Report on the Banality of Evil* (New York: Penguin Books, 2006 [Viking Press, 1963]), 10.

23. Shula Hirsch, *An American Housewife in Israel* (New York: The Citadel Press, 1962), 84–85.

24. Lederhendler, *New York Jews and the Decline of Urban Ethnicity*, 61.

25. See, for example, Steven T. Rosenfeld, *Irreconcilable Differences?: The Waning of the American Jewish Love Affair with Israel* (Hanover and London: Brandeis University Press, 2003).

26. Staub, *Torn at the Roots*, 45–75.

27. Meyer Levin, "After All I Did for Israel," *Commentary* 12, no. 1 (July 1951): 58.

28. Ibid., 58, 57.

29. Halter, *Shopping for Identity*, 7.

30. For a classic study of the intersection of Jewish consumption and politics, see Paula E. Hyman, "Immigrant Women and Consumer Protest: The New York City Kosher Meat Boycott of 1902," *American Jewish History* 70 (1980): 91–105.

31. Eli Lederhendler has presented a rare challenge to this narrative, arguing that, in fact, the Six-Day War had a less momentous effect on Jewish life in America in political, cultural, and communal terms, than is popularly believed. "The Six-Day War offered . . . Jewries [in pluralist-democratic countries] the opportunity to make use of the event (or not) as they saw fit," he writes, an opportunity that did not "call into question any basic change in their status as citizens and co-nationals." Lederhendler, "Introduction: The Six-Day War and the Jewish People in the Diaspora," in *The Six-Day War and World Jewry*, ed. Eli Lederhendler (Bethesda, MD: University Press of Maryland, 2000), 7.

32. For a particularly rich and insightful reassessment of the relationship between the early postwar period and the post-1960s era in American Jewish history, including the similarities and differences between each era's reckonings with the Holocaust and also Israel, see Diner, *We Remember With Reverence and Love*, 365–90.

BIBLIOGRAPHY

MAJOR ARCHIVAL COLLECTIONS CONSULTED

America-Israel Cultural Foundation (New York)

American Jewish Archives

> B'nei Akiva of North America, Nearprint Special Topics
> Hashomer Hatzair Records
> Union of Reform Judaism Records
> Women of Reform Judaism Records

American Jewish Historical Society

> Jewish Student Organizations Collection

Hadassah Archives

> Hadassah Israel Education Services Reports 1950–1974
> Hadassah Vocational Education Records
> Young Judaea Collection

Israeli Dance Institute (New York)

Library of the Museum of Modern Art

> William Seitz correspondence (Israeli Art scrapbook, vol. 2)

New York Public Library

> New York World's Fair 1965–1965 Corporation Records, 1959–1971

New York Public Library for the Performing Arts

> Dance Collection

Archives of the 92nd Street Y

> Education Department Records

Yeshiva University Museum

    Papers of Kathryn M. Yochelson

YIVO Institute for Jewish Research

    Records of the Labor Zionist Organization of America

PERIODICALS AND NEWSPAPERS CONSULTED

American Jewish Year Book
American Judaism
Art Digest
Book Review Digest
Christian Century
Commentary
Congress Weekly/Congress Bi-Weekly
Dance Magazine
Forverts
Furrows
Haboneh
Hadassah Newsletter/Hadassah Magazine
Hora
Israel Economic Horizons/ American-Israel Economic Horizons
Israel Life and Letters
Jewish Book Annual
Life
Los Angeles Times
Midstream
New York Herald Tribune Weekly Book Review
New York Post
New York Herald Tribune
New York Times
New Yorker
Publishers' Weekly
The Reconstructionist
Recreation
Religious Education
Saturday Review of Literature/Saturday Review
Time
Tog
United Synagogue Review

Viltis
The Washington Post-Times Herald
Women's League Outlook
Young Judaean

SELECTED PRIMARY SOURCES

Alpert, Carl. "An Experience in Cultural Relationships." *The Reconstructionist*, June 26, 1942, 12–14.

"An American Synagogue for Today and Tomorrow: Statements Made at Conference of the Union of American Hebrew Congregations." *Architectural Record* 102, no. 3 (September 1947): 99.

Ardon-Bronstein, Mordecai. "Art: Its Function in Israel." *Hadassah Newsletter* 33, no. 5 (January 1953): 13.

Arendt, Hannah. *Eichmann in Jerusalem: A Report on the Banality of Evil*. New York: Penguin Books, 2006 (Viking Press, 1963).

Banin, Sylvia Satten. "Israel Makes It America Buys It." *Hadassah Newsletter* 38, no. 2 (October 1957): 2, 15.

Bar-David, Molly Lyons. "Israel Crafts: A Rich Inheritance." *Hadassah Newsletter* 33, no. 1 (September 1952): 6, 14.

———. *My Promised Land*. New York: G. P. Putnam's Sons, 1953.

Barkan, Ida M. "Memories of the Future." *Women's League Outlook* 33, no. 1 (Fall 1962): 10.

Beliajus, Vyts. "Folk Dance Toward Brotherhood." *Religious Education* 53, no. 1 (January/February 1958): 60–61.

Berger, Elmer. *Judaism or Jewish Nationalism: the Alternative to Zionism*. New York: Bookman Associates, 1957.

Berk, Fred. "A Dissenting Point of View: About Folk Dance." *Dance Magazine* 31 (December 1957): 90–91.

———. *Guide for the Israeli Folk Dance Teacher*. New York: American Zionist Youth Foundation, 1979.

———. "Staging Folk Dance." *Dance Magazine* 36 (May 1962): 68–69.

———, and Lucy Venable. *Dances from Israel in Labanotation*. Dance Notation Bureau, 1963, rev. 1967.

Berkowitz, Michael. *Zionist Culture and West European Jewry Before the First World War*. New York: Cambridge University Press, 1993.

Bikel, Theodore. *Theo: The Autobiography of Theodore Bikel*. New York: HarperCollins, 1994.

Bliss, Edward Jr., ed. *In Search of Light: The Broadcasts of Edward R. Murrow, 1938–1961*. New York: Alfred A. Knopf, 1967.

Bloomfield, Bernard M. *Israel Diary*. New York: Crown Publishers, 1950.

Boroff, David. "Jewish Readers and Jewish Writers." *Congress Bi-Weekly*, December 19, 1960, 3–5.

Breslau, David, ed. *Adventure in Pioneering: The Story of 25 Years of Habonim Camping*. New York: The CHAY Commission of the Labor Zionist Movement, 1957.

Brown, Esther. "New Vitality From Ancient Roots." *Dance Magazine* 28 (February 1954): 39–41, 51, 58–59.

Burrows, Millar. *Palestine Is Our Business*. Philadelphia: Westminster Press, 1949.

Buxton, Frank W. "Cultural Lend-Lease." *Israel Life and Letters* 7, no. 5 (May 1951): 15.

Chochem, Corinne. "Artists in Search of Their People." *The Reconstructionist*, February 7, 1947, 21–23.

———, and Muriel Roth. *Palestine Dances!* New York: Behrman's Jewish Book House, 1941.

Clawson, Mary. *Letters from Jerusalem*. London and New York: Abelard-Schuman, 1958.

Cohen, Ethel S. "The Disharmony Between Israeli and American Jewish Composers." *The Reconstructionist*, April 20, 1951, 23–25.

"The Crisis in Zionism." *Life*, February 17, 1961, 34.

"A Cultural Explosion." *Life*, October 18, 1954, 38.

Davis, Moshe. "The Dance: What It Means to Me—A Religious Interpretation." *Dance Magazine* 31, 6 (June 1957): 22.

———. "Letters on Hebrew Culture." (In Hebrew) *Niv* 3, no. 1 (Tishrei 5699 [September 1938]): 9–11.

———. "Letters on Hebrew Culture." (In Hebrew) *Niv* 3, no, 2 (Cheshvan 5699 [October 1938]): 4–5.

———. "Letters on Hebrew Culture." (In Hebrew) *Niv* 3, no. 3 (Kislev 5699 [November 1938]): 2–4.

———. "Letters on Hebrew Culture." (In Hebrew) *Niv* 3, no. 4 (Tevet 5699 [December 1938]): 7–8.

Duker, Abraham G. "The Impact of Zionism on American Jewry." In *Jewish Life in America*, edited by Theodore Friedman and Robert Gordis, 301–21. New York: Horizon Press, 1955.

Duncan, Donald. "The Views of a Church." *Dance Magazine* 32 (September 1958): 67–68.

Dunner, Joseph. *Republic of Israel: Its History and Promise*. New York: Whittlesey House, 1950.

Eisenstein, Ira. "What Concerts Do to Israelis." *The Reconstructionist*, December 1, 1950, 14–16.

Eliot, George Fielding. *Hate, Hope and High Explosives: A Report on the Middle East*. Indianapolis: Bobbs-Merrill, 1948.

Essrig, Harry, and Abraham Segal. *Israel Today*. New York: Union of American Hebrew Congregations, 1964.

Ethridge, Willie Snow. *Going to Jerusalem*. New York: Vanguard Press, 1950.

Fierst, Miriam, and Lili Eller. "Who Is She?: An Appraisal of the Composite Hadassah Member." *Hadassah Newsletter* 39, no. 2 (October 1958): 9, 14.

Freehof, Florence E. *Guide for Israeli-Jewish Folk Dancers*. New York: Bloch, 1963.

———. *New Dances From Israel*. New York: Bloch, 1960.

———. *Tips on Teaching Folk Dancing*. New York: Bloch, 1948.

Garcia-Granados, Jorge. *The Birth of Israel: The Drama As I Saw It*. New York: Knopf, 1948.

Gelatt, Roland. "Bogus Best Sellers." *Saturday Review of Literature*, March 26, 1949, 20–22.

Gildersleeve, Virginia. *Many a Good Crusade: Memoirs*. New York: Macmillan, 1954.

Glazer, Ruth. "The Jewish Object: A Shopper's Report." *Commentary* 12 (July 1951): 63–67.

Glicksberg, Charles I. "'Israelization of the American Tourist." *Congress Bi-Weekly*, May 25, 1959, 20–21.

Goldberg, J. J., and Elliot King, eds. *Builders and Dreamers: Habonim Labor Zionist Youth in North America*. New York: Herzl Press, 1993.

Goodman, Jerry. *Ptsah B'Zemer: A Basic Selection of Hebrew and Yiddish Folk Songs*. New York: United Synagogue of America Youth Commission, 1964.

Goodman, Percival, and Paul Goodman. "Modern Artist as Synagogue Builder: Satisfying the Needs of Today's Congregations." *Commentary* 7 (January 1949): 233–41.

Gordon, Albert Isaac. *Jews in Suburbia*. Boston: Beacon Press, 1959.

Gradenwitz, Peter. "Israeli Music in America." *Commentary* 8 (July 1949): 76–79.

Greenberg, Betty D., and Althea O. Silverman. *The Jewish Home Beautiful*. New York: The Women's League of the United Synagogue of America, 1950 (1941).

Greenberg, Clement. "Art." *The Nation* 166 (March 1948): 84–85.

Gruber, Ruth. *Exodus 1947: The Ship that Launched a Nation*. (Formerly titled *Destination Palestine*.) New York: A. A. Wyn, 1948; New York: Random House, 1999.

———. *Israel Without Tears*. New York: A. A. Wyn, 1950.

———. *Witness: One of the Great Foreign Correspondents of the Twentieth Century Tells Her Story*. New York: Schocken Books, 2007.

Halperin, Samuel. *The Political World of American Zionism*. Detroit: Wayne State University Press, 1961.

Handlin, Oscar. "America Recognizes Diverse Loyalties: 'External' Ties Are Not Necessarily Dangerous." *Commentary* 9 (March 1950): 220–26.

Heckscher, August. *The Public Happiness*. New York: Atheneum, 1962.

Herman, Jerry, with Marilyn Stasio. *Showtune*. New York: Donald I. Fine Books, 1996.

Hirsch, Shula. *An American Housewife in Israel*. New York: The Citadel Press, 1962.

Holmes, John Haynes. *Palestine To-day and To-morrow: A Gentile's Survey of Zionism*. New York: Macmillan, 1929.

Kallen, Horace M. "The American Function of the American Fund." *Israel Life and Letters* (January/February/March/April 1952): 15.

———. *Frontiers of Hope*. New York: H. Liveright, 1929.

Kaplan, Mordecai M. *Judaism as a Civilization: Toward a Reconstruction of American-Jewish Life*. New York: Macmillan, 1934; Philadelphia: Jewish Publication Society, 1994.

Katz, Shlomo. "Shepherd Songs (Notes in Midstream)." *Midstream* 6, no. 2 (Spring 1960): 26–28.

Kaufman, Gert, and Dvora Lapson. *New Israeli Dances*. New York: The Jewish Education Committee of New York, 1948.

Kramer, Hilton. "How Good Is Israeli Art?" *Commentary* 39 (February 1965): 62–65.

Kraus, Richard. *Folk Dancing: A Guide for Schools, Colleges, and Recreation Groups*. New York: Macmillan, 1962.

Lapson, Dvora. "Dance in the Jewish School." *The Reconstructionist*, December 28, 1951, 23–26.

————. *Dances of the Jewish People: Israeli and East European Dances*. New York: Jewish Education Committee Press, 1954.

————. "The Jewish Dance." *The Reconstructionist*, May 26, 1944, 13–17.

Lekis, Lisa. "Folk Dance Flourishes in California!" *Dance Magazine* 29 (January 1955): 39–43.

Levi, Shonie B., and Sylvia R. Kaplan. *Across the Threshold: A Guide for the Jewish Homemaker*. New York: Farrar, Straus, and Cudahy and the National Women's League of the United Synagogue of America, 1959.

Levin, Meyer. "After All I Did for Israel." *Commentary* 12 (July 1951): 57–62.

Lilienthal, Alfred. *What Price Israel*. Chicago: H. Regnery, 1953.

Lipman, Eugene J., and Myron E. Schoen, eds. *The American Synagogue: A Progress Report; Proceedings, Second National Conference and Exhibit on Synagogue Architecture*. New York: Union of American Hebrew Congregations, 1958.

List, Kurt. "The Folk Revival in Jewish Music: A Report on the 1948–1949 Season." *Commentary* 8, no. 5 (November 1949): 481–86.

————. "Jewish Music on Records: A Guide for Listeners." *Commentary* 2 (September 1946): 240–48.

————. "Music." *American Jewish Year Book* 51 (1950): 228–33.

McDonald, James G. *My Mission in Israel*. New York: Simon and Schuster, 1951.

McGill, R. E. *Israel Revisited*. Atlanta: Tupper and Love, 1950.

McNaspy, C. J. "Culture Explosion." *America*, December 3, 1960, 340–42.

Meir, Golda, and Judith Krantz. "At Home in Jerusalem." *Good Housekeeping* 145 (July 1957): 68–71, 177–82.

Michaels, Ruth Gruber. "Israel Fashions in U.S.A." *Hadassah Magazine* 48, no. 2 (October 1966): 8, 28.

"Modern Drama, Art, Music, Dance Expressing Faith at San Francisco Biennial." *American Judaism* 15, no. 2 (Winter 1965–66): 12–14.

National Women's League of the United Synagogue of America. *Proceedings of the Biennial Convention, 1950–1952*. New York: National Women's League, 1953.

Myers, Therese. "Israel Dances in America. *Recreation* XLVI-A, no. 3 (June 1953): 152–54.

Pekarsky, Nell Ziff. "Shopping, Swapping, *Shepping Nahas* in Israel." *Hadassah Newsletter* 32, no. 6 (March 1952): 6.

Plaut, James S. "Seven Painters of Israel." *Carnegie Magazine* 27, no. 3 (March 1953): 86–89.

Poster, Herbert. "Literature." *American Jewish Year Book* 51 (1950): 201–10.

Prime, William C. *Tent Life in the Holy Land*. New York: Harper and Bros., 1857.

Reiss, Lionel S. "A Letter on Art in Israel." *The Reconstructionist*, April 18, 1952, 27–28.

————. "Oils and Watercolors by Israeli Artists at Y.M.H.A., New York." *The Reconstructionist*, December 26, 1952, 27–28.

Rhapsody: The Music and Dance of Israel. Canadian Broadcasting Corporation, 1959.

Ribalow, Harold U. "Zion in the Book Stores." *Jewish Frontier* 19, no. 1 (March 1952): 16–19.

Ronnen, Meir. "Art in Israel," *Midstream* 10, no. 3 (November 1964): 51–62.

Rudavsky, Mordkhe. "James Grover McDonald" (In Yiddish). *Der amerikaner* (The Jewish American) 46, no. 38 (July 9, 1948): 2.

St. John, Robert. *Shalom Means Peace.* Garden City, NY: Doubleday, 1949

Sargeant, Winthrop. "Musical Events (Yemenite Hoedown)." *New Yorker,* January 18, 1958, 92–93.

Schack, Sarah C. "Every Day in Every Way . . ." *Midstream* 3, no. 2 (Spring 1957): 106–10.

Schack, William. "Art Worth Celebrating: Two Tercentenary Shows of Jewish Painting and Sculpture." *Commentary* 20 (October 1955): 335–42.

———. "Israeli Painting: After Twenty-Five Years." *Commentary* 15 (June 1953): 593–601.

———. "Synagogue Art Today: I: Something of a Renaissance." *Commentary* 20 (December 1955): 548–53.

Schonberg, Harold C. "Speaking Out (The National 'Culture Explosion' is Phony)." *The Saturday Evening Post,* July 13, 1963, 10, 14.

Schreiber, Ben Zion. "The Brandeis Camp Institute, An American Jewish Educational Institution." *The Reconstructionist,* May 13, 1949, 7, 15.

Seitz, William C. *Art Israel: 26 Painters and Sculptors.* New York: The Museum of Modern Art, 1964.

Sklare, Marshall, and Joseph Greenblum. *Jewish Identity on the Suburban Frontier: A Study of Group Survival in the Open Society.* New York: Basic Books, 1967.

Sklare, Marshall, and Benjamin B. Ringer. "A Study of Jewish Attitudes toward the State of Israel." In *The Jews: Social Patterns of an American Group,* edited by Marshall Sklare, 437–50. Glencoe, IL: The Free Press, 1960.

Sonnenfeld, Herbert, and Pierre van Paassen. *Palestine: Land of Israel.* Chicago: Ziff-Davis, 1948.

Steinberg, Leo. "Bible-Age Relics and Jewish Art." *Commentary* 16 (August 1953): 164–66.

Stone, I.F. *This Is Israel.* New York: Boni and Gaer, 1948.

Swisher, Viola Hegyi. "'In the Light of a Kindred Humanity.'" *Dance Magazine* 41 (March 1967): 46–49.

Synagogue Architects Consultant Panel of the Union of American Hebrew Congregations. *The American Synagogue: A Progress Report; Proceedings, Second National Conference and Exhibit on Synagogue Architecture,* edited by Rabbi Eugene J. Lipman and Myron E. Schoen. New York: UAHC, 1958.

Taylor, Margaret Fisk. "Creative Rhythmic Movement as a Religious Education Art." *Religious Education* 53, no. 1 (January/February 1958): 47–51.

Teplitz, Miriam. "'To See Ourselves As Others See Us': The Experience of our National Program Chairman at a Church Family Encampment." *Women's League Outlook* 28, no. 2 (December 1957): 12, 14.

"This Culture Boom: How Real Is It?" *Changing Times* 19, no. 10 (October 1965): 37–40.

Thompson, Dorothy. "America Demands a Single Loyalty: The Perils of a 'Favorite' Foreign Nation." *Commentary* 9 (March 1950): 210–19.

Thomson, William McClure. *The Land and the Book.* New York: Harper & Bros., 1859.

Toast of the Town: The Israel Anniversary Show. CBS, May 13, 1959.

Toffler, Alvin. *The Culture Consumers: A Study of Art and Affluence in America.* New York: St. Martin's Press, 1964.

Udin, Sophie A. *Palestine and Zionism: A Three Year Cumulation, January 1946–December 1948: An Author and Subject Index to Books, Pamphlets and Periodicals*. New York: Zionist Archives and Library of Palestine Foundation Fund, 1949.

Uris, Leon. *Exodus*. Garden City, NY: Doubleday, 1958.

Vester, Bertha Spafford. *Our Jerusalem, An American Family in the Holy City—1881–1949*. Garden City, NY: Doubleday, 1950.

Weiss-Rosmarin, Trude. "The Plight of the Jewish Book." *Jewish Spectator* 17, no. 9 (October 1952): 5–6.

Weizmann, Chaim. *Trial and Error: The Autobiography of Chaim Weizmann*. New York: Harper and Brothers, 1949.

Werner, Alfred. "Art—Israel's New Frontier." *Judaism* (Spring 1958). Reprinted in *Art in Judaism: Studies in the Jewish Artistic Experience*, edited by Robert Gordis and Moshe Davidowitz, 98–105. New York: National Council on Art in Jewish Life, 1975.

———. "Melting Pot: The Third Phase." *Arts Magazine* 39, no. 4 (January 1965): 40–45.

Wischnitzer-Bernstein, Rachel. "The Problem of Synagogue Architecture: Creating a Style Expressive of America." *Commentary* 3 (March 1947): 51–55.

Yochelson, Kathryn M. "Golden Threads: Discovering Israeli Art." In *Fruits of a Lifetime: The Kathryn Yochelson Collection of Israeli Art*, edited by Gabriel M. Goldstein and Kathryn M. Yochelson, 9–61. New York: Yeshiva University Museum, 2002.

Young, T. Cuyler. *Near Eastern Culture and Society: A Symposium on the Meeting of East and West*. Princeton: Princeton University Press, 1951.

Zelomek, A. W. *A Changing America: At Work and Play*. New York: Wiley, 1959.

SECONDARY LITERATURE

Abrams, Nathan. *Norman Podhoretz and Commentary Magazine: The Rise and Fall of the Neocons*. New York: Continuum, 2010.

Ambos, Kai, ed. *Eichmann in Jerusalem: Fifty Years After*. Berlin: Duncker u. Humblot, 2012.

Arndt, Richard T. *The First Resort of Kings: American Cultural Diplomacy in the Twentieth Century*. Dulles, VA: Potomac Books, 2005.

Balint, Benjamin. *Running Commentary: The Contentious Magazine that Transformed the Jewish Left into the Neoconservative Right*. New York: PublicAffairs, 2010.

Band, Arnold J. "Popular Fiction and the Shaping of Jewish Identity." In *Jewish Identity in America*, edited by David M. Gordis and Yoav Ben-Horin, 215–25. Los Angeles: The Wilstein Institute of the University of Judaism, 1991.

Berkowitz, Roger, Jeffrey Katz, and Thomas Keenan, eds. *Thinking in Dark Times: Hannah Arendt on Ethics and Politics*. New York: Fordham University Press, 2010.

Brautbar, Shirli. *From Fashion to Politics: Hadassah and Jewish American Women in the Post World War II Era*. Boston: Academic Studies Press, 2012.

Breines, Paul. *Tough Jews: Political Fantasies and the Moral Dilemma of American Jewry*. New York: Basic Books, 1990.

Brilliant, Richard, ed. *Facing the New World: Jewish Portraits in Colonial and Federal America*. New York: Prestel, 1997.

Brown, Michael. *The Israeli-American Connection: Its Roots in the Yishuv, 1919–1945*. Detroit: Wayne State University Press, 1996.

Brubaker, Kristi Dawn. "Dance Festivals in the Church of Jesus Christ of Latter-day Saints." MA thesis, UCLA, 2000.

Carnes, Mark C. *Secret Ritual and Manhood in Victorian America*. New Haven and London: Yale University Press, 1989.

Chiswick, Barry. "The Labor Market Status of American Jews: Patterns and Determinants." *American Jewish Year Book* 85 (1985): 135–38.

Cohen, Lizabeth. *A Consumer's Republic: The Politics of Mass Consumption in Postwar America*. New York: Alfred A. Knopf, 2003.

Cohen, Naomi W. *American Jews and the Zionist Idea*. Jerusalem: KTAV Publishing House, 1975.

Cull, Nicholas J. *The Cold War and the United States Information Agency: American Propaganda and Public Diplomacy, 1945–1989*. Cambridge: Cambridge University Press, 2008.

Davis, John. *The Landscape of Belief: Encountering the Holy Land in Nineteenth-Century American Art and Culture*. Princeton: Princeton University Press, 1996.

Diner, Hasia R. "Before 'The Holocaust': American Jews Confront Catastrophe, 1945–62." In *American Jewish Identity Politics*, edited by Deborah Dash Moore, 83–116. Ann Arbor: The University of Michigan Press, 2008.

———. *The Jews of the United States, 1654 to 2000*. Berkeley: University of California Press, 2004.

———. *We Remember With Reverence and Love: American Jews and the Myth of Silence After the Holocaust, 1945–1962*. New York and London: New York University Press, 2009.

———, Shira Kohn, and Rachel Kranson. "Introduction." In *A Jewish Feminine Mystique?: Jewish Women in Postwar America*, edited by Hasia R. Diner, Shira Kohn, and Rachel Kranson, 1–12. New Brunswick, NJ, and London: Rutgers University Press, 2010.

Dobkowski, Michael N., ed. *Jewish American Voluntary Organizations*. New York: Greenwood Press, 1986.

Edwards, Bob. *Edward R. Murrow and the Birth of Broadcast Journalism*. New Jersey: John Wiley and Sons, 2004.

Elazar, Daniel J. *Community and Polity: The Organizational Dynamics of American Jewry*. Philadelphia: The Jewish Publication Society, 1995.

Emery, Edwin. *The Press and America: An Interpretive History of the Mass Media*. Englewood Cliffs, NJ: Prentice-Hall, 1972.

Emery, Michael. *On the Front Lines: Following America's Foreign Correspondents Across the Twentieth Century*. Washington, DC: The American University Press, 1995.

Erdman, Harley. *Staging the Jew: The Performance of an American Ethnicity, 1860–1920*. New Brunswick: Rutgers University Press, 1997.

Fellow, Anthony R. *American Media History*, 2nd ed. Boston: Wadsworth/Cengage Learning, 2010.

Fishman, Aleisa R. "Keeping Up with the Goldbergs: Gender, Consumer Culture, and Jewish Identity in Suburban Nassau County, New York, 1946–1960." PhD diss., American University, 2004.

Friedman, Murray, ed. *Commentary in American Life*. Philadelphia: Temple University Press, 2005.

Furman, Andrew. *Israel Through the Jewish-American Imagination*. Albany: State University of New York Press, 1997.

Gal, Allon, and Alfred Gottschalk, eds. *Beyond Survival and Philanthropy: American Jewry and Israel*. Cincinnati: Hebrew Union College Press, 2000.

Ganin, Zvi. *An Uneasy Relationship: American Jewish Leadership and Israel, 1948–1957*. Syracuse: Syracuse University Press, 2005.

Goldsmith, Emanuel S., Mel Scult, and Robert M. Seltzer, eds. *The American Judaism of Mordecai M. Kaplan*. New York: New York University Press, 1990.

Goldsmith, Peter D. *Making People's Music: Moe Asch and Folkways Records*. Washington, DC, and London: Smithsonian Institution Press, 1998.

Golombek, Tobias. "A New Approach in Jewish Education." *Hamigdal* 2, no. 7 (June 1942): 6–7.

Goodman, Ruth R., with Ruth P. Schoenberg. "Dance: Israeli Folk Dance Pioneers." In *Jewish Women in America*, edited by Paula E. Hyman and Deborah Dash Moore, 294–300. New York: Routledge, 1998.

Goren, Arthur A. "Celebrating Zion in America." In *Encounters with the "Holy Land": Place, Past, and Future in American Jewish Culture*, edited by Jeffrey Shandler and Beth S. Wenger, 41–59. Hanover and London: University Press of New England, 1997.

———. "Epilogue: On Living In Two Cultures." In *Divergent Cultures: Israel and America*, edited by Deborah Dash Moore and S. Ilan Troen, 333–50. New Haven: Yale University Press, 2001.

———. *The Politics and Public Culture of American Jews*. Bloomington: Indiana University Press, 1999.

Gorny, Yosef. *The State of Israel in Jewish Public Thought: The Quest for Collective Identity*. New York: New York University Press, 1994.

Greenberg, Gershon. *The Holy Land in American Religious Thought, 1620–1948: The Symbiosis of American Religious Approaches to Scripture's Sacred Territory*. Lanham, MD, New York, and London: University Press of America, 1994.

Greene, Daniel. *The Jewish Origins of Cultural Pluralism: The Menorah Association and American Diversity*. Bloomington: Indiana University Press, 2011.

Greenstein, Howard R. *Turning Point: Zionism and Reform Judaism*. Chico, CA: Scholars Press, 1981.

Gross, Nachum T. "The Economic Regime during Israel's First Decade." In *Israel: The First Decade of Independence*, edited by S. Ilan Troen and Noah Lucas, 231–41. Albany: State University of New York Press, 1995.

Hackett, Alice Payne, and James Henry Burke. *80 Years of Best Sellers, 1895–1975*. New York: R. R. Bowker, 1977.

Hahn, Peter L. *Caught in the Middle East: U.S. Policy Toward the Arab-Israeli Conflict, 1945–1961*. Chapel Hill: University of North Carolina Press, 2004.

Hajdu, David. *Positively 4th Street: The Lives and Times of Joan Baez, Bob Dylan, Mimi Baez Farina and Richard Farina*. New York: North Point Press, 2001.

Halamish, Aviva. "American Volunteers in Illegal Immigration to Palestine, 1946–1948." *Jewish History* 9, no. 1 (Spring 1995): 91–106.

Halevi, Nadav. "Perspectives on the Balance of Payments." In *The Israeli Economy: Maturing Through Crises*, edited by Yoram Ben-Porath, 241–63. Cambridge and London: Harvard University Press, 1986.

Halpern, Ben. "The Americanization of Zionism, 1880–1930." *American Jewish History* 69 (September 1979): 15–33.

———. *The Idea of the Jewish State*. 2nd ed. Cambridge: Harvard University Press, 1969.

Halter, Marilyn. *Shopping for Identity: The Marketing of Ethnicity*. New York: Schocken Books, 2000.

Harap, Louis. *The Image of the Jew in American Literature: From Early Republic to Mass Immigration*. Philadelphia: The Jewish Publication Society of America, 1974.

Heald, Morrell. *Transatlantic Vistas: American Journalists in Europe, 1900–1940*. Kent, OH, and London: The Kent State University Press, 1988.

Heilman, Samuel. "Jews and Judaica: Who Owns and Buys What?" In *Persistence and Flexibility: Anthropological Perspectives on the American Jewish Experience*, edited by Walter P. Zenner, 260–79. Albany: State University of New York Press, 1988.

———. *Portrait of American Jews: The Last Half of the Twentieth Century*. Seattle: University of Washington Press, 1995.

Heinze, Andrew R. *Adapting to Abundance: Jewish Immigrants, Mass Consumption, and the Search for American Identity*. New York: Columbia University Press, 1990.

Hertz, Richard C. *The Education of the Jewish Child: A Study of 200 Reform Jewish Religious Schools*. New York: UAHC, 1953.

Hixson, Walter L. *Parting the Curtain: Propaganda, Culture, and the Cold War, 1945–1961*. New York: St. Martin's, 1997.

Hyman, Paula E. "Immigrant Women and Consumer Protest: The New York City Kosher Meat Boycott of 1902." *American Jewish History* 70 (1980): 91–105.

Ingber, Judith Brin. *Shorashim: The Roots of Israeli Folk Dance*. New York: Dance Perspectives Foundation, 1974.

———. *Victory Dances: The Story of Fred Berk, A Modern Day Jewish Dancing Master*. (In Hebrew and English) Tel Aviv: Israel Dance Library and Minneapolis: Emmett Publishing, 1985.

Jackson, Naomi M. *Converging Movements: Modern Dance and Jewish Culture at the 92nd Street Y*. Hanover: University Press of New England/Wesleyan University Press, 2000.

Jacobson, Matthew Frye. *Barbarian Virtues: The United States Encounters Foreign Peoples at Home and Abroad, 1876–1917*. New York: Hill and Wang, 2000.

Jick, Leon. "The Reform Synagogue." In *The American Synagogue: A Sanctuary Transformed*, edited by Jack Wertheimer, 102–104. Hanover and London: Brandeis University Press and the University Press of New England, 1987.

Joselit, Jenna Weissman. "Bezalel Comes to Town: American Jews and Art." *Jewish Studies Quarterly* 11, no. 4 (2004): 354–65.

————. "The Jewish Home Beautiful." In *The American Jewish Experience*, edited by Jonathan D. Sarna. 2nd ed., 236–44. New York and London: Holmes and Meier, 1997.

————. *The Wonders of America: Reinventing Jewish Culture, 1880–1950*. New York: Hill and Wang, 1994.

Kanof, Abram. "The Tobe Pascher Workshop 1956–1986." In *Moshe Zabari: A Twenty-Five Year Retrospective*, edited by Nancy M. Berman, 6–17. New York: The Jewish Museum and Los Angeles: The Hebrew Union College Skirball Museum, 1986.

Katz, Emily Alice. "Introducing Israeli Art: Communal and Critical Encounters in Postwar America." *Images: A Journal of Jewish Art and Visual Culture* 3, no. 1 (2009): 47–56.

————. "It's the Real World After All: The American-Israel Pavilion—Jordan Pavilion Controversy at the New York World's Fair, 1964–1965." *American Jewish History* 91, no. 1 (March 2003): 129–55.

————. "Pen Pals, Pilgrims, and Pioneers: Reform Youth and Israel, 1948–1967." *American Jewish History* 95, no. 3 (September 2009): 249–76.

————. "That Land Is Our Land: Israel in American Jewish Culture, 1948–1967." PhD diss., The Jewish Theological Seminary, 2008.

Kaufman, Menahem. "Envisaging Israel: the Case of the United Jewish Appeal." In *Envisioning Israel: The Changing Ideals and Images of North American Jews*, edited by Allon Gal, 219–53. Detroit: Wayne State University Press, 1996.

Kelman, Ari Y. "Hear Israel," *Tablet Magazine*, January 7, 2011, http://www.tabletmag.com/jewish-arts-and-culture/music/55172/hear-israel.

Kenaan-Kedar, Nurith, ed. *Modern Creations from an Ancient Land: Metal Craft and Design in the First Two Decades of Israel's Independence*. (In Hebrew and English) Tel Aviv: Eretz Israel Museum and Jerusalem: Yad Itzhak Ben-Zvi, 2006.

Kirshenblatt-Gimblett, Barbara. "Kitchen Judaism." In *Getting Comfortable in New York: The American-Jewish Home, 1880–1950*, edited by Susan L. Braunstein and Jenna Weissman Joselit, 76–105. New York: The Jewish Museum, 1990.

————. "Sounds of Sensibility." *Judaism* 47, no. 1 (Winter 1998): 49–78.

Klein, Christina. *Cold War Orientalism: Asia in the Middlebrow Imagination, 1945–1961*. Berkeley: University of California Press, 2003.

Klein, Shira. "An Army of Housewives: Women's Wartime Columns in Two Mainstream Israeli Newspapers." *Nashim* 15 (2008): 88–107.

Kolsky, Thomas A. *Jews Against Zionism: The American Council for Judaism, 1942–1948*. Philadelphia: Temple University Press, 1990.

Koner, Pauline. "Cochem, Corinne." In *Jewish Women in America*, edited by Paula E. Hyman and Deborah Dash Moore, 226. New York: Routledge, 1998.

Krasner, Jonathan. *The Benderly Boys and American Jewish Education*. Waltham: Brandeis University Press, 2011.

————. "Israel in American Jewish Textbooks, 1948-Present." Paper presented at Midwestern Jewish Studies Association Conference, 2003.

————. "The Limits of Cultural Zionism in America: The Case of Hebrew in the New York City Public Schools, 1930–1960." *American Jewish History* 95, no. 4 (December 2009): 349–72.

Lazarowitz, Arlene. "Different Approaches to a Regional Search for Balance: The Johnson Administration, the State Department, and the Middle East, 1964–1967." *Diplomatic History* 32, no. 1 (January 2008): 25–54.

Lederhendler, Eli. "Introduction: The Six-Day War and the Jewish People in the Diaspora." In *The Six-Day War and World Jewry*, edited by Eli Lederhendler, 1–9. Bethesda: University Press of Maryland, 2000.

———. *New York Jews and the Decline of Urban Ethnicity, 1950–1970*. Syracuse: Syracuse University Press, 2001.

———. "The Ongoing Dialogue: The Seminary and the Challenge of Israel." In *Tradition Renewed: A History of the Jewish Theological Seminary, vol. II—Beyond the Academy*, edited by Jack Wertheimer, 177–270. New York: The Jewish Theological Seminary of America, 1997.

Lipstadt, Deborah E. *The Eichmann Trial*. New York: Nextbook/Schocken, 2011.

Little, Douglas. *American Orientalism: The United States and the Middle East Since 1945*. 3rd ed. Chapel Hill: The University of North Carolina Press, 2008.

Long, Burke O. *Imagining the Holy Land: Maps, Models, and Fantasy Travels*. Bloomington: Indiana University Press, 2002.

Manor, Dalia. *Art in Zion: The Genesis of Modern National Art in Jewish Palestine*. London: Routledge/Curzon, 2005.

Marchand, Roland. "Visions of Classlessness, Quests for Dominion: American Popular Culture, 1945–1960." In *Reshaping America: Society and Institutions, 1945–1960*, edited by Robert H. Bremner and Gary W. Reichard, 163–90. Columbus: Ohio State University Press, 1982.

Mart, Michelle. *Eye on Israel: How America Came to View Israel as an Ally*. Albany: State University of New York Press, 2006.

———. "Tough Guys and American Cold War Policy: Images of Israel, 1948–1960." *Diplomatic History* 20, no. 3 (Summer 1996): 357–80.

McAlister, Melani. *Epic Encounters: Culture, Media, and U.S. Interests in the Middle East, 1945–2000*. Berkeley: University of California Press, 2001.

McDannell, Colleen. "Interpreting Things: Material Culture Studies and American Religion." *Religion* 21, no. 4 (1991): 371–87.

———. *Material Christianity: Religion and Popular Culture in America*. New Haven and London: Yale University Press, 1995.

Medoff, Rafael. "Recent Trends in the Historiography of American Zionism." *American Jewish History* 86, no. 1 (1998): 117–34.

Melvin, Patricia Mooney. "Building Muscles and Civics: Folk Dancing, Ethnic Diversity and the Playground Association of America." *American Studies* 24, no. 1 (Spring 1983): 89–99.

Meyer, Michael A. *Response to Modernity: A History of the Reform Movement in Judaism*. Detroit: Wayne State University Press, 1988.

Meyerowitz, Joanne. "Beyond the Feminine Mystique: A Reassessment of Postwar Mass Culture, 1946–1958." In *Not June Cleaver: Women and Gender in Postwar America, 1945–1960*, edited by Joanne Meyerowitz, 229–62. Philadelphia: Temple University Press, 1994.

Miller, Julie, and Richard I. Cohen. "A Collision of Cultures: The Jewish Museum and the Jewish Theological Seminary, 1904–1971." In *Tradition Renewed: A*

History of the Jewish Theological Seminary, edited by Jack Wertheimer, 310–61. New York: The Jewish Theological Seminary, 1997.

Mintz, Alan. "The Divided Fate of Hebrew and Hebrew Culture at the Seminary." In *Tradition Renewed: A History of the Jewish Theological Seminary, vol. II—Beyond the Academy,* edited by Jack Wertheimer, 81–112. New York: The Jewish Theological Seminary of America, 1997.

Moore, Deborah Dash. "Bonding Images: Miami Jews and the Campaign for Israel Bonds." In *Envisioning Israel: The Changing Ideals and Images of North American Jews,* edited by Allon Gal, 254–67. Detroit: Wayne State University Press; and Jerusalem: The Magnes Press, 1996.

———. "Hadassah." In *Jewish Women in America: An Historical Encyclopedia,* edited by Paula E. Hyman and Deborah Dash Moore, 576–77 and 579–81. New York: Routledge, 1997.

———. "A Synagogue Center Grows in Brooklyn." In *The American Synagogue: A Sanctuary Transformed,* edited by Jack Wertheimer, 315–19. Hanover and London: Brandeis University Press and the University Press of New England, 1987.

———. *To the Golden Cities: Pursuing the American Jewish Dream in Miami and L.A.* Cambridge: Harvard University Press, 1994.

Morgan, David. *Visual Piety: A History and Theory of Popular Religious Images.* Berkeley: University of California Press, 1998.

Morris, Benny. *Righteous Victims: A History of the Zionist-Arab Conflict, 1881–2001.* New York: Vintage, 2001.

Mullins, Paul R. *Race and Affluence: An Archaeology of African America and Consumer Culture.* New York: Kluwer Academic/Plenum Publishers: 1999.

Novick, Peter. *The Holocaust in American Life.* Boston: Houghton Mifflin, 1999.

Ochs, Vanessa L. *Inventing Jewish Ritual.* Philadelphia: The Jewish Publication Society, 2007.

Olin, Margaret Rose. *A Nation Without Art: Examining Modern Discourses on Jewish Art.* Lincoln: University of Nebraska Press, 2001.

Orsi, Robert. *The Madonna of 115th Street: Faith and Community in Italian Harlem.* New Haven: Yale University Press, 1985.

Patterson, James T. *Grand Expectations: The United States, 1945–1974.* New York and Oxford: Oxford University Press, 1996.

Pellegrini, Ann. "Whiteface Performances: Race, Gender, and Jewish Bodies." In *Jews and other Differences: The New Jewish Cultural Studies,* edited by Jonathan Boyarin and Daniel Boyarin, 108–49. Minneapolis: University of Minnesota Press, 1997.

Persico, Joseph E. *Edward R. Murrow: An American Original.* New York: McGraw-Hill, 1988.

Prell, Riv-Ellen. "Community and the Discourse of Elegy: The Postwar Suburban Debate." In *Imagining the American Jewish Community,* edited by Jack Wertheimer, 67–90. Hanover and London: Brandeis University Press and the University Press of New England, 2007.

———. *Fighting to Become Americans: Jews, Gender, and the Anxiety of Assimilation.* Boston: Beacon Press, 1999.

Radway, Janice A. *A Feeling for Books: The Book-of-the-Month Club, Literary Taste, and Middle-Class Desire*. Chapel Hill: The University of North Carolina Press, 1997.

Raider, Mark A. *The Emergence of American Zionism*. New York: New York University Press, 1998.

Rains, Stephanie. "Celtic Kitsch: Irish-America and Irish Material Culture." *Circa Art Magazine* 107 (Spring 2004): 52–57.

Raphael, Jacob H. "Israel in the Classroom." *The Jewish Teacher* 18, no. 3 (March 1950): 15–25.

Regev, Motti, and Edwin Seroussi. *Popular Music and National Culture in Israel*. Berkeley: University of California Press, 2004.

Reinharz, Shulamit, and Mark A. Raider, eds. *American Jewish Women and the Zionist Enterprise*. Waltham: Brandeis University Press, 2005.

Riesman, David. *The Lonely Crowd: A Study of the Changing American Character*. New Haven: Yale University Press, 1950.

Roginsky, Dina. "Sixty Years to the First Dalia Conference, 1944–2004: Changes in Israeli Folk Dance." *Dance Now* 11 (November 2004): 92–99.

Rosenfeld, Steven T. *Irreconcilable Differences?: The Waning of the American Jewish Love Affair with Israel*. Hanover and London: Brandeis University Press, 2003.

Rubin, Joan Shelley. *The Making of Middlebrow Culture*. Chapel Hill: The University of North Carolina Press, 1992.

Sacks, Adam. "Hannah Arendt's Eichmann Controversy as Destabilizing Transatlantic Text." *AJS Review* 37, no. 1 (2013): 115–34.

Sanua, Marianne. "The Esco Fund Committee: The Story of an American Jewish Foundation." In *America and Zion: Essays and Papers in Memory of Moshe Davis*, edited by Eli Lederhendler and Jonathan D. Sarna, 117–160. Detroit: Wayne State University Press, 2002.

Sarna, Jonathan D. *American Judaism: A History*. New Haven: Yale University Press, 2004.

Saunders, Frances Stonor. *The Cultural Cold War: The CIA and the World of Arts and Letters*. New York: New Press, 1999.

Scult, Mel. *Judaism Faces the Twentieth Century: A Biography of Mordecai M. Kaplan*. Detroit: Wayne State University Press, 1993.

Segev, Tom. *The Seventh Million: The Israelis and the Holocaust*. Translated by Haim Watzman. New York: Hill and Wang, 1993.

Shandler, Jeffrey. *Adventures in Yiddishland: Postvernacular Language and Culture*. Berkeley: University of California Press, 2006.

———. "Producing the Future: The Impresario Culture of American Zionism before 1948." In *Divergent Jewish Cultures: Israel and America*, edited by Deborah Dash Moore and S. Ilan Troen, 53–71. New Haven: Yale University Press, 2001.

———. "What Is American Jewish Culture?" In *The Columbia History of Jews and Judaism in America*, edited by Marc Lee Raphael, 348–49. New York: Columbia University Press, 2008.

———. *While America Watches: Televising the Holocaust*. New York: Oxford University Press, 1999.

———, and Elihu Katz. "Broadcasting American Judaism: The Radio and Television Department of the Jewish Theological Seminary." In *Tradition Renewed: A*

History of the Jewish Theological Seminary, edited by Jack Wertheimer, 363–401. New York: The Jewish Theological Seminary, 1997.

———, and Beth S. Wenger. "'The Site of Paradise': The Holy Land in American Jewish Imagination." In *Encounters With the "Holy Land": Place, Past, and Future in American Jewish Culture*, edited by Jeffrey Shandler and Beth S. Wenger, 11–40. Hanover and London: The University Press of New England, 1997.

Shapira, Anita. "Golda: Femininity and Feminism." In *American Jewish Women and the Zionist Enterprise*, edited by Shulamit Reinharz and Mark A. Raider, 303–12. Waltham: Brandeis University Press, 2005.

Shapiro, Edward S. *A Time for Healing: American Jewry since World War II*. Baltimore: Johns Hopkins University Press, 1992.

Shapiro, Laura. *Something From the Oven: Reinventing Dinner in 1950s America*. New York: Viking Penguin, 2004.

Shay, Anthony. *Choreographing Identities: Folk Dance, Ethnicity, and Festival in the United States and Canada*. Jefferson, NC, and London: McFarland, 2006.

———. *Choreographic Politics: State Folk Dance Companies, Representation, and Power*. Middletown, CT: Wesleyan University Press, 2002.

Silver, M. M. *Our Exodus: Leon Uris and the Americanization of Israel's Founding Story*. Detroit: Wayne State University Press, 2010.

Simmons, Erica B. *Hadassah and the Zionist Project*. Lanham, MD: Rowman and Littlefield, 2006.

Sorin, Gerald. *Tradition Transformed: The Jewish Experience in America*. Baltimore: Johns Hopkins University Press, 1997.

Sperber, A. M. *Murrow: His Life and Times*. New York: Freundlich Books, 1986.

Spiegel, Nina. "Jewish Cultural Celebrations and Competitions in Mandatory Palestine, 1920–1947." PhD diss., Stanford University, 2001.

Staub, Michael E. *Torn at the Roots: The Crisis of Jewish Liberalism in Postwar America*. New York: Columbia University Press, 2002.

Stein, Rebecca L. "'First Contact' and Other Israeli Fictions: Tourism, Globalization, and the Middle East Peace Process." In *Palestine, Israel, and the Politics of Popular Culture*, edited by Rebecca L. Stein and Ted Swedenburg, 259–87. Durham and London: Duke University Press, 2005.

Stock, Ernest. "Philanthropy and Politics: Modes of Interaction between Israel and the Diaspora." In *Israel: The First Decade of Independence*, edited by S. Ilan Troen and Noah Lucas, 699–711. Albany: State University of New York Press, 1995.

Stowe, William W. *Going Abroad: European Travel in Nineteenth-Century American Culture*. Princeton: Princeton University Press, 1994.

Svonkin, Stuart. *Jews Against Prejudice: American Jews and the Fight for Civil Liberties*. New York: Columbia University Press, 1997.

Tebbel, John. *A History of Book Publishing in the United States, vol. IV, The Great Change, 1940–1980*. New York and London: R. R. Bowker, 1981.

Urofsky, Melvin I. *We Are One! American Jewry and Israel*. Garden City, NY: Anchor Press/Doubleday, 1978.

Vogel, Lester I. *To See A Promised Land: Americans and the Holy Land in the Nineteenth Century*. University Park: The Pennsylvania State University Press, 1993.

Wall, Wendy L. *Inventing the "American Way": The Politics of Consensus, from the New Deal to the Civil Rights Movement.* New York: Oxford University Press, 2008.

Wertheimer, Jack. "American Jews and Israel: A 60-Year Retrospective." *American Jewish Year Book* 108 (2008): 3–79.

———. "The Conservative Synagogue." In *The American Synagogue: A Sanctuary Transformed,* edited by Jack Wertheimer, 123–32. Hanover and London: Brandeis University Press and the University Press of New England, 1987.

Whitfield, Stephen J. "Value Added: Jews in Postwar American Culture." In *A New Jewry? America Since the Second World War, Studies in Contemporary Jewry: An Annual VIII,* edited by Peter Y. Medding, 68–84. New York and Oxford: Oxford University Press, 1992.

Whyte, William H. *The Organization Man.* New York: Simon and Schuster, 1956.

Wiese, Christian. "'No Love of the Jewish People'?: Robert Weltsch's and Hans Jonas's Correspondence with Hannah Arendt on 'Eichmann in Jerusalem.'" In *German-Jewish Thought Between Religion and Politics: Festschrift in Honor of Paul Mendes-Flohr on the Occasion of His Seventieth Birthday,* edited by Christian Wiese and Martina Urban, 387–432. Berlin: De Gruyter, 2012.

Wolf, Rebecca Boim. "'It's Good Americanism to Join Hadassah': Selling Hadassah in the Postwar Era." In *A Jewish Feminine Mystique?: Jewish Women in Postwar America,* eds. Hasia R. Diner, Shira Kohn, and Rachel Kranson, 65–86. New Brunswick and London: Rutgers University Press, 2010.

Wolffsohn, Michael. *Israel: Polity, Society, and Economy, 1882–1986: An Introductory Handbook.* Translated by Douglas Bokovoy. Altlantic Highlands, NJ: Humanities Press International, 1987.

Wong, Janay Jadine. "Synagogue Art of the 1950s: A New Context for Abstraction." *Art Journal* 53, no. 4 (Winter 1994): 37–43.

Zalmona, Yigal. "History and Identity." In *Artists of Israel: 1920–1980,* edited by Susan Tumarkin Goodman, 27–46. New York: The Jewish Museum, 1981.

Zipperstein, Steven J. "*Commentary* and American Jewish Culture in the 1940s and 1950s." *Jewish Social Studies,* New Series 3, no. 2 (Winter 1997): 18–28.

Zollman, Joellyn Wallen. "Shopping for a Future: A History of the American Synagogue Gift Shop." PhD diss., Brandeis University, 2002.

Zucker, Bat-Ami. *U.S. Aid to Israel and Its Reflection in* The New York Times *and* The Washington Post, *1948–1973: The Pen, the Sword, and the Middle East.* Lewiston, NY: The Edwin Mellon Press, 1992.

INDEX